MW00514090

A BUBBE MEISE

A Bubbe Meise

A Grandmother's True Story

Hinda Rotenberg Miller

Copyright © 2014 Hinda Miller
Published by Hinda Miller

All rights reserved. No part of this publication may be reproduced, stored in a retrieval system or transmitted, in any form, or by any means, electronic, mechanical, recorded, photocopied, or otherwise, without the prior written permission of both the copyright owner and the above publisher of this book, except by a reviewer who may quote brief passages in a review.

The scanning, uploading, and distribution of this book via the Internet or via any other means without the permission of the publisher is illegal and punishable by law. Please purchase only authorized electronic editions and do not participate in or encourage electronic piracy of copyright-able materials. Your support of the author's rights is appreciated.

Designed by Vince Pannullo
Printed in the United States of America by RJ Communications.

ISBN: 978-0-578-14217-3

CONTENTS

DEDICATION

To Michael who has helped me to become the woman I wanted to be

and

To Lyla who reminds me who I have always been

Life must be lived forward, but it can only be understood backward.

Søren Kierkegaard

Looking for the answer to the question "Who am I?" with the intellect is like flying to the moon in search of your belly button.

Reflections of the One Life, Scott Kiloby

The names and identifying characteristics of many characters in my book have been changed. All the incidents described are true, but some events have been compressed, consolidated or otherwise changed to protect the identities of the people involved. Dialogue is as close as possible to conversations that actually took place, as best my memory serves me.

A *"bubbe meise"* literally translated from the Yiddish means a grandmother's story. When I was a little girl, to hear a *"bubbe meise"* was to hear a fable, a fiction, an old wives' tale, certainly nothing true. But inside each *"meise"* sometimes there was also a lesson, something you could learn from, like the moral of one of Aesop's fables. I'm no Aesop, but I have stories to tell and what I learned from my experiences.

One at a time my grandchildren have come to me with their questions, starting when they're seven or eight years old. Emma asks, "Bubbie, what were you like when you were my age?" Isabel inquires, "What did you like best about school?" Watching television one day with Teddy, he asks "What programs did you watch?" Dustin wonders "What books did you read when you were a kid?" Nate and Matty ask "What was my mother like when she was a little girl?" Inevitably all of them have one question in common: "How old are you, Bubbie?"

"Seventy-five years old," I tell them, almost five times the age of the oldest one. As a result of living that many years, I have many stories to tell them about my childhood, my family, of meeting and marrying their Poppa, of the pleasure of welcoming their parents to the family and my work outside the house as well.

Each of those experiences added to my accumulated "wisdom." Now, looking back, I remember not only what learned along the way, but the values I developed from my adventures. These are what I want to share with them, and also with you.

BLUE-EYED BABY

MY real name is Hinda. Because it's uncommon, I've often been asked "How did you get that name?" Hinda is an old-fashioned name chosen for me because Jewish families like mine name their children to honor a beloved deceased relative. My father's mother, Hinda, died in Poland before my birth in 1939. I was a third daughter and last child. When I was little I overheard the story of the night I was born. Daddy went to tell my mother's parents about my arrival, walking up the steps to their apartment on Kelly Street in Rochester, New York and saying "It's just another girl." *Just another* girl? Didn't Daddy want me? It was many years before I learned that he had also uttered five more words, words which made me feel so much better, "but is she ever beautiful!"

To me my sisters were G-d's[1] greatest creations. They made my life richer, safer, more expansive and happier. They were 11 and seven when I was born, a real live baby doll for them to play with. I also was a novelty for them; none of their friends had a sibling so young. Frances Mae was beautiful, with strawberry blond hair and caramel-colored eyes that seemed to twinkle. When I was little I couldn't pronounce her name. It came out sounding like "Feshie" or "Fedgie." She was Fedgie or Fedg to everyone from them on, except Mummy who called her Fran. Lyla Renèe had gorgeous hazel eyes and dark flowing locks. My sisters moved with confidence and had many friends. They wore makeup, nail polish, and jewelry.

I, the blue-eyed baby of the family, the only one lacking a middle name, had short fly-away mousy-brown hair and an impish grin. I felt like the misfit runt of the family: short, skinny, with scabbed knees, bitten nails, disheveled clothes and frequently dirty smudges on my face. I made myself even smaller by hunching my shoulders. I suppose I might have been called cute in a way, but my sisters were truly beautiful.

Because of the age differences between them and me, I didn't usually spend

---

[1] While Jews are allowed to say G-d's name aloud, out of respect for G-d's holiness, they are not allowed to write it in its entirety in any language on anything that might later be discarded.

a lot of time with them. The exception was after dinner when they remained in the kitchen to clean up. Mummy expected them to clear the table and do dishes every night. They traded off who washed and who dried. I pulled up a chair to watch and listen, never taking my eyes or ears from them. I was thrilled to be there in their presence. As they did dishes, they sang ballads made popular in the 1940s. One would start a song and the other would join her, favoring songs by the Dorsey band crooner, Frank Sinatra, such as, "I'll Never Smile Again."

As they sang and cleaned up, Fedgie beamed smiles at me, encouraging me with a nod of her head to join in. With her smile for encouragement, I learned the lyrics fast. I loved being part of their teenage world. Fedg's personal radiance felt better than food, motion pictures, or chocolate ice cream. I yearned for it more than for anything else.

Fedg appeared to enjoy having me around. Of course she was accustomed to having a younger sister; I don't think she remembered a time before Lyla was born. She also had all the privacy she wanted when she didn't want me around. Her big sunlight bedroom with a double bed and yellow wallpaper was in the back of the house and was hers alone. Lyla, on the other hand, had no such escape. She had to share her blue-papered room with one closet with me.

My sisters sometimes played checkers, Monopoly or Sorry with me when they had time, but they were usually too busy with homework, girlfriends and boyfriends. Sometimes, when Fedg didn't have a full night of homework, she would seek me out for a card game, usually Gin Rummy, Fish or War. "How's school?" she'd ask, looking at me as if she expected a real answer rather than the usual "Fine." No one else, not my parents nor Lyla, ever asked me about school expecting an answer which might lead to a longer conversation. With them it was just something they were supposed to ask. Fedgie really wanted to know.

"It's really fun, Fedg," I'd answer.

"Tell me about what happened today," she'd say.

Excitedly I told her about my American history unit, for example, and then I added, with a huge smile "But you know that I already knew about all that!"

She gave me a wink and a smile because she had seen me reading ahead and looking into our 20 volumes of *The Book of Knowledge* with my questions. But I went beyond just answering questions. I read these volumes with passion, as certain as only a child can be, that if I read every page of every volume and I remembered what I read, that I would be the smartest girl in the world. I would know everything there was to know, everything I might need to know for a lifetime.

Fedgie didn't seem to mind having me underfoot. As the eldest, she had experienced only four years as an only child before Lyla came along. Mummy sometimes asked both of them to let me tag along when they went out with their friends. Fedgie didn't seem to mind, but Lyla most certainly did. Maybe it was because she got the lion's share of the sister-sitting.

I was only seven when Fedg went away to college. I eagerly awaited the letters that Mummy shared with the rest of us at dinnertime. Long distance calls were expensive so Fedg called home only every few weeks. My folks let me take the phone, but we always said the same things, "What's new with you?" "How are you?" I grew tongue-tied when I spoke with her, the only time I was ever at a loss for words. I didn't want to talk to her long-distance; I wanted her home.

While I missed her a lot, I benefited from her absence by getting her room for my own. What joy! I could listen to my favorite programs on the little radio which sat on the table next to the bed. That beloved radio was carved from wood and featured the figures of Snow White and the Seven Dwarfs. Late at night in spring and summer, when I was supposed to be sleeping, I would lie there listening to programs. Mummy or Daddy must have known what I was doing; who else would have turned off the radio after I fell asleep?

When Fedg went to college things got a little better between Lyla and me. But only a little better.

Many times I heard Mummy ask Lyla to take me with her and I saw her wince at Lyla's reply:

"Does she have to come?" Lyla complained. "She's such a pain."

Mummy scowled and replied, "She is not a pain. I'm ashamed of you, Lyla Rotenberg! Hinda is your sister."

Under her breath Lyla would mutter, "She may be my sister, but she's still a pain!" Lyla had been the family's "baby" for seven years before I was born. Did she resent my arrival? Was she jealous of me? Did she regard me as an intruder? She sure acted that way.

On many Saturday afternoons, primary-school me went with high-school Lyla downtown on a city bus to meet her friends at one of the many downtown movie houses. One week, after seeing a double feature at the RKO Palace Theatre on Clinton Avenue, Lyla and I left her friends to catch our bus home. We held hands to cross Main Street. The passersby roughly jostled us, causing our hands to separate. We were apart in the crowd. I couldn't see her, and I was terrified. I stood still in the crosswalk, certain I was lost forever.

I croaked out her name, "Lyla?" And then I screamed, "*Lyla*! Where *are* you?" I'm sure it was only a second or two before she found me, but it felt like forever. She hugged me tightly to her body.

"You scared me half to death!" she said. And then, just so I wouldn't think she liked me any better, she added, "What would I have told the folks if I lost you? You can be such a pain some days."

No matter. I never loved Lyla more than at that moment.

She and I shared the same passion; we both loved to sing and perform. I would watch her with her friends as they created and prepared original shows to perform outdoors for an audience of relatives and neighbors. I wanted to do that, too!

I craved attention as far back as I can remember. Every night at the dinner table, Mummy and Daddy chatted with my sisters about their school activities, such as drama club or sports. They laughed together, my parents asking question after question. I laughed, too, even though I didn't really understand what they were talking about; I just wanted to belong, but didn't feel as if I did. No one asked me anything or wanted to know more about my life. When I tried to share my day of what I did in school or afterwards, climbing trees, riding my bike or playing ball with my friends, they would listen and laugh briefly, but change the subject. After a while I didn't even try to talk, except to ask, "May I please have some more mashed potatoes?" I became hungrier for attention than for all the tasty dinners Mummy would make. I wanted to be as special as my sisters. I wanted someone to listen to me.

To my family I may have appeared to be a confident child, happy in my own skin, but inside that skin I was trying to shine, to out-achieve my sisters. No one seemed to notice my fingernails bitten to the quick from insecurity.

When I was 11, I decided I wanted to be on the radio. Al Sigl was then a very popular radio personality in Rochester and well-known today for the umbrella agency of service programs bearing his name. Besides announcing the news each weekday in his peculiar screechy voice, he also hosted a Saturday morning children's amateur hour on radio, an early pediatric version of "America's Got Talent." Any child who wanted to audition for the show was invited to try out and perform. If you were chosen, you were asked to come back and sing, or recite your poem, or tell your story, on Mr. Sigl's program. There were no prizes, just the honor of being "on the air."

I practiced day and night singing one of the most popular songs of the day, "A Bushel and a Peck." If my parents had heard it one more time, I think they would have sent me off to live on some farm! As I practiced, I accompanied my song with gestures, although totally aware that they weren't needed for radio.

One weekday afternoon after we returned from school, Lyla offered to take me downtown on a bus for an audition at Al Sigl's studio. I couldn't believe Lyla was going to help me and had volunteered to take me after all her belly-aching about having to take me to the movies, but I was grateful because, otherwise, I couldn't have gone. I also couldn't believe I was finally going to be a star! My "specialness" would be known to one and all! My dream was coming true. The studio was on an upper floor of the Rochester Savings Bank downtown on Chestnut Street. My sister and I took the elevator to the third floor and entered a room where other children were sitting, most of them accompanied by a parent. Lyla tried to make conversation with me as we awaited my turn, but I concentrated on remembering the lyrics to my song. They called out names one at a time for auditions.

Finally, it was my turn. Lyla stayed behind as I was led away. The man escorting me took me to a room as small as a closet empty except for a microphone standing in the middle. He asked me to stand in front of the mike as he adjusted it to my height, bringing the talking part even with my nose. He said he was leaving and that when I saw a signal from the glass booth in front of me, I was to say my name and then sing my song. I looked around and could see a few men behind the glass in the distance, but didn't know if Mr. Sigl was one of them.

The man left and closed the door behind him. I saw the signal and said my name. When I tried to sing, my throat froze. "All I want is a bushel and a peck, a bushel and a peck and a hug around the neck..." That's about as much as I managed to croak out before I said, "I want to leave - now." The man who brought me to the room took me back to my sister.

"What's happened? Are you going to be on the show" Lyla asked, excited to hear about what went on.

I shook my head, but I couldn't speak. I hung my head. I was so embarrassed. Sensing something was wrong, Lyla didn't say anything. We went down the elevator and left the building in silence. I kept thinking that Lyla took the time to bring me downtown and I had failed. Finally, on the bus ride home, I told her what happened.

She never mentioned it again.

Our parents, Herbert and Muriel Rotenberg, struggled to give my sisters and me the childhoods they had not experienced.

Until I was about 10, I don't think I heard my parents' accents, nor did I notice that they were just a bit old-fashioned. As I grew older, however, I noticed subtle differences from listening to the parents of my friends' American-born parents with nasal "Roch-ster" accents. I became somewhat ashamed that my parents were the only ones with foreign accents. I didn't want them to stand out in any way.

Both of my parents were immigrants, Dad from Ivansk, Poland and Mum from Nikolayev in the southern Ukraine. They met in Rochester in the 1920s, briefly courted and were married. They were thrilled to be Americans, but I felt detached from some early history and important events celebrated in school. The Pilgrims had come to America 300 years before my family did. The Revolutionary War and the Founding Fathers? My ancestors lived in Europe. The Civil War? Still not here. My family's American history didn't begin until Woodrow Wilson was President. I didn't feel as truly "red, white & blue" as my friends, although my parents were intensely patriotic.

As I began to discover things about myself as I grew, things which made me "me" and not just another little girl, I couldn't imagine what Mummy had been like when she was my age, living in another country before making the journey to America. I pestered her with questions about what her life was like when she was young, who did she play with, why she came to Rochester and many more things Finally, in answer to all of these questions, she agreed to sit down with me and discuss her early years. We sat in the living room, browsing through old photo albums. The pictures were nice, but something was missing.

"Why aren't there any early pictures of you or Aunt Min?" I asked. "What did your house look like? Your neighborhood? Didn't you take any pictures?"

Mum thought about my questions. "You know, I never thought about it until just now." She paused. "I wonder if we even had a camera... Well, even if we did, film was very expensive, and we were very poor."

"How poor were you? What do you remember about your early years in the

Old Country, Mummy? I'd love to know some things about you when you were a little girl."

She began, smiling a bit as she began to share: "When I was young, maybe six or seven and Aunt Min a few years younger," she began, "we lived in the small town of Nikolayev. My Pa, your Zaide, received a letter from an older sister who was already living in Rochester. She had left for America before I was even born. She wrote that if Pa wanted to come, she was willing to sponsor him for American citizenship."

I jumped in. "So you came here in 1912, when you were really young?"

Mummy laughed at my impetuousness. "No, Hinda, it wasn't that simple. You have to be patient and listen to the whole story." She continued, shaking her head from time to time as she recalled memories. "There were funds for only one passage, something like $25 or $50, a fortune in those days. My parents, your Bubbie and Zaide, talked about it and reluctantly decided that he would go alone, work as a tailor for Bonds, a large clothing company in Rochester, and save for our boat tickets."

"So you all followed him after he saved the money?" I looked at her hopefully, expecting a happy conclusion.

She smiled at me. "Again, not that simple. By the time Pa had saved enough to send for us, the World War, the first one, had started. No one could travel in or out of Europe for five years."

"Oh," I groaned. "You must have missed him so much. How did you manage?"

Mummy recalled that Zaide had left them with some of his savings, and her mother, sister and she were able to get by only if they were frugal. They cultivated a small garden and traded their vegetables for their neighbors' eggs and cheese.

The first years of the War passed without fighting near their village. However, the Russian Revolution, which had begun in 1917, literally came right to their front door. Mum was eleven when they woke up one night to the sound of hard pounding.

"Get up! Get up! Let us in," ordered gruff voices in Russian outside the door. My mother had an ear for languages. As a youngster, she knew a little Russian and was fluent in Yiddish, Polish, and Ukrainian, so she knew what they were saying.

Frightened, but with little choice, the women let the soldiers in.

"Bring food and drink," yelled the strangers. "Take our uniforms and fix all rips and tears. Sew on missing buttons."

My mother, her sister and their mother fed the men and then, while the women worked all night sewing by firelight, the soldiers slept in their beds. Night after night, for two years or so, as armies advanced and retreated, the same orders were repeated. Sometimes it was the Reds, sometime the Whites. Grateful that this was all the soldiers required, the vulnerable women complied willingly.

Eventually both World War I and the Russian Revolution ended. In 1920, Zaide was able to bring the remaining family to Rochester, where he worked as a tailor in what Mummy told me was a flourishing clothing industry. She showed me pictures from their first years in America. I laughed at the frumpy clothes and old-fashioned hairdos. My Bubbie looked really old although she was probably less than 50 at the time the picture was taken. The picture I liked best showed Bubbie, Zaide, Aunt Min and Mum standing on the porch of their first rental house in Rochester, a family reunited. Although their expressions were somber, they were finally all together.

They chose new names to suit the new country. My grandmother Sura became Sarah, my grandfather Nachem, Nathan. Mum's sister Mara became Minnie, and she herself went from Michaeyla[2] to Muriel. "Along with my old world name, I also tried to shed anything not strictly American. I insisted on speaking only English, except with my parents, with whom I spoke Yiddish."

"What else did you do or not do to make you more American?" I asked, fascinated by the story of my mother's metamorphosis.

"After a day's work as a seamstress, I attended night school to improve my language, math and history skills. I watched what the other girls wore and adapted to their styles. As soon as I could afford to buy new clothes, I dressed in the American style -- skirts, silky blouses, heeled shoes and cotton stockings. Before we came to Rochester, I never had owned a garter belt or even a bra."

I loved picturing my Mum as a young woman, no longer what they called a greenhorn. So this was the woman my father met and married.

I had a much harder time getting my father to share his early years with me. When I was in high school, I lied and told him I needed this background information from him for a school project. Reluctantly, he agreed to share.

We sat in the den one night after dinner. Daddy also had family photos he had received through the years from his brothers and sisters. He started by telling

---

[2] Pronounced me-kha-ay-lah

me he had been one of 14 children. He showed me photos of his brothers and sisters, some from their weddings and many with their own children. Daddy pointed out who was who. His voice grew soft when we came to a picture of his younger brothers and sisters: Kalman, Chana, Malka, Leah, Mayer, Isserle. His eyes became misty and his voice trembled a bit. I could tell that he had been especially close to them.

Daddy sat quietly for a few minutes to compose himself. His face was solemn. He didn't look at me at all. It was obvious he was lost in his memories. I sat respectfully waiting for him to begin. Finally he looked up at me and said, "This is very hard to say, Hinda, so this is the one and only time we are going to talk about it, okay? Remember what I tell you because I don't want to talk about this again."

"Thank you, Daddy." I attempted to say more.

He raised his hand to cut me off. After a deep sigh, he began: "I had a wonderful childhood. My father was greatly revered in our little town. As his son, I was also given respect. At five years old I began to study at *cheder*, the Jewish school, because we weren't allowed in the public schools. But there was no real anti-Semitism, you understand. We got along with everyone. After school I helped my father in his tanning business and when I came home, I helped my mother with the younger children. My father was almost old enough to be my grandfather. He had six older children with two previous wives who died before he married my mother. I was my mother's oldest. She helped raise the youngest of my father's other children."

He paused, took a deep breath and began again. "Where we lived was called Poland, which was sometimes an independent country, but most of the time was under Russian rule. When I was 18, I was arrested for not reporting for induction into the Tsar's Army. We weren't at war at that time, but all young men who were healthy had to serve in the Army. My mother bravely went to the jail where I was held and bribed the soldier in charge to get me out. I don't know what she gave him, but whatever it was it worked."

I didn't dare interrupt, but my mind was racing with questions. *Where did she get the money? How did she find out you were arrested?*

He continued, "She gave me a basket of food, whatever money she still had, a passport, a map and a brief tearful embrace. Mama told me to run as fast as I could, never look back, and try to reach relatives who lived in Canada. I never said goodbye to my father, brothers, sisters or anyone. I never saw any of them again."

Daddy began to cry, letting the tears stream down his face without wiping them. I sat there, wanting to comfort him and not knowing how. More questions raced through my head: *Where had the passport come from? Did your family know this day would come and you would have to leave? Were your brothers also called for service? Were they also arrested?*

He paused to compose himself. "I followed a trail known to other young Jewish men fleeing Army service. To this day I couldn't tell you what cities or towns I traveled through on my way to Danzig[3] on the Baltic Sea. There I booked passage to Quebec. It took me maybe four or five months before I arrived safely in Toronto to stay with my Uncle Luzar, my father's older brother. He died before you were born, but we always see his son, Cousin Max, when we're in Toronto. After a few months in Canada I decided to come to Rochester to work with my older half-brother, Izzie, the only other member of my immediate family who left Poland." He stopped. He didn't look at me. He just sat quietly. I could tell that was all he was going to say.

"Thank you, Daddy. I'm so proud to be your daughter." He stood up abruptly and left the room without another word. I was overwhelmed. I went to my room and curled up into a ball on the bed, reviewing everything he told me. He had left his whole family behind. He never saw them again. He couldn't even say good-bye. I knew my father in an entirely new way. He was brave, strong, clever and resourceful. All those years away from his family, always keeping them in his heart. I never got answers to the rest of my questions. As the years passed, they became less important.

After hearing Daddy's story I recalled something that had happened when I was six or seven. The Second World War had ended less than a year before. The phone rang and my father answered it.

"Yes, this is Herbert Rotenberg." He paused and listened. "Yes, I originally come from Ivansk. Yes, I asked you to find out about my family still living there." Another moment passed as he listened. His voice erupted. "What? *What did you say?*" I watched as he dropped the phone and crumpled to the floor, howling, gushing tears.

"Mummy, what's happening? What's wrong with Daddy?" I was so frightened. I had never seen him like this. Mum took the receiver and said to whomever

---

[3] Today Danzig is known as Gdansk

called, "Will you please repeat what you told my husband?" She listened for a while, murmured "thank you," hung up slowly as tears fell down her face.

She knelt down beside Daddy, hugging him and cooing, "Herb, it's what we already suspected. We knew this. We knew…"

He was inconsolable.

My sisters and I gathered near them, watching our parents together in sorrow. I asked my sisters what was wrong and was told to "hush." We left the room to give our parents some privacy. Fedg enveloped me in her arms, but didn't answer my questions. I know now what I couldn't guess then - that call let Daddy know that his hopes were unrealistic, his fears confirmed. No more Isserle. No Kalman. No Mayer, Malka, Leah or Chana. Our family eventually learned the terrible name and its purpose: Treblinka, an extermination camp.

Daddy was despondent and, as I learned later, felt directly responsible for the deaths of two of his sisters. Chana and Leah had each had written him a letter describing young men who wanted to marry them and asking for his advice. In both cases he answered that the man did not appear to have good prospects and that his sister should not accept the marriage. Both of those young men came to America. Both survived the Nazis. Daddy felt personally responsible that he did not "save" Chana and Leah.

A few years later, survivors from Ivansk visited us and told Daddy that his brothers and brothers-in-law had contracted with non-Jewish neighbors to hide their families. Then the men went to the hills to fight with the partisans. Despite being handsomely paid, those neighbors did not shelter my aunts and cousins. They turned them over to the Nazis as soon as the Germans appeared in town.

After Daddy's departure from Poland in 1920 and before World War II, he and his family in Poland had kept in touch by mail. They knew of his courtship of and marriage to my mother as well as when my sisters were born. Grandmother Hinda sent beautiful sterling silver candlesticks as a wedding present. I noticed dents in one of them and asked Mummy why she didn't have it repaired.

She smiled as she answered. "This is the way they came to us. They came with love, good wishes and these dents. They make them unique and remind me of the long way they traveled to our home."

Those candlesticks are still dented and still beautiful. I use them every week for the Shabbat lights and for the major holidays. As I kindle the candles, I recite the traditional prayers and ones entirely from my own heart, asking for blessings on our entire family, thanking G-d for what we have already received.

I carry Ivansk with me every day.

THE OUTDOORS WAS MY HOME

OUR family lived in the downstairs apartment of a large green Tudor-style house on Rochester's northeast side, ours having ten rooms, counting both the back and front parlors. Our home, off St. Paul Street on Huntington Park, had shiny oak parquet floors in the living and dining rooms. Area rugs in both rooms left the corners exposed to display decorative inlaid designs. The kitchen was huge, with a separate pantry to one side and a sewing room to the other. Heat came from a coal furnace in the cellar and iron radiators in every room. Those radiators were handy for drying wet snowsuits and mittens in the wintertime. The five of us shared one large bathroom. Many times, especially before school or at bedtime, my sisters and I shared the room – Lyla in the shower, Fedg at the sink and me in the bathtub. My favorite feature of our house was the large front closet which opened into another, smaller closet, my special space for hide-and-seek.

We knew every neighbor. In warm weather people sat on their front porches or stoops, took casual strolls up or down the street and exchanged pleasantries with those they encountered. We had a brick patio two steps up from the front walk, with room for a few chairs; other neighbors had porches large enough to hold dining tables, chairs, and even cushy sofas. Families brought out radios to their patios or porches and, if space allowed, played board games. Youngsters were allowed to run around with their friends after school until suppertime, and even afterwards, as long as we came home when the street lights came on. As much as I loved my house, the outdoors was my real home.

Within our house, I was only the little sister with no special distinctions to force my parents to focus on me. But outside the door, on Huntington Park, I became special. I was the only girl on a street full of boys my age. My companions were Burt, Davy and Steven, boys who wanted to play baseball or kickball, climb trees or roofs, hike, ride bikes, and invent messy activities. I wanted to do those things, too. In the vernacular of the day I was a tomboy and I was happy being called one. It made me different from my sisters.

I considered myself the guys' match, always rambunctious and ready to climb a tree or a rooftop at any moment. However, as a typical girl in the 1940s, I was dressed in highly starched dresses which were hand-laundered and crisply ironed. My mother expected me to be the lovely little girl my sisters had been; I was a different kind of girl. I liked games boys played. I didn't mind getting dirty. My parents tried to tame me.

One day Mrs. Rogalsky, a neighbor, saw me on my way down the street to see one of my friends. She waved hello and then slowly shook her head from side to side, and said "Hinda, your mother dressed you so very beautifully today. You're not going to get yourself filthy dirty again, are you?"

"I'll try not to," I answered with a wishful grin. Most days I forgot that promise as soon as the guys and I headed for an adventure – climbing trees, digging for China or roller skating. While my playmates wore play clothes, I had to wear those dumb dresses. No wonder my knees were scraped and skinned, my shins bruised, my elbows scratched, and that beautiful clothing sometimes ruined. It didn't help that my fingernails were also bitten down to the quick, a habit I developed early and didn't give up until I was many years older.

"Mummy," I'd beg, "please, please, please can I wear pants like the other kids?"

Always the same stern reply in the same stern voice: "Hinda Rotenberg. You are a little girl. Boys wear pants. Girls wear dresses. Now run along and stop this nonsense."

I tried to stay neat and clean. I really did. But as the guys and I climbed trees or dug forts or played tag, somehow I lost track of keeping clean and concentrated on keeping up. I wasn't defiant; I was distracted. Daddy spanked me once after Mummy dressed me up for a fancy family event and I had escaped the house, managing to destroy my shoes, my dress and the shiny curly hairdo which had taken her an hour to set right.

Huntington Park was a street well named. A lateral park ran down the middle, giving young bike riders a loop to circle again and again. The park had small trees, bushes and grass. Everyone, owners and renters alike, took good care of their own properties. The street had a fine look and feel to it although we who lived there were of very modest means.

Ride around the park without holding onto the handlebars? No problem. I never flinched when we climbed Davy's garage roof, although I was leery to venture down. For the most part, no dare was too scary for me to accept.

My one and only fear was of Handy, our neighbor's dog. That giant Doberman pinscher tried to frolic with me almost daily, but what he considered frolicking, I considered menacing. Every week or two I climbed to the highest branches of the nearest tree to avoid his nips. The wind blew me from side to side up there. Yet it was less frightening up there than to risk his jowls. If I didn't appear at the table for dinner, someone would come looking for me, to rescue me from my lofty perch.

"Did Handy tree you again, Hin?" Lyla would laugh. Then her smile would fade. "He's just trying to be friendly. He won't harm you."

I wasn't taking any chances.

With the guys, I played our version of baseball, running pretend bases in an open field. Most of the time, however, we played in "The Jungle," an area next to my house with undeveloped land filled with trees, weeds and giant granite boulders. Hide-and-seek was especially fun there because of all of the places to hide. And if weather forced us indoors, and we were at my house, the closet inside the closet in my front hall made a great hiding place, at least until I used it too many times and was found right away.

There were days when I fervently wished to be a boy, if only because their plumbing equipment would have suited me better. I was always too preoccupied by play to take time out to use a bathroom. I just held my water as long as I possibly could. When this happened at home or at school, someone would usually spot me jiggling from side to side and suggest I use a bathroom.

"Okay. I'll be right back. Don't let anything happen while I'm gone."

Outside there were no such reminders. I'd be playing in the woods and suddenly realize that I had to go, and I had to go right then! I wouldn't be able make it home. My playmates got used to my yelling, "Turn around and don't peek. I gotta go."

Despite trying not to, I always managed to pee on my shoes and socks, something that I knew wouldn't happen if I could direct my flow like a boy. Since they peed in the woods, they didn't think it unusual that I did too.

When I was six, a girl my age moved in on our street. Her name was Rosemary, and she lived in the opposite direction from the houses of the rest of my friends. Rosemary was short with delicate bone structure and long blonde curly hair, the bluest of eyes and rosy skin. If I had a doll, I imagined she would have looked just like Rosemary, complete with frilly dress, lacy socks and Mary Jane shoes.

Our friendship was doomed from the start. She acted like a girl and wanted to play dolls with me. Ugh. But what really killed any chance of friendship was the day we were sitting on a lawn about halfway between her house and mine.

She asked me, "Do you believe in G-d?"

"Sure."

"And Jesus?"

"Who?"

"Don't you know who Jesus is?" she asked, staring at me in disbelief.

"No."

"Don't they talk about Him at your church?"

"I don't go to church. I go to synagogue," I answered proudly.

Her eyes widened and she screamed, "Oh, you killed our Lord. You killed our Lord." That being said, she jumped up and ran home at top speed.

What? Killed someone? She's crazy. I ran home, too.

Bursting in the door, I yelled to Lyla and Mummy, the only ones home, "Rosemary said I killed someone named Jesus. Why does she think I killed someone?"

Whatever they were doing before I burst through the door, they looked at each other and stopped what they were doing. Mummy ushered me into the living room, a serious place for serious discussions. Sitting between them on the sofa, I turned from one to the other, expectantly.

Lyla began to explain, "Christians believe that a man named Jesus Christ was the Messiah, you know, the one we refer to as the *mosheach*[4], who will someday come to save the world. A man named Jesus lived and died almost 2,000 years ago." She paused. "He died a horrible death and some Christians blame the Jews for it."

I waited.

Seeing the expression of hesitation on my face, Mum assured me, "It's not true. Jews didn't do it. It's nothing for you to worry about."

I wasn't quite convinced, but if Mum said not to worry, I wasn't going to worry.

I never played with Rosemary again.

---

[4] Mo-she-akh, the Hebrew word for messiah

Just up the street from my house, on the other side of The Jungle, was a house subdivided into apartments. Miss Lane, who lived upstairs, was what my mother called a maiden lady. She worked downtown as a secretary for some large company. I met her when I was about seven and liked to visit her in nice weather on her front porch. She welcomed my late afternoon visits and asked me questions about school and my friends. My parents didn't mind my going there because they agreed that she was nice.

Mummy told me, "Hinda, as long as I know where you are, you may go to anyone's house on the street." She paused. "But when you're at Miss Lane's, don't eat anything."

I agreed without hesitation or questions.

One day Miss Lane invited me to bake cookies with her. I was worried because I remembered I wasn't supposed to eat anything, but how could I not eat cookies made with my very own hands? So I ate them, and they were good! Nothing bad happened.

The next time I saw Miss Lane, she talked about what a good little baker I was – and a good little eater, too! She went inside to get something for me to taste. I figured nothing bad happened when I ate the cookies so what could happen if I ate what she offered me? She came out with a slice of something which looked like salami, I tasted it and it was good, real good! I had another piece and another.

When I got home I wasn't hungry for dinner. Mummy teasingly asked, "Where did your appetite go?"

I confessed that I had eaten a little something at Miss Lane's house.

The shouting began: "What did she give you?" "What did it look like?" "What did it taste like?"

"It looked and tasted like salami," I said, amazed at all this fuss.

There was a whole lot of "Oh, my G-d." My family assumed from my description that I had eaten ham, the biggest no-no of all for a little girl being raised kosher. I knew ham was a no-no, but I had no idea what it looked like. I was eventually allowed to go back to visit Miss Lane, but my mother called her first to ask, please, not to feed me.

My youngest years coincided with the Second World War. Because of it, there were limitations on what we could buy. Each family had ration cards for such staple items as sugar, coffee, and butter and women could no longer buy nylon stockings because, we were told, nylon was needed to make parachutes for the Army Air Corps. We also had ration cards for gasoline, but that wasn't a hardship because Daddy didn't drive our old car any more than absolutely necessary. We couldn't buy a new car or new appliances because all steel was also dedicated to the war effort.

My best friend in the whole wide world lived right down the street. Burton Kolko was part of my life from as far back as I can remember. We were four months apart in age, almost to the day. He was the oldest of three sons in an observant Jewish family who lived a dozen or so houses aways from ours. Mrs. Kolko referred to me as her "almost daughter," and my parents seemed to consider Burt their "extra child." When I went to visit Burt, I didn't knock on the door or ring the bell: I just walked in; he did the same at our house.

Burt and I walked to and from school together every day, twice, because we came home for lunch. From Kindergarten to seventh grade, we had all the same teachers. After school four days each week, we went to Hebrew School together, on Sundays to Sunday school, and every Saturday to "junior congregation" services.

We watched television together and read the same books so we could talk about them. Every Halloween we went trick or treating together and shared our treats. We even had the same piano teacher. Poor Mr. Falkoff taught us duets in the hopes that he could get each of us to practice more because we got to practice together.

When we fought, our fights were epic. Everyone up and down Huntington Park knew when we were on the outs. I was the touchy one, the one whose emotions were close to the surface, but there were times he got mad, too. We fought about absolutely anything, but we fought differently. I exploded; he grew silent and glared. We were both stubborn. Something as simple as talking about baseball statistics could set us off.

"I think it was when Mel Ott was with the Yankees," I said. I smacked my forehead. "No! I mean the New York Giants. I meant the Giants!"

Burt gloated, "Ha! That's a girl for you. She doesn't even know the difference between the Yankees and the Giants."

Oh boy. Insult me because I'm a girl? I saw red. "You aren't my friend anymore! I don't wanna play with you," I screamed. I raised my chin high and turned away from him. I crossed my arms across my scrawny chest.

"Well, if that's the way you're gonna be, and you can't take a joke, then I don't wanna be with you either!" he retorted.

Days went by without walking to school or playing together. We left hateful messages for each other in envelopes with the other's name in big black letters. Dirty looks eventually softened as the days went on.

Mummy asked me, "Are you going to stay mad forever?"

"No," I answered haughtily, "just until he learns his lesson."

Eventually one of us would break the icy silence and we became best pals again, never referring to the fight. By the time we made up, I had usually forgotten what the fight was about anyway.

Because television was new entertainment in the 1940s, programs were shown only after 5:30 pm., and children my age mostly listened to the radio. At noontime, when Mummy and I would eat lunch, an announcer would ask "Can a young girl from a little mining town in the West be successful as the wife of a wealthy and titled Englishman?" and then one of the daily soap operas would begin. On weekends we heard Lamont Cranston and "The Shadow Knows." On weekdays we had Superman, followed by Captain Midnight, and Tom Mix. I hated to miss even one episode of these three. I collected Ovaltine labels and sent away for a secret decoder ring so I could figure out Captain Midnight's secret messages to his fans.

Just before I turned six, my world was jolted by news I heard while listening to that radio. On an April afternoon in 1945, my program was interrupted by the bulletin that President Franklin Roosevelt had died at his winter home in Warm Springs, Georgia.

I rushed into the kitchen to tell the rest of the family. "The President is dead!" I screamed, tears running down my face.

"Oh, stop acting smart, Hinda," said my father. "That's not funny. At all!"

"I'm not being funny. It's true! I wouldn't make up stuff like that! Come into the living room and listen for yourself."

Franklin Roosevelt's sudden demise was the first death I remember knowing about. He had been President so long that my sisters didn't remember anyone else having held that office.

Lyla whined, "What will happen to America now?"

Fedgie worried, "Can we still win the War?"

I got my first civics lesson that afternoon. We were going to have a new President. Automatically when a chief dies, the next guy in line takes over. Vice President Harry S Truman was President now.

Daddy left each weekday morning for work in our only car. On Sundays he drove Mummy to buy supplies from distant stores. Weekdays she walked to neighborhood stores to buy whatever else we needed. I frequently accompanied my mother to the grocery store. Mr. Less, the owner, was generous with his treats.

"Hi honey," he'd say to me with a broad smile and a twinkle, "Would you like some halvah?" He knew my answer. When had I ever turned down halvah?

Halvah, which came plain, marbleized and even chocolate-coated, was the best treat ever, a Middle Eastern candy made from pulverized sesame seeds and sweeteners. I never met a halvah I didn't adore and devour.

"Thank you, Mr. Less. Thank you so much."

Much of what else we needed came right to our door: The milkman delivered almost daily, leaving milk in glass bottles with whole fresh cream floating at the top. Joe, the egg man, delivered dozens of farm fresh eggs every two weeks, collecting his receipts and making change from a bulging scratched leather purse hanging from his belt. The ice man lumbered in periodically with huge chunks of ice for our ice box.

During good weather months, an older gentleman drove his horse-drawn cart up and down the street calling out "Huckster, Huckster." My mother joined the neighbors to pick over and purchase recently harvested produce. Volumes of fruits and vegetables almost weighed down the cart. Mummy let me do some of the choosing. My favorites were deep red cherries in old worn straw baskets. I loved to stick my hand in and grab some, sometimes splashing cherry juice on me and my clothes. In season, there was nothing I liked more than choosing sweet corn from large wooden crates. Their season began in late July or early August with golden corn, transitioning into the yellow and white varieties. Sometimes the huckster even let us hitch a ride on his cart or feed a carrot to his horse.

When I was about eight, and Daddy was away on a trip, Mummy asked me to do a favor.

"Hinda, would you please run upstairs and return this plate to Mrs. Lapides?" she asked. The Lapides family lived in the upstairs apartment of our house.

I returned the plate and waited in the kitchen while Mrs. Lapidus went to get something for Mummy from another room. There in front of me on the counter were some purple candies -- a temptation I couldn't resist. Grape was my favorite flavor of sweets.

I stealthily took a few and put them in my pocket. I hurried out, my task complete. I wanted to share these colorful jellybeans with my pals. The only friend I could find was Davy.

"Hey, I've got candy. Want some?" I asked.

Davy never turned down food, especially sweets.

We went to the park and started eating the candies. They weren't sweet. In fact they were kind of sour.

"Do you like the taste of these?" I asked, feeling a little sick to my stomach.

"No! They're awful," Davy answered. "And I don't feel so good."

We both ran home, throwing up purple glop along the way. Purple stains on my hands and mouth alerted my parents that something awful had happened. I shrieked in pain. They called an ambulance and asked me what I had eaten. Lyla found uneaten pieces in my pocket and gave them to the ambulance driver when they arrived. I was so scared and so sick. Also embarrassed. I vomited all over the nice man who kept me company in the back of the ambulance. I kept apologizing between barfs. I guess he had seen worse because he was nonchalant about it.

At the hospital, despite my vomiting, I had to have my stomach pumped to make sure all that candy was out of my system. Davy got the same treatment. When Mummy and Davy's parents arrived, they stayed with us in a large waiting room. I was glad Daddy was away on a trip and couldn't see me. Davy and I slowly sipped some liquid that would settle our stomachs. We snuck peeks at each other, but we didn't talk. What could we say? Just before we left, the doctors came to tell us that what we had swallowed wasn't candy; it was a prescription for foot fungus. Not candy at all! When we got home Mummy made me go upstairs and apologize to Mrs. Lapidus for stealing. I was crying, and she was very sweet about it, but I knew from the frown on her face that I had disappointed her.

I begged Mum not to tell Daddy when he got home from his business trip, but she said she had to. As always, he came home with a present for each member of the family. Mine, quite by coincidence, was a toy ambulance. I never played with it.

Burt was shocked when he heard I had stolen something. "I can't believe that you would do that!" he said in amazement. "Your parents must have been very angry. You're lucky you got sick so they wouldn't punish you…"

Lucky? No punishment? Let him try having his stomach pumped out!

That incident was one of very few times I did something without Burt. Sometimes your best friend can keep you out of trouble.

When I was eight or nine I began to read the children's books that my sisters had left behind. I couldn't go through them fast enough. Some, like the Jill Drew and Bobsey Twins stories, were too girly for me. I preferred adventure, detective or animal stories. I shared them with Burt, who didn't have older siblings to supply them. Soon we ran out of choices at home and dove into our meager school library. Fortunately, we also had a public library four or five city blocks away.

On the way home from school one day, I asked Burt the question I asked about every two weeks. "Do ya wanna go to the Lincoln Library?" I asked with a hopeful smile.

"Yeah. I'm really ready to get some new books," he'd say. "Let's ask one of our fathers to drive us when he gets home or, hey, do you think we could walk there by ourselves?"

"Let's ask."

With permission, from then on every few weeks Burt and I walked to the Lincoln branch, returned our old loans, browsed through the shelves and finally, reluctantly, made our choices. During the stroll home we discussed what we had chosen that day and what we'd get the next time. Sometimes we borrowed books both of us liked and traded them before they were due.

Burt and I were not only best friends, but protective of one another as well. If someone said something bad about him in my presence, I quickly defended him. I felt sure he did the same for me. As we neared the end of sixth grade, we learned that the school was about to appoint a new Standard Bearer and Daughter-of-the-Flag, choosing the highest achieving boy and girl entering seventh grade for these honors and special duties. Those chosen led all school assemblies in the Pledge of Allegiance. Burt's parents were both American-born. Mine were not, so achieving this patriotic goal may have been more important to me than to him. Even so, I didn't want to be chosen if he wasn't, and vice versa. We pledged eternal friendship even if only one of us got the honor. On the second to the last day of school, we received word that both of us were to be next year's honor attendants! Everyone celebrated on Huntington Park that night.

My neighborhood supplied everything I needed. My best friend lived down the street. I had the lateral park for playing in and riding around on my bike. I went to "The Jungle" for tree-climbing and hide-and-go-seek and to the open lot behind our house for baseball and tag. I was cared for by not only my family, but also by warm neighbors. Anything I needed was either on my street or only a few blocks away -- our school, the library, the synagogue. What more did I need?

A SCHOOLGIRL ON A MISSION

WHEN I turned five and readied to start school, Fedgie and Lyla decided that "Hinda" was just too ethnic a name for me. My parents had named both of them for deceased relatives from the Old Country, Fruma and Leah respectively, but my sisters had been given Anglicized versions of those names at birth. When I was born my parents didn't look for a modern American equivalent of my grandmother's name; I was given it "as is." My sisters selected "Helene" for my school name, and my parents liked the sound of it. I remembered thinking it was neat to have another name. My relatives and most of the neighbors, however, still called me Hinda. I answered to both. Fedgie made a ditty of my names, sing-songing, "Hinda-Helene, Hinda-Helene," and smiling at me, as if it were a joke we shared.

I had always wanted to be something more than my sisters. I wasn't certain what the "more" was, but I wanted to be best at something. No one actually compared me to them or found me unequal to them in any way. I did that myself. The one thing I knew at an early age was that I was smart. Could I become the smartest Rotenberg girl? If I were ever going to catch up to my sisters or perhaps even to surpass them in some way, I suspected that learning a lot of stuff would help me. Therefore, it was with a happy heart and a skip in my step that I prepared to go to school with what no one else had -- an alias.

A week before school began, all the mothers and five-year-olds from my neighborhood were invited to Number Eight School. I picked out my best dress that morning and asked Mummy to take a long time brushing and curling my hair. I wanted to make a good impression. After all, this was the start of my new career, that of a schoolgirl.

Mummy and I walked to school hand in hand, with me just a little ahead of her, actually sort of pulling her along with me. I couldn't wait. Down Huntington we went, turning left on Harris Street and then right onto Avenue B. On the corner, there it stood: an enormous brick two-story school, Carthage School

Number Eight. We entered the building through the Conkey Avenue main entrance and were greeted by two women.

"Hi," I told them. "I'm Helene Rotenberg," trying out my new name on strangers for the first time. "I'm here for Kindergarten training."

Mrs. Evans, who turned out to be the school's principal, looked at me and laughed at my choice of words. "Hello, Helene." Then she turned to my mother and said, "It's so nice to meet you, Mrs. Rotenberg. I don't think we've met before."

"No, we haven't," Mummy answered. "We moved into this neighborhood only three years ago. Our older daughters went to Twenty-two School."

I turned to look at the other woman, a plumpish pink-skinned lady with fluffy white hair, who was smiling. "Welcome, Helene. I'm your teacher, Mrs. Judd," she said, as she pinned a nametag on me. "I know we'll have a good time learning together. Now go down the stairs on the left and you'll find our room at the bottom. I'll be there in just a few minutes after I've greeted all the other children."

Again pulling Mummy, I headed for the stairs. I couldn't wait to see my new room! However, when we got down there, it didn't look like I thought it would. There were no rows of desks and chairs. The only signs that it was a classroom were a few posters on the wall, a chalkboard, and large alphabet letters clipped to a wire circling the room. Some other children and their mothers sat in rows on folding chairs. I waved to kids I knew and stole glances at the ones I didn't. Burt and his mother were already there. He and I grinned at each other.

Once Mrs. Judd arrived with the last of the kids, she explained that our real furniture would be in place before the first day of school. Whew! I hated to think we would have to sit in these chairs all day. Mrs. Judd also talked about what we would be learning. She promised art projects and plays, music lessons and history stories. It sounded pretty good. Time flew by; it felt like only minutes until Mummy and I walked out of the school with Burt and Mrs. Kolko to head back to Huntington Park.

"So what do you think?" I asked him.

"I think I'm going to like it. We're together. That's good."

"I like it already! I can't wait for the first real day!"

On the day school started I raced through breakfast and ran down the street to Burt's house. "Hey, Burt! Ready yet?" I yelled as I knocked on his front door. "Let's go!"

"I'm coming,'" he yelled back and then appeared as the door opened. We both had smiles a mile wide. This was going to be great!

When we got to school, retracing the route we had taken with our mothers the week before, we entered the main door and found our room. We waited in the hallway with the other kids because the door was locked. As we gathered there, we laughed and yelled "hellos" as each one showed up. I knew some of them already, but it didn't matter. My best friend was at my side.

After Mrs. Judd arrived and opened our classroom door, Burt and I walked into our room, looking at each other and nodding an unspoken understanding. We would always go to school together, always learn together, and always be friends. I was almost vibrating in excitement. Mrs. Judd interjected in a soft, but commanding voice, "Children, why don't you all sit down on your mats, and we can begin."

I quickly scanned the room. It was filled with floor mats, long low tables with little chairs, and easels. There were no desks! Oh no! A desk was the very symbol of being a student. If there were no desk for me, maybe I wasn't a real student. How would I ever be like my sisters? I wanted to cry. I looked at Burt with alarm. Was he disappointed, too? He was smiling. Maybe it would be okay. Burt and I found mats next to one another. We sat on them and looked at our teacher in expectation.

The first day began with Mrs. Judd reading us a story. Later we sat in circles on the floor, relearning letters of the alphabet and numbers I already knew. I didn't mind. In mid-morning, Mrs. Judd told us it was naptime. I hadn't taken a nap since I was little. Who still takes naps at five years old? I thought I was all grown up since I went to school! She told us to use one of the multi-colored mats to rest upon. I lay there and tried to guess what we might do next and how long it was going to be until I knew as much as my sisters. I was sure it would take years and years, especially if we had to interrupt the learning for naps!

It took me a while, but I found there were advantages to going to this school, even though I had no desk. Number Eight belonged to me alone. I didn't have to share it with anyone else in my family. Because Fedgie and Lyla had attended a different grade school, my teachers didn't compare me with them at all. At home I was the third girl; in school I was just me.

In first grade, my new teacher, Miss Meyers, helped me perfect my printing in a lined black and white covered notebook. I loved when we began to write and recognize whole words and were soon able to read books, even if there were only a few words on each page. It was a start.

Miss Meyers taught me first and then second grade, too. We discovered math -- first addition, then subtraction. She taught us the times tables as well. Burt and I drilled each other on them walking to and from school until we had them totally memorized.

When I wasn't learning as much as I could, I tried to attract the attention I wished I got at home. One day when we were studying Colonial America and Miss Meyers was talking about some Revolutionary War heroes, like George Washington, I whispered under my breath, just loud enough for those near me to hear, "President Washington said to his horse, 'Hi ho, Silver, awaaaaay!'" The kids who heard covered their mouths to hide their smiles, but I heard their squelched laughter and it made me feel good.

Many times Miss Meyers would hear either my wisecracks or the snickering and stop the lesson. "I'm very disappointed in you, Helene," she said in front of the other kids. "Not only are you not paying attention, but you're keeping the other children from learning."

"I'm sorry, Ma'am," I answered, truly sorry, at least for the moment. I was ashamed when she scolded me for talking out of turn, but I didn't stop doing it. I was proud I could make my classmates laugh. When the next tempting situation arose, I jumped in with a wisecrack. I couldn't help myself. I was willing to risk getting in trouble just to have that fleeting sense that I was someone worth listening to.

My third grade teacher, Mrs. Levy, greeted us every morning with a welcoming smile. She wore variations of the same outfit: a long skirt and an oversized blouse. She had shoulder-length, dark blondish hair parted in the middle and curled under into a page boy style. In my eyes she looked elegant.

Her desk was in the front corner of our room with a chair behind it, but she never sat there. She chose to sit in a low chair in front of the room, putting her head at our level. Sometimes she knelt at our sides to help while we did individual work. I loved everything about her.

One day, she asked us, "Who do you admire the most?"

My classmates chimed in:

"My rabbi."

"The President."

"Teachers."

I answered, "My parents."

After she gave each of us a chance to answer she then asked, "And what do they all have in common?"

"Is it because they're special?" Donny asked.

"Yes, that's it," answered Mrs. Levy. "But in what way are they special?"

Hmm. I thought of something: the people we were mentioning were good people. Is that what they have in common, I wondered?

Mrs. Levy gave us the answer: "The people you mentioned, all of them are really good and decent people."

I was right!

"I want to teach you children to grow up to be like them, to be more than just book-learning smart," she continued. "I want you to be good people as well."

To encourage good behavior, Mrs. Levy explained a reward system. Every Friday after lunch there would be a special ceremony. All well-behaved students would receive a golden felt triangle to pin to their outfits. They could wear them for the entire next week. If you behaved, you would keep it. If you didn't, you had to surrender it at the ceremony the following Friday and go without this badge of distinction for the next week.

I wanted one.

During that next week, each time I itched to whisper something to Burt or pass funny notes to other classmates, I'd catch myself. What if Mrs. Levy hears and doesn't give me a golden badge?

On the first Friday Mrs. Levy called my name to receive the golden badge. I smiled from ear to ear. I felt special, although there were others also rewarded. I wore it home and told my parents what it meant. They congratulated me. I could tell by their smiles they were proud. I wore my badge pinned to whatever I was wearing every day, including on the weekend. I stopped in front of every mirror I passed to see myself reflected wearing that gold badge.

The next week at school, even with the triangle as incentive, I just couldn't stop myself from making jokes and talking out of turn.

During the badge ceremony, Mrs. Levy announced that some students no longer deserved to wear a golden badge. She called the names one by one of those who had to relinquish them. Suddenly I heard, "Helene, please come forward and turn in your triangle."

No! My heart sank. Stunned, I walked slowly to the front of the room, my head lowered, feeling the eyes of my classmates on me. My hands shook as I unpinned my badge and placed it on her desk. She said, "Thank you, Helene. I hope you will do better next week."

I couldn't look at her or my classmates either. I raced back to my desk, crossed my arms on it and buried my burning hot face in them. I lost my special honor, and, when I got home, I would have to tell my parents. I was pained, but I knew deep down inside that I had brought this shame on myself. The ceremony finally ended and we went on to do some arithmetic review.

Near the end of that day, Mrs. Levy stopped by my desk and softly asked me to remain in the classroom after everyone left. My heart beat a little faster. Maybe she changed her mind about taking back the golden badge?

The final bell rang. I sat at my desk and didn't move. As I slumped at my desk, Mrs. Levy knelt beside me and hugged me hard. "Helene, what happened?" she whispered. "I know you're disappointed, but I am, too."

I broke into tears. She hadn't changed her mind. I sniffed in my tears and confessed, "I'm so very sorry, Mrs. Levy. I promise I'll be good from now on."

"I know you will." Mrs. Levy held me until my tears stopped. "You know, Helene, you're an exceptional young lady, but you have to learn to listen and respect rules. Don't always try to be the center of attention." I nodded, but was too choked up to talk.

When I got home I explained my situation to my parents and got through the next week without my beloved badge of honor. I hardly ever looked in the mirror that week.

I tried hard to remember what Mrs. Levy told me. I was less of a wise guy and more of an obedient student. Once I even saw her wink at me! She noticed that I was on my best behavior. I won my triangle back the next week, never to relinquish it the rest of the year. I wanted to please Mrs. Levy, not only because of the badge, but because I admired her and yearned for her approval.

Fourth grade brought Miss Burns, a short, thin woman whose gray hair made her look ancient, and with her also came learning to write in cursive, using pens and inkwells, reading chapter books, and being challenged with more complicated math and science.

Miss Burns didn't use golden triangles to encourage good behavior. She used a good story. If every single one of us was well-behaved during the day's lessons, she would stop regular lessons at 2:45 pm, 15 minutes before afternoon dismissal, and read to us.

Towards the end of each school day I watched the clock on the front wall, muttering to myself, "Only ten more minutes. Eight more. Five." I listened to every click of that clock. It seemed to slow down as we waited for our lessons to end and the magic of stories to begin.

On the days we were all obedient, we sat silently with our hands folded atop our desks while Miss Burns read from books about adventures, fantasies and exploration. My favorite book that year was *Nobody's Boy*. Remi, the subject of the book, is a young French boy who is tossed from one home and one place to another. I waited through each school day, anxious to hear about his latest adventure.

On days when someone misbehaved, and we lost the privilege of being read to, we let the offender know that we didn't appreciate being punished for his or her actions. We'd shoot them "dagger looks" or give them the silent treatment. I was ruthless with anyone who stole that pleasure from me: "Why'd ya have to be such a clown? Because of stupid you, I have to wait a whole 'nother day to find out what happens!" In one year I had gone from the girl who had acted out all the time to the one who expected everyone else to behave.

Every year, each grade level was in charge of presenting a school-wide assembly for schoolmates as well as their parents and grandparents. In the lower grades, we sang songs and students who could dance, baton twirl or play an instrument performed. I usually sang with the class or recited a poem I had memorized. But in fourth through seventh grades, we were expected to prepare something more artistic.

I knew that many of the previous fourth grades had put on a play. Miss Burns had an idea. She told us, "You're a very creative class. I think it would be a good idea for you to write an original play to perform."

While many of my classmates moaned and groaned, I loved the challenge and was eager to try. Miss Burns divided us into small groups to discuss what we could do. In my group, no one spoke for a while. Suddenly I had an inspiration: "What if we take an event from history, something we know something about but not everything? We could make up what might have been said and done."

"I don't get it," Marsha said.

The idea wasn't perfectly formed in my head, but I thought fast. "Well," I

said, improvising as I spoke, "there are many historical events we've studied." I
paused. "Maybe we could write about Betsy Ross sewing the first flag, or what
it was like when they wrote the Declaration of Independence. What do you
think?"

"It might be fun to put our words in Washington's mouth," laughed Donny.

"Or in Jefferson's," added Brenda.

Miss Burns listened to suggestions from each of the planning groups. She
liked the Betsy Ross idea and I was put in charge of the writing team. A lot of
my ideas and my words made it into the final script, but I always put in dialogue
invented by my classmates so they wouldn't resent me.

I wanted to play Betsy, but casting the play was a group decision. How could
I get them to choose me? I had already memorized most of the lines, having
written many of them myself. Thank goodness when it came time to cast roles,
my classmates seemed to think I would be perfect. We agreed on a final script
and casting, followed by two weeks of rehearsals. We scrounged the school's
wardrobe room and our closets at home for costumes. The only outside prop we
needed was an original thirteen star American flag.

We presented our play on a Friday morning in February, just before a school
holiday for George Washington's birthday – how appropriate! The other classes
applauded, but our visiting relatives clapped the loudest. My mother, who knew
little early American history, told me, "I'm very proud that my 100% American
daughter could create such a play!"

That first play I wrote led to others in fifth, sixth and seventh grades, and I
also wrote skits for Sunday school. I wrote about many subjects, but I was sometimes uneasy when I wrote about Plymouth Rock, the American Revolution, or
Gettysburg. My ancestors didn't come here with the Pilgrims. They didn't fight
in the Revolution or the Civil War. I forced myself to remember that I was an
American and this *was* my history. As I pretended to be these characters from
history, I began feeling more authenticity, "more red, white and blue."

Through these years of grade school, Burt and I would walk home to
Huntington Park noontime to have lunch with our mothers. My lunch was
usually a sandwich, but in wintertime, it was accompanied by a bowl of soup,
usually tomato. For winter my parents always bought me two snowsuits, usually
one navy and the other dark green. When I came home for lunch and removed

the one I wore to school that morning, it went onto the radiator in the kitchen to dry so that I could use it after school to play.

Mum and I didn't talk much during lunchtime. We listened to the radio which, after a short news break by Al Sigl, ran 15-minute serial dramas. I remember "Our Gal Sunday" and "The Romance of Helen Trent." These lunchtime programs illustrated the lives of young women, trying to make something of themselves in the world and their best solution always seemed to be to become someone's wife. My mum and the mothers of my friends had realized their goal of doing exactly the same thing. I didn't question their lack of ambition to become anything else until 1949 when Mrs. Clark, my fifth grade teacher, expanded my thinking.

She called us to attention one morning, saying "Today we're going to talk about what you'd like to be when you grow up. Later, we'll do research on how you can achieve your goals." She went around the room and asked, "What would you like to be someday?"

I thought about it. My mother was a wife and a mother. The ladies on the radio were trying to become wives. Fedgie was married and Lyla was going steady with a high school boyfriend. I thought that was my future, too. When Mrs. Clark called on me, I answered, "When I grow up I want to be married."

"That's not a proper answer, Helene" Mrs. Clark asserted, scowling a bit.

"It isn't?" I was embarrassed to have given a wrong answer and sank down in my seat.

"No," she said, "you have to pick a *real* profession, a job you get paid to do, something you think you'd be good at and also, hopefully, something you'd enjoy."

I thought about what she said. I puzzled over another response while my classmates offered their ideas such as teaching, fighting fires, nursing, working with animals, and other jobs. Mrs. Clark had said something I'd enjoy, something I thought I was good at, and something "professional."

I raised my hand again, and Mrs. Clark called on me a second time.

"I want to be a writer," I stated firmly, "a really great writer."

She smiled. "That's a good goal, Helene."

I wasn't clear what I would write. I had already written plays, but maybe I could also write poetry or short stories. Even a novel. Just as long as it was something special, something that everyone would read and admire. How I would go about becoming a writer was unclear though.

For inspiration, I decided to read books written by women writers. I had loved *Black Beauty* by Anna Sewell and *Little Women* by Louisa May Alcott. And Helen Keller! If she could write a marvelous book while both blind and deaf, what would be my excuse for not doing so? I had a direction. I was going to be writer.

Everyone would know my name.

Sixth grade brought Burt and me to Mrs. Mindell, who taught us the prescribed curriculum and more. She was different from earlier teachers. Sometimes, if she saw we were getting antsy and needed a break, she would take us out of the classroom into the hallways to dance. On other days she insisted we memorize funny obscure poems or sing French songs. What endeared her to us most was when she told us what to do when unexpected company arrived at our house. "Take every dirty dish, pot, pan, dish towel, whatever and put them into your oven and shut the door. No one ever looks there," she said.

We giggled. Who wouldn't love a teacher like that?

That year Burt and I were cast in a play together. As he came onto the stage into what was supposed to be my parlor, I was to ask him to hold a skein of wool between his hands as I wound it into a ball. Everything went well in dress rehearsal, but during the actual performance, I couldn't find the yarn. I recited the lines which came before the wool-winding dialogue and quickly thought ahead. With a little wink to Burt, I skipped two pages of dialogue and gave him the cue for the line he was supposed to say after the wool was rolled. He picked up my cue and went on with the rest of the scene.

When the curtain came down, Mrs. Mindell came up to me, with a look of bewilderment on her face. "Why did you skip ahead and leave out lines?" She didn't seem angry, just confused.

"I couldn't find the wool and that conversation would have made no sense without it."

"So you just left out that part?" She smiled from ear to ear.

"Yep."

"I should have known you would have a good reason," she said. "Good girl. That was the right thing to do. And Burt was quick to catch on, too."

Mrs. Mindell thought I was a genius, even if the audience of students, teachers and parents got a much shortened version of *The Courtship of Miles Standish*.

At Number Eight School, for as long as anyone could remember, your choice of teachers for seventh grade was Miss L. or Miss M, the Rausch sisters. Their classrooms were across the hall from one another. Burt and I got Miss M.

She was somewhat of a letdown after the zaniness of Mrs. Mindell, but she helped us develop good skills as we looked ahead to high school. She gave us homework for the first time: research papers, essays, take-home tests.

The biggest change that year was as the result of my being in the right place at the right time. My classmates and I frequently gathered at someone's house for a party. What we called a party was enjoying soft drinks and popcorn, listening to records and trying to master dancing. On one particular night, I was sitting out a dance on the arm of a soft chair. My friend Audrey was sitting in the chair itself and as she leaned forward and her white buttoned shirt fell away from her body, I saw an amazing sight!

I leaned down and in a hoarse whisper in her ear asked, "Are you wearing a bra?"

She grinned and nodded.

If she had one, I had to have one, despite no visible signs of my needing one. When I got home I insisted that Mummy take me downtown to buy me a bra. To her credit she didn't laugh. We went downtown to one of the major department stores, McCurdy's. Mummy put me in the hands of a tender-hearted saleswoman who had been through this before with other 12 year olds. I practically walked on air out of the store with my first bra, a size zero. It was a start.

One morning that year, as I came into the kitchen to eat breakfast, Daddy turned to me with a smile.

"I figured out a great job for you when you grow up!" He was so excited, he almost yelled. "You should be a foreign correspondent!" My parents had known that my fifth grade teacher had started me thinking about a career in writing.

My face fell.

Daddy saw my reaction. "What's wrong?"

"Why would you want me to do that?" I asked with a tremor in my voice.

"Hinda, think about it. You love to write and you love adventure. This woman who your mother and I heard last night... she was so excited about her work." They had gone to a lecture by a nationally known newspaper woman. "I don't understand. I thought you liked to write."

"Oh yes, I do. I love it. But I don't want to do it far, far away! "

Daddy understood. "Oh dear one, I didn't mean the 'foreign' part. I guess I used the words together because I heard them together. I meant the 'correspondent' part, you know, being a reporter and having your name attached to every story you write. You'd like that, wouldn't you?"

"Oh yes, Daddy. I'd love to be famous. But only if it means not being far away from family."

In high school I continued to write. To encourage me my parents read almost everything I wrote, every essay, every short story, every article for the school newspaper. In 1955, when I was 16, I worked half-days in the office of my father's furniture store during the summer, answering phones and keeping the accounts. Every afternoon, we listened to a particular radio station.

One day the disc jockey talked about the new movie *High Society* and announced a contest for the best promo of 25-words or less. "Hey, writer," Daddy yelled from across the showroom in a bantering tone. "Why don't you enter this contest? I bet you can win it."

I smiled. "Well, I could try." I sat down right then and there and composed my entry: "With Grace Kelly, Bing Crosby, Frank Sinatra and Louis Armstrong, how can this movie fail to entertain and satisfy the public?" I send it in to the radio station immediately, without even reading it to Daddy first.

Two weeks later my name was announced as the winner and a week after that I was sent the long-playing record of the soundtrack. The prize was nice, but my father's swelled chest and huge smile were even better. Every time I played that record I remembered the warm feeling of being recognized as a writer.

I wasn't like Fedgie, and I wasn't like Lyla. No, I was the one who could write well, the one who might eventually get the best education, the highest degree, the most important job.

EVERY SWING OF THE BAT

IN the spring of 1948, when I was in third grade, a representative from our local baseball team came into our classroom. He explained a little bit about our local baseball team and told us that when our Rochester players got more experienced, they would go "up" to the major leagues, in our case to the St. Louis Cardinals. Our team was known as Red Wings because it was another way of describing a cardinal. This man explained that there was a special program for school children called the Knot Hole Gang. If we joined, we could see many games for a total of only one dollar. The words "Knot Hole," we learned, meant openings in wooden fences formed from knots in the wood through which anyone could spy on the other side. Our Knot Hole experience, however, would bring us into the ballpark to where the action was. We could see real professional baseball for the first time!

On our way walking home that day, Burt and I talked about our Red Wing visitor and what he said.

"Well, what do you say?" I asked him. "Do ya wanna sign up?"

"Are you kidding? Of course I'll sign up, but ha-ha, you can't 'cause you're a girl!"

"Wanna bet?" I challenged him. The Knot Hole Gang was originally formed for boys only, but girls were now welcome. "Ha-ha yourself! You didn't listen hard enough. I can too sign up," I said, defiantly.

His face lit up as he confessed, "I woulda felt so bad if we didn't go together."

With joyous anticipation, we brought in our money and signed up for the Knot Hole pass. We could now go to ten Knot Hole-designated day games at Red Wing Stadium for free!

It was the custom in those days that all city public schools closed at noon before the first Knot Hole game so that any kid who wanted to go wouldn't have to miss it. As an exception to our usual attire, we were allowed to wear play clothes to school that day: shorts and tee shirts if it was warm enough, dungarees and sweaters if it was still cool - and we carried mitts, if we had them, and sported Red Wings ball caps. No dress for me – yay!

School buses lined up near the doors of the school waiting to take us to the ball park. Although they took us to the game, parents were responsible for getting us back home. Burt and I wanted to walk home after the game and our parents gave us permission. From Red Wing Stadium to Huntington Park was a distance of less than two miles.

It was hard to concentrate on lessons that first Knot Hole day. All I could think about was The Game. Finally the bell rang for lunch, releasing us from school. Burt and I ran and literally jumped on the bus, sitting together and grinning at each other, anticipating the adventure ahead. In less than 20 minutes we arrived at Red Wing Stadium.

Once we showed our Knot Hole passes and pushed through the turnstiles, aromas from the grills and popcorn machines overwhelmed us. We ran past the food vendors, squeezing past grown-ups to get to the bleachers near left field where Knot Hole kids were supposed to sit. We didn't mind sitting on benches even in the blazing sun. We thought that we had the best view of the stadium and we could see the players to the best advantage. We looked out onto the playing field. It was huge. The fences, covered with advertising slogans from local businesses, seemed miles away. Over them, we could see the large industrial buildings which ringed the neighborhood.

"When do they start the game?" I asked our group leader, one of the teachers from school.

"Not for a while, Helene, but soon they'll come out to do warm-ups and maybe even take batting practice," she answered.

I was stunned. "They have to *practice*?"

She smiled. "Helene, if you ever want to be really good at something, you have to practice. Just like homework from school which helps you to know your subjects better."

I never thought of that. I had heard on the radio that our team this year was better than any other previous Red Wing team. Hmmm. As great as they were, even the best players had to practice. Playing sports was more than just natural talent.

When the players took the field for warm-ups, there were only about 400 people in the 10,000 seat stadium. Our rousing cheers were so loud that the players looked over at us, smiled broadly and waved. We grinned and waved back.

The Red Wing players threw the ball around the bases, then from the outfield into the infield. One of the coaches hit balls to the different base players to simulate grounders. After fifteen minutes or so, the other team took the field and went through the same routine.

We ate our lunch while we waited for the real game to begin. My classmates, except for Burt, me and a few other Jewish kids, went into the concourse to get hot dogs from the concession stand. Ballpark hot dogs weren't kosher so our mothers had packed lunch for us, crackers, bananas and peanut butter & jelly sandwiches. We bought lemonade, popcorn and, before the game was over, ice cream scoops for dessert.

I watched all the players, but I paid special attention to the big hitters, Russ Derry and Steve Bilko. My eyes were even more focused on Eddie Kazak, the shortstop. He positioned himself between second and third base, and it seemed that most infield hits went in his direction. He also caught many, if not most, of the pop-ups. To me, Eddie was the most involved, most important person on the entire field. There was no doubt which position I wanted to play from then on. Hinda Helene in the middle of the action. I liked the sound of that!

Once it began, the game seemed to whoosh by. Before we realized it, the seventh inning break arrived and we stood to sing "Take me out to the Ball Game." Burt and I had our arms around each other's shoulders and swayed in time to the music. Within a half hour, the whole game was over, a win – hurray! – for the Red Wings.

Burt and I rehashed the game on our walk home, oblivious to everything around us.

Remembering a big play, I asked, "Did you see how Bilko got under that fly ball? He was practically running all the way out to right field. I thought he was going to hit the fence."

Burt said, "Yeah, but what about Hal Rice? He almost hit for the cycle![5]" We were so proud we knew baseball lingo.

A few blocks later, I'd add, "You know, Ray Yochim was throwing cheddar[6] until they took him out. I was happy to see him pitch for us, but he sure did have a bad day."

---

[5] A batter hits, in any order, a single, double, triple and home run in the same game

[6] Easy to hit pitches

This had been real baseball, not the made-up game we played on the lot behind my house. There were rules about how many players, how many strikes, balls, outs and innings. There were definite positions and specific jobs for each player. We had watched and we had learned. It didn't take us long to learn how to read the scoreboard, what symbols we would use to fill out a scorecard during a game, or what a crooked number[7] was. After that first Knot Hole game we pretended to be the players we saw.

"Going back, back, back and I've got it. What a can of corn![8] Yowee!" Burt always saw himself as an outfielder, catching long flies and directing action from center field. He also sometimes pretended to be the play-by-play announcer: "And Rotenberg throws to first and catches the runner off base. Heeeeeee's out!"

Burt and I hardly finished rehashing the game and sharing our fantasies before we arrived home to Huntington Park, eagerly awaiting our next outing.

---

[7] Any number larger than 1

[8] Easy catch

HIYA G-D

"**WHAT'S** this?" I was four or five and walking out of the door to play with the neighborhood boys. For the first time I noticed a metal cylinder about five inches long attached near the top of the doorpost.

Mummy was nearby and heard me. "That's our *mezuzah*." She came to stand in the doorway with me.

I tried out the word: "Meh-zoo-zah." I liked the feeling it made in my mouth when I said it. "What's it for? What does it do? Why is it there?"

Mummy chuckled at my questions and was eager to explain. "If you sit down for a minute, I'll tell you." I sat. "Every Jewish home has a *mezuzah* on its outside doorpost to remind us that we are G-d's people," she said, as I listened intently. "Many people kiss their fingertips and touch it when they leave or come back."

"Really? And every Jewish home has one?"

"Yes. Every one."

"Wow." Somehow that didn't seem enough of an explanation.

"You'll learn much more about the *mezuzah* when you start Sunday school."

When I went to visit people I thought about what Mummy had told me and started paying attention to their doorposts. Burt's house had one on every outside door and even on some inside doors. Steven's house had them. So did Davy's.

Our *mezuzah* was too high up for me to touch, but I starting waving to it as I walked by. Maybe G-d liked "hiya" waves as much as kisses.

When I was a few years older, I learned that the *mezuzah* casing wasn't the important part. Inside was a special handwritten Hebrew scroll with words from the central prayer of Judaism: "Hear, O Israel, the Lord is our G-d, the Lord is One." It was the same short prayer I was taught to say in Hebrew every night before I went to bed. The *mezuzah* also contained the part of the Torah that Jews recite in all services: "You shall love G-d with all your heart, with all your soul and with all your strength...."

Being Jewish was something I didn't have to think about -- it was my family, my neighborhood, my heritage. As the child of immigrant Americans, I couldn't always relate to histories of Bunker Hill or Gettysburg, but I got deep meaning from our unique Jewish customs.

When I was about nine or ten I even developed my own relationship with G-d. One evening after dinner Mummy told me she and Daddy had someplace to go.

"How would you feel about staying alone for an hour or so? The Lapiduses are right upstairs if you need anything."

She let me think about it for a minute.

"Oh sure," I told them. "Go ahead. I'll be fine." I was a Big Girl, capital B, capital G. I got into my jammies and settled myself in my bed with the radio on and a book on my lap. Until that year, if my parents went out, one of my sisters was always there. Now one of them was married and the other in college. There was only me.

The first five minutes after I heard the door close and the car pull out of the driveway, I was fine. Ditto the next ten. But over the next half hour, I became uneasy – then scared – then terrified. I was even too frightened to leave my bed, even to walk down the hall and go up the stairs to the Lapiduses.

I hated being alone. I thought and thought about what to do and the answer came in a flash – of course! I could ask G-d to keep me company, G-d who I had been taught was always there for us if we were ever in need. I was a good little Jewish girl, attending Hebrew school and Sunday school and also going to Shabbat services on Saturdays. But I had never before seriously thought of G-d Almighty as a companion.

I considered what I should do. Should I pray? I didn't know a prayer for asking for company. I decided just to say in my own words what I was feeling. Out of respect for G-d, I sat up in bed.

"Hello, G-d. I hope you're listening. Hi. I'm a pretty good girl and I thought I was a brave girl, too, but I'm all alone and scared. Could you, would you, uh, if you have time, I mean, keep me company? Please?"

I lay down and waited for something to happen. At first I didn't sense anything. Then, slowly, I began to feel very calm, like I knew that nothing bad was going to happen to me. Was G-d giving me that feeling? I didn't know, but I thought so. I just started feeling better and better.

I sat up again in my bed and whispered, "Thanks, G-d."

The next morning my parents told me that when they came home, they looked in on me. They said I was cuddled up in my blankets, sound asleep, with a smile on my face. I never shared with them what had happened when they left me alone and how I coped. But I was never again afraid of being left home alone. I knew I wouldn't really be alone.

The only grandparents I knew were my mother's parents, Bubbie and Zaide Ackerman. I considered them ancient, although they were probably only in their fifties or early sixties when I was born. Zaide always wore a suit, dress shirt and tie; Bubbie wore stockings and cotton house dresses with buttons from hem to neck. No makeup. They both had on orthopedic shoes.

Although they sometimes babysat when my parents were away, they didn't play with me. Bubbie and Zaide spoke very little English, and we didn't speak their languages: Yiddish, Polish, Russian and Ukrainian. Conversations between us were acted out in pantomime.

Zaide's love for our family shone forth from his every pore, the way he looked at us, and the way he followed me especially from room to room when he came to visit. He didn't care if I was reading, putting together a jigsaw puzzle, or practicing piano. I think that I was giving him back the years he had missed with my mother and Aunt Min when he was in America and they were stuck in the Ukraine. Zaide almost never came to see us without some trinket he had found or bought: a "not real gold" ring, a plastic yo-yo, an almost new ball. His eyes gleamed as he presented his gifts.

"Hindele," (little Hinda) he'd say, "Ikh hob dikh lib (I love you)."

"A dank deer (thank you), Zaide," I'd respond as I hugged him tight. He'd hug me back and hold on just a second longer than I did.

One year near the time we celebrate Passover I thought of something I thought might please him. As the youngest child, I was given the responsibility to ask the Four Questions at the Seder.[9] I asked Mummy if she would teach me how to ask them in Yiddish. I'll never forget Zaide's shocked but smiling face as I rose and turned to him, saying *"Zeide, ich vil de fregen der Feir Kashes* (I want to ask the Four Questions.)

---

[9] The Four Questions, which appear at the start of the Seder ask: Why do we eat only matzah? Why do we eat bitter herbs? Why do we dip vegetables twice in salt water? And why do we recline as we eat? The answers, which also answer the question why this night of Seder is different from all other nights, make up the rest of the formal recitation.

One April Sunday, when I was a month short of my twelfth birthday, the phone rang during lunch. Mummy answered the phone and began sobbing. Someone from a hospital told her that Zaide was there. A Good Samaritan had found him lying in the street near his apartment and called an ambulance. My parents rushed to pick up Bubbie and Aunt Min and dashed to the hospital, but they arrived too late. It hurt me terribly that Zaide, that sweet and loving man, was alone and not with his dear, dear family when he died. I missed him so much. I wanted to hug and kiss him once more and tell him how much I loved him.

As I was not quite 12, I wasn't allowed to go to his funeral. Besides, someone had to stay home with Fedg, then in her eighth month of pregnancy. She wasn't allowed to go for superstitious reasons, bringing the Evil Eye on her unborn baby or some such nonsense. Fedgie and I spent the time sharing memories of Zaide and celebrating his life in our own way.

The proximity of new life in our family following a death was transforming. Until that time I never thought about the fact that no one, not even me, lives forever. I thought about the impact such a modest man like Zaide had made on the world. What impact would I make?

I always wanted people to like me. I wanted people to smile when they thought about me. But, most of all, I wanted to make a difference in the world. My young ego wished that when I died, it would be a great loss to those who knew me. I wanted people I didn't even know to mourn me. My ego was boundless; I just had to make something worthwhile of my life.

For the next few months Bubbie came to live with us. She was not a happy woman, usually sour-faced and full of complaints. I didn't like being around her very much, and I was ashamed that I didn't.

However, one afternoon during the time she was staying with us, I was playing jacks on the living room floor and she sat on the couch watching me. She and I were the only ones home. I decided to try to develop some positive connection with her.

"Bubbie," I asked, "Do you have a middle name?" I don't know what inspired me to ask this question as I myself had never been given one. It took a lot of pantomime and acting out until she finally seemed to understand what I was asking.

"Yah," she answered, smiling. That smile in itself was a gift. "Me nomen Sarah Shprinze."

"Shprinze? (sh'prin-tzah)"

"Yah."

"Shprinze?" I began to roll on the floor with uncontrolled laughter. It was the funniest name I'd ever heard. Bubbie was at first was shocked by my gales of laughter, but after a few minutes, when I just couldn't stop, she joined in. It was wonderful to share laughter with her.

When my parents came home, they found us sitting side-by-side on the couch, looking through old photo albums. That was the closest we had ever been, physically and emotionally. We had another Bubbie-and-me experience the next year when I got the mumps. Each time Bubbie came into the bedroom to see me, she'd go through the same routine: she'd sit at the foot of the bed and stare at me until she knew she had my attention. Then she'd puff out her cheeks with air, as if in imitation of what I looked like. It always made me laugh and softened my feelings for her just a bit.

Bubbie went back to her own apartment for a few years, but eventually she became too frail to live alone. Her last five or six years were spent in progressively intense levels of care in an old-age home. I watched her make my mother's and Aunt Min's lives pretty miserable with demands and dissatisfactions about everything.

"Dis food, feh!," she said, indicating her displeasure.

Mum or Aunt Min would then bring her homemade food.

"Mine-a tochters, (my daughters) ich lieb (I like) gansa (a lot of) chicken mit (with) skin (or without) skin" whichever was the opposite of whatever they brought. She would not be satisfied. Mummy cried almost every time she came home from visiting Bubbie. When she eventually died, I found I couldn't mourn her. I was relieved. At least now she wouldn't hurt Mummy any more.

Forty years later when my daughter Caralyn delivered her first child, she asked what I wanted her daughter to call me. Instantly I said, "Bubbie."

My sister Lyla couldn't believe it. "Why would you choose that name when memories of our own Bubbie are so negative?"

I was adamant. "That name needs redemption."

While Daddy's immediate family stayed in Poland, many first cousins immigrated to Canada. Our family made pilgrimages two or three times a year to visit them in Toronto.

We always stayed with Daddy's first cousin on his mother's side, Dubra

Goldhar, who had fled Poland after Daddy, but, thank G-d, before the Second World War broke out. She was more like an aunt than a cousin to me. She had lost brothers and sisters during the Holocaust, except for one surviving brother who also lived in Toronto with his family. Daddy and Dubra were very much like siblings, into each other's business all the time, but warm, loving and accepting of each other most of the time. She was a very large-bodied woman who was always, but always, jolly. She managed to hug me not just when I came and left, but whenever she was near me. I loved those hugs. I was enfolded inside her meaty arms, held up against her very ample chest and heard cooing murmurs in my ear. Then she kissed my face about a dozen times. I didn't know which I loved more, the attention she gave me or the food she served. She was an outstanding cook and her delicious meals and scrumptious desserts were a gift to those she loved. Dubra's husband, Moishe, was a small quiet man, sweet and gentle, with not much to say to little children, but he looked at us with shining eyes. We knew he loved us.

My parents spoke mostly Yiddish with Dubra, Moishe and Dubra's brother Duvid Eisen and his wife, Chavela. The Goldhars and the Eisens emigrated as grown, married adults, unlike my father who had come in his teens. They were less fluent in English than Daddy, and their Polish/Yiddish accents were very strong. They revered my parents, called them "The Americans" as if that were a great honor. Even after twenty-some years in Canada, the Goldhars and Eisens had remained more "green," much more like new immigrants than citizens of the New World.

My Canadian family loved me just because I was "Hartzke's *tochter*," Herb's daughter. I didn't have to do anything to win their approval except breathe and show up. Most of my memories of Toronto start and end with food. The wafting aromas of brisket, *tzimmes, knaidlach, and kishke*[10] emanating as we walked in the Goldhar's door reminded us of our traditional Eastern European Jewish heritage. Dubra prided herself on being able to make all Old World recipes superbly.

My father had many good qualities and talents and I loved him dearly, but, unfortunately, he was a dreadful driver. I hated to go any major distance in a vehicle he was driving. I was generally okay with city driving, but those trips to Toronto were awful. Daddy never kept even pressure on the accelerator so there was constant jerking back and forth of the car. Within an hour of leaving Rochester, I was so nauseous that I begged Daddy to pull over on the highway

---

[10] Baked carrot pudding, matzah balls and stuffed intestine

and let me out so that I could heave up breakfast. I usually arrived at the Goldhars both very hungry and very cranky.

With a stomach empty from misadventures on the road, I was always ready to eat everything put on my plate. However, I couldn't let myself eat too much because after dinner I had to perform.

As a little girl, listening with my sisters to records of Big Bands and popular singers, I fell in love with the voice of Al Jolson, especially when the movie *The Jolson Story* came out and I could relive his life on the big screen. I knew all of his hits, but my favorite one was "April Showers." I liked the lyrics which express the idea that after something bad happens (rain,) something good could come of it (flowers.) After dinner at the Goldhars, I was always asked to perform my rendition of "April Showers" along with original dance steps and hand gestures.

The family sat around the living room, on the sofa, chairs and ottomans, my young cousins on the floor, in expectation for this twice-yearly performance. I faced them and began to sing.

"When April showers," gesturing the rain coming down, "may come your way, they bring the flowers that bloom in May," pantomiming picking them. The part I liked best was towards the end. "So keep on looking for the bluebird," my hand flat across my eyebrows, looking from side to side like a sailor, "and listening for his song," cupping my ear, "whenever April showers come along." Applause, applause from my faithful family audience. I must have done that number twice a year every year until they or I thought enough was enough.

Before we left Toronto we always visited one of the many Jewish bakeries. Many Polish Jews had settled in Toronto so there were constant customers for the tastes of "back home." Whatever else we bought, our purchases always included blueberry muffins. No bakery in Rochester, Jewish or secular, produced anything like them!

While in Toronto for a weekend, we also visited Daddy's relatives on his father's side, our cousins Max and Sarah Rotenberg. Max's father, Luzar, and Daddy's father, Yehudah, had been brothers. It was to Uncle Luzar's house that Daddy had come when he first arrived in Toronto when he fled Poland. Max was at least 15 years older than my father so he knew some Rotenberg family history which Daddy didn't know because he was so much younger. It was literally at Max's feet that I learned more about life in Ivansk, about my grandparents and Daddy's brothers and sisters. Many years later I interviewed my father about his early years. After he shared what he remembered, I was able to tell him some of what I had learned from Cousin Max.

Max had told me that his Uncle Yehudah, my grandfather, was a religious, wise, and prosperous man. He said merchants in Ivansk, both Jewish and Christian, came to his uncle for advice and that he was the unofficial mayor of the town. Many years later I found among my father's possessions an oil painting of my grandfather's headstone which had been sent to Daddy. The monument appears impressive, surely evidence of the family's wealth and power. Framed, this artistic legacy hangs in my front foyer.

My grandfather impressed his children, my father included, with family pride. Although Daddy left home forever at age 18, he reflected the strong values of that ancestral household, values such as honesty, friendship, education, and loyalty, and the importance of family. Daddy was extremely proud of his good name and reputation and raised us to value our own.

Being part of my family made being Jewish instinctive, like throwing a baseball up in the air and catching it easily on its way down. The traditions of Judaism pervaded my house from front door to the rear. They were also with me in the food I ate, at the synagogue nearby, playing, studying, learning, growing.

We kept a kosher home, keeping meat and dairy foods separate from one another. It didn't feel unusual to me. Burt's, Steven's, Davy's families all kept kosher homes as well. We had two sets of dishes, silverware, pots and pans, as well as two additional sets for the eight days of Passover. We weren't allowed to eat pork, shrimp, lobster or other shellfish. We ate only kosher cuts of animals raised and slaughtered according to centuries-old specifications. Before setting the table, I always asked Mummy what we were having for dinner so I used the correct plates and silverware.

Because our level of *kashruth* (keeping kosher) was strict, visiting rabbis and other dignitaries could come to our home for food and housing without worrying about being exposed to anything *treyf* (not kosher). I was proud that we were so observant. I felt that by keeping kosher, I was really showing that I loved G-d with my heart, my soul and my whole body.

Many times, especially before I started going to school, I walked with my mother hand-in-hand to Strassman's Meat Market two blocks away to get fresh chickens, one for the Friday night soup and one for roasting. Both chickens were plucked, cleaned and ready to use, the fattier soup meat already cut into pieces to fit into our soup pot. What made our soup especially delicious was that it included the chicken's feet and any raw eggs the chicken hadn't laid. Who would get a foot? There were, after all, only two and they were juicy to suck on. Who would get an egg? I usually got at least one. There were definite advantages in being the baby of the family!

It made sense that I grew to love baseball and Judaism at the same time; to me they were neighbors. Our house on Huntington Park backed up to an empty lot which the neighborhood kids had turned into a giant baseball field. Beyond it were a set of rickety stairs leading to the parking lot of our synagogue, Beth Joseph Center, which was on St. Paul Street.

I loved learning to read and write Hebrew. It's a language with a unique alphabet, and it was like cracking code to figure out the words. On Saturdays I went to religious services in the basement of my synagogue with friends my age, the junior congregation. One of the oldest boys, usually someone 14 or 15, led the service, but we were all expected to take part by reading some prayers aloud.

Sunday school reinforced what I already had learned at home about the Bible, the history of the Jewish people and a love of Israel. It always ended with a school-wide assembly and the singing of both the Star-Spangled Banner and *Hatikvah* (the Hope), the Zionist anthem. *Hatikvah* spoke of an intense yearning for a Jewish homeland.

In 1948, after the State of Israel was created, some of the words to *Hatikvah* were changed to reflect the creation of that homeland. The first time we sang the new version, Burt was standing next to me at the assembly. We exchanged glances, then grabbed each other's hands.

"I have chills," I said, trembling.

Burt squeezed my hand. "Let's go there together, okay?"

"Okay."

"Promise?"

"I promise."

The creation of the Jewish state occurred only a few years after six million Jews were killed during World War Two simply because they were Jews. Even at nine years old I understood the difference it made to me as a Jew that there was a place where Jews could not be forced to leave or to die.

For most of my early years, both of my parents were active in our synagogue,

Beth Joseph Center. If Daddy wasn't at his furniture store or at home, we knew to reach him at Beth Joseph. Mummy went to every Sisterhood meeting and prepared food and baked goods whenever they were needed. How proud I was to be their daughter! They taught me not only about our faith, but how to make it alive in the world.

Our family generally had a light "lunch and learn" midday on Sunday. The meal was generally eggs, bagels, salads, sometimes lox, white fish or tuna fish. But more important it was time to review with Daddy the lessons learned that morning at Sunday school. As I grew older, I joined this Show and Tell.

One Sunday, when it was my turn, my father asked, "Well, Hinda, what did you study today?"

"Well, we talked about Jonah."

"But what did you learn?"

This was the real question. I strived to have a good answer for Daddy, something intelligent, something impressive. No one else spoke. My sister, my mother and Daddy waited for something half-way bright to fall from my lips.

"Well," I answered, "everyone talks about when Jonah went into the sea and was swallowed up by a big fish, but we studied a different part of the story today." And then I told the rest of the story, about what happened to Jonah after he came out of the sea, about going on to Nineveh to preach to the sinners.

Daddy nodded and asked me, "Why do you think the second part of the story is important?"

"G-d wanted Jonah to learn about caring for all people, even those who aren't the best citizens," I replied. I was glad that I had paid attention and absorbed this other lesson.

"You listened, Hinda. I'm proud of you."

It was a great feeling to get Daddy's praise. I continued to listen closely in Sunday school every week so that I would get more of it. I wanted him to always be proud of me.

Going to Sunday school also gave me a way to regain confidence behind a radio microphone. When I was 11 and in sixth grade, our Sunday school class was invited to present a short musical play about the holiday of Purim on radio station WSAY. I was given a leading role, that of the secretly Jewish queen of Persia, Queen Esther. I didn't even think about my earlier failure behind a microphone. On a live broadcast I sang my heart out, a cappella, asking "What shall I do? The king knows not that I am a Jew," with many more woeful lyrics indicating that I might have my head cut off if the king got mad. I think I was so into the operetta that I scarcely thought about the microphone or the live audience. Maybe it was because I was sharing the experience with friends. Or maybe I had just grown up a bit.

One Sunday night when I was about 14, Mum was away so Daddy and I were on our own for dinner out at the Maplewood Restaurant. I sat there, gaping, when he ordered a steak. I struggled to keep quiet, but I couldn't.

I stared at him and then whispered "Daddy, does Mum know that you eat *treyf*[11]?"

He chuckled. "Yeah, she knows. She doesn't like me to do it so I don't when she and I are out together, but I didn't think you'd mind."

I didn't. It actually relieved me of some of the shame I had for doing the very same thing. I thought everyone in the family, except me, kept *kosher* even away from our house. Without my parents' knowledge, I had experimented with forbidden foods. Many days my friends and I walked to Howard Johnsons for lunch. They almost always ordered a hot dog. After a while I, too, ordered one, "with mustard and relish, please." I didn't feel especially sinful, but I wasn't very proud of myself either. What a relief to know that Daddy, too, ate *treyf* away from home!

From the time I began to date in high school, I dated only Jewish boys. It was expected by my family and me that I would someday marry a Jewish man, have a *kosher* home, and raise Jewish children. That's what generations of our family had done. In high school I dated guys I knew through school or Temple youth activities. They knew I was Jewish, and I knew the same about them.

College life was different. Although I always thought my name, Hinda Rotenberg, sounded Jewish, some of the people I met didn't know I was. One handsome Columbia sophomore, who helped move my possessions into the dorm when I arrived as a freshman, was tall and blond, with blue eyes that twinkled. He was definitely attractive, but when he asked me to have coffee with him, I gulped hard before I answered.

"I'm sorry, Al. I'd love to, but, you see….um, well, I'm Jewish and I only go out with Jewish guys," I answered and blushed at the same time.

I blushed an deeper shade of red when he told me, "Hinda, not only am I

---

[11] Unkosher food

Jewish, but I'm preparing to go to rabbinical school!" Whoops. I had wrongly assumed he wasn't Jewish and he had correctly assumed I was. We laughed about it.

Not every misunderstanding about my Jewishness made me laugh. Early in my freshman year, Lynn, one of the girls on my dorm floor, came to my room and, with a somber expression on her face, said she had to talk to me privately.

"Should we go out for a walk?" I suggested. I looked at my roommate who, although as curious as I about what this was leading to, said "Stay here. I'll go to the library."

The minute the door closed and Lynn and I were alone, she blurted out, "Phyllis says you're Jewish. What are you going to do about it?"

I did some fast thinking. Lynn obviously wanted me to deny it. I wasn't her idea of what a Jew was supposed to be like and, whatever she thought Jews were like, it wasn't a good thing to be. I recalled she had come from Lookout Mountain, Tennessee. Maybe she'd never known a Jew before she came north.

I took a deep breath and dove in. "I am Jewish, Lynn." I smiled widely. "Have been my whole life."

"But you don't seem Jewish at all. You're just like me..." she sputtered and ran out of words. She lowered her eyes to the floor and wouldn't look at me, acting as if she wanted to be anywhere but in my presence. Still looking at the floor, she said, "I'm sorry." She started moving toward the door of my room.

I looked at her, still smiling, and tried to keep my cool. "Wait a minute, Lynn. You and I have to talk about this. I don't know what you think a Jew acts or looks like. I *am* like you and I'm also different. Can't we talk this out?"

Reluctantly she sat down in my desk chair and I plopped on the edge of my bed. She hung her head and didn't say anything, so I plunged ahead. "Lynn, I know that where you come from, there aren't many Jews, maybe none. You have no experience with Jewish people. I understand that you think we're somehow different, but how? In what ways do you think Jews are different?"

"Hinda, I'm so embarrassed..." she began, still looking down instead of at me. "Maybe we should forget I ever brought this up." She stood up to leave. I persuaded her again to stay and talk this out with me.

She began to talk, hesitantly at first and then gathering speed as she spoke. This time she looked directly at me. "When I first got here to college, I met so many different girls in the dorms from all over the country, you included. They acted and dressed like me, wore just a little makeup. They were so much like me that I assumed they were like me in every way. When classes started, I met the commuter girls and they were all from New York City and the suburbs. They had accents and well, this is terrible, but..." she faded off.

"Keep going." I tried to encourage her. "You're doing fine."

"Well, frankly, their voices were loud, their gestures too big, almost theatrical, exaggerated. They all wear trendy clothes and carry huge pocketbooks and..." She paused, and then in a rush finished, "They all seemed to have names like Goldstein and Cohen and Schwartz."

I was quiet for a minute or two, thinking how to phrase what I needed to say. "So, because I talk moderately, don't use a lot of makeup, carry a big pocketbook, or wear the most fashionable clothes, you assumed I was Christian?"

She nodded. I could see from her slumped shoulders and failure to make eye contact that she was embarrassed and wished she had never started this conversation.

"Lynn, I'm glad you came to me. We're learning a lot from each other. You are learning that Jews come in all shapes, voices and make-ups. I'm learning that I can teach people who have never known a Jew that we are not a stereotype. No one wants to be judged by one trait. Would you want people to think you're a "hillbilly" because you come from Tennessee?"

She shook her head.

"Well, I don't want people to think I'm alien or unworthy because I'm a Jew."

"Oh. I never thought of it like that," she said. "I'm so embarrassed."

"No need to be. Let's talk some more. I want us both to feel better about things before you leave." I persuaded her to stay.

Fifteen minutes more of conversation and a few hugs later, all was well between us. We both walked away from our talk together having learned a lot. From my experience with Lynn, one thing I learned was that, unfortunately, my Jewish identity would make me anathema to some people.

HEAVEN ON EARTH

JULY and August were my two favorite months of the year because they were summer camp season. I could get as dirty as I wanted and was encouraged to cheer loudly and sing boisterously. Of course I could also play sports and climb trees. It was heaven-on-earth.

In 1946, the summer I was seven, my mother was scheduled to undergo surgery and my parents didn't want me around during her convalescence. They decided that I should go with my sisters to the Rochester Jewish community's overnight camp on Seneca Lake for a few weeks in July. My sister Fedgie, then 18, would be a senior counselor that summer and Lyla, age 14, a junior counselor.

I had attended a Jewish-sponsored summer day camp when I was five and six years old, but never overnight camp. I had wonderful memories of day camp, especially of a junior counselor named Joanie. Her beautiful smile in my direction always made me feel special.

Although an overnight camper was supposed to be at least eight years old for Camp Seneca Lake, those in charge made an exception for me because both of my sisters were going to be there. I also wouldn't be the only seven-year-old in my bunk. I was told that seven-year-old Wendy Phillips, the daughter of the camp director, would be there too. If I needed some assurance, Wendy, who had come to Seneca Lake with her parents since she was a baby, would be there.

My camp experience started before I even left home. My mother and I had to match what I already had to the list of clothes and equipment the camp sent home. How many pair of shorts, tee shirts, sweat shirts, long pants, or dungarees did I have to bring? Could I have a new shiny flashlight of my very own? Parents delivered their children and their camp trunks plus duffle bags to the JYM&WA (Jewish Young Men's and Women's Association), predecessor to the JCC (Jewish Community Center), on a morning in June soon after school ended.

Once the luggage was loaded and I swapped kisses and hugs with my parents, I was ready for my brand new adventure. As I boarded the bus, I had only one thought in mind: Which one is Wendy? A smiling, freckle-faced, flaming red head grinned up at me.

"Sit here," she said, patting to the empty seat beside her. "You're Hinda, right? My parents told me we were going to be together. Aren't you excited?"

"Am I ever!" I replied. I was on my way to overnight camp, and already made a new friend.

"Goodbye. Goodbye," my parents called out as the bus pulled away. "Have a great time and don't forget to write!" This last request was, of course, very important to Mummy and Daddy; they had packed preaddressed postcards and a pen with my other possessions.

I learned that there were four villages at the camp: Mohawk for the older boys, Seneca for the younger boys, Cayuga for the older girls and Onondaga for the younger girls. At that time cabins were reserved for only the youngest campers; the older ones slept in platform tents.

Wendy and I were placed together in one of the two first-timers' cabins in Onondaga. Camp officials may have thought they were helping me adjust to camp by assigning me to the cabin where Lyla was a junior counselor, but I worried about it. This sister who had resented my presence at home was now stuck with me. Would she treat me any better at camp?

The first day she seemed sisterly, placing her hand on my shoulder from time to time, raising her eyebrows as if questioning was I okay. Things got different in a big hurry.

"Okay, girls, line up and we'll go to the mess hall for lunch," she'd say. "Hinda, why don't you hurry up? We're all waiting for you…" Or, if I hurried, "Do you always have to be first in line? Why don't you give someone else a chance?"

I was confused and angry. Was she my big sister, my counselor or my biggest obstacle to fun? I couldn't talk it out with Fedgie. She was off in Cayuga, which seemed miles and miles away. After less than a week of Lyla's criticisms and my frustration and tears, the senior counselor in our cabin asked us to try to work out our differences. We were left alone in the cabin one afternoon while everyone else went to arts and crafts.

I got my two cents in first. "I wish I had never come here! You're mean!"

"I treat you just like I treat everyone else. You can't get special attention just because you're my sister."

I stamped my foot hard on the floor of the cabin. "You do not! You don't treat me like the others! You treat them nice and you act... like you hate me!" I exploded. "You do hate me. And I hate you, too! " I broke into gushing tears.

Lyla pulled back, her mouth dropping. She really didn't know how much she was hurting me. She may have thought she was doing a good job, but I didn't.

"I'm sorry, Hin," she said in a soft voice, reaching out for me. She hugged me tightly and wouldn't let go. I resisted at first, keeping my body rigid, but it just felt so comforting to be hugged by Lyla, even if I was angry with her, that I relaxed and hugged her back. Finally, I pulled away and looked at her, still wet-eyed but expectant.

She looked at me, thoughtfully. "Maybe we should separate, you know, be in different cabins," she suggested. "Then we could still see each other, but not get angry every day."

I hastily agreed. We told the senior counselor our decision; she agreed it was for the best. Later that day Wendy and I exchanged places with first-time girls from the other cabin. I easily left my sister, but didn't want to leave my new best friend!

Camp was rustic. Every day brought a fight with bugs, both in our cabin and on the way to the bathroom sheds at the end of the village where the toilets, sinks and showers were. Bug spray became another good friend. There was no outdoor lighting, so at night, my flashlight was a constant companion. Going anywhere in camp, to mess hall, rec (recreation) hall, flagpole, or campfire meant traversing uneven trails. When it rained, no one was wimpy enough to carry an umbrella. I had to wear an oversized plastic poncho. Not only didn't it keep all the rain out, it left me soaked in my own sweat!

Days after camp began I met the counselor in charge of the Nature Lodge. He came into our village one day, yelling, "M.I.C, M.I.C." which stood for man in camp, a requirement for announcing a male's entry into a girl's village. If a girl entered a boy's village, she had to yell "W.I.C."

Dressed in khaki shorts and shirt, tall socks, and mountain shoes with Indian-style jewelry hanging from his neck and on his wrist, he gathered us in the center of the village, introduced himself as Ron, and formally shook hands with each one of us as we said our names. I thought it was so grownup to shake hands with a counselor.

"I am in charge of your nature time at camp. I need to know more about you before I make up the schedule," he said and then paused, smiling. "By the way," he asked," is anyone here afraid of snakes?"

All of us rapidly nodded our heads.

Ron smiled. "Well, you just shook hands with one and nothing bad happened, right?"

"What snake?" we said, almost in unison and stepped back from him.

He held out his arm and what we thought was his bracelet slithered around his wrist and up his arm. He held it out to us. We had backed away, but a few of us, me included, came forward and touched the creature. It was cool to the touch, and its skin was rough. At that moment, I lost whatever fear I had of snakes, toads and frogs.

Meals in the mess hall were all *kosher*, like at home, and were preceded with traditional prayers said or sung in unison. After the evening meal, we also said blessings in thankfulness for our meal. I joined in saying the blessings, even when the food wasn't to my liking.

Every Friday night, it was traditional for all campers and counselors to dress in all white pants or shorts and t-shirts or shirts. After dinner, at the start of the Sabbath, campers strolled from the mess hall to the fire cycle at the waterfront for Sabbath services. On rainy nights we went to the rec hall instead. On Saturdays our activities were more sedate and non-competitive, honoring the Sabbath, although we could swim, play games, and hike.

I adored being at camp. I loved feeling free from the city, parental supervision and normal routine. I shared fun and new things to do, played games and kidded around with old friends, such as Burt who was also at camp, and new friends like Wendy.

My favorite activities at camp were based at the waterfront, not just swimming and diving, but watercraft lessons also. In my first years the counselors took us out in rowboats, heading south on the lake to a stand selling ice cream cones. Sometimes we just rowed out into the lake just for the view. We had to wear life vests until we passed an upper-level swimming test.

When my two weeks were coming to an end, I begged to stay two more and my parents agreed. My dirty clothes went home in a duffle bag with one of the counselors on her day off, and came back to me clean and ready for the rest of the month. That was the first and only summer I stayed for only four weeks. My parents and I agreed that henceforth I could enjoy the whole eight weeks that camp was in session.

Every summer I learned something new. One year I learned to paddle a canoe, first in fours with a counselor in the stern, then in pairs and eventually solo. I absolutely loved canoeing with its effortless gliding that felt like gentle breathing, each stroke accompanied by a deep exhalation. I loved the solitude of the solo canoe. After sleeping, eating, doing crafts, and playing sports with eight or ten other girls, it was my only solitary time.

My favorite time of the camp summer was always Color War. In mid-August every year, campers were divided into two teams which competed against each other for points. Competitions were varied so they could include younger as well as older campers: writing cheers, singing songs, foot races, baseball games, tag, swimming contests, tennis and volleyball games, and one-to-one tetherball. Everyone worked hard for the points so as to not let their team down. The winning team got a special dinner and a trip to town for a movie.

Color War in 1951, the year I was 12, ended differently for me. While Norma, one of my friends, and I raced down a trail to a campfire for our team, I tripped and fell. I was about to get up when I noticed the stunned look on my friend's face. Then I saw the red mark on the rock my head had hit. I put my hand to my forehead, and it came away with blood. I looked up.

Norma had frozen where she was standing, staring at me in fright.

"I think you'd better get a counselor," I managed to croak out before I blacked out.

I awoke to feel the strong arms of Marshall, one of the senior counselors, carrying me to his car. I tried to thank him before I blacked out again. When I came to again I was on a gurney in the Emergency Room of Soldiers and Sailors Hospital in Penn Yan. A young doctor looked down at me.

"How do you feel?" he asked.

"Woozy."

"I've got to do a little sewing, if you don't mind," he continued.

"Sure, go ahead." I grinned. "But please count the stitches so I can tell my friends how many I got!" He agreed and then gave me a shot of something. After that I felt the pull of the needle as he sewed me up, but felt no pain. I must have dozed off. The next thing I remember is waking up to my parents' anxious faces.

"What are you doing here?" I asked, still groggy, but grinning to let them know I was okay.

Daddy smiled back at me, but his smile was shaky, and he looked nervous.

"Your mother and I decided we'd go for a little drive, and this is where we wound up. Maybe you'd like to join us on the return trip?" he said. *Oh dear.* That's when I realized that I wouldn't be going back to camp to tell my friends about my stitches. I was going home, a good choice actually when I realized I was still dizzy and had a huge headache.

At home Mummy told me, "From the time we got that phone call from camp about your accident, we were both very frightened. I wanted to talk about it, but not your father. After he asked for driving directions to the hospital, he didn't say another word until he answered your question about what we were doing there."

During my recovery of about a week or so, I was antsy to get back to camp. There were only a few days left in the season by the time I was declared well enough.

"May I please go back to camp?" I begged. "I want to say goodbye to my friends. I could even pack up my own things. Please?"

Mum and Lyla took me up there for the day, arriving in time for lunch. I got to see all of my friends and show off the eleven stitches of my Color War wound. Norma was scared to look me in the face, but I gave her a hug and told her I was so glad she was there with me. I couldn't imagine what would have happened if I had been alone.

The following summer Wendy and I were among ten girls chosen for a special trail-blazing weekend in a wilderness site. Since we had to make all of our own meals over a fire in rustic pots and pans, we also had to gather and chop all of the firewood for those fires. We were given special instructions on outdoor chores.

"Ladies," instructed one of the counselors, "Always, always, always, look behind you when you chop wood. You never know who or what will have come up behind you."

A second counselor warned, "And remember never, never, never walk behind someone chopping wood. They may not be able to see you."

A day or so later, as I stood chopping wood, I felt powerful. I loved being chosen to perform a physical activity. I glanced briefly behind me. All clear.

"Ow!" Wendy yelled. I turned behind me at the sound of her voice. She was on the ground, holding her head.

"What happened?" I asked, "Why are you down there? What's wrong with your head?"

"Hinda, you just whacked me in the head with that axe. I hope you didn't take my eye out!"

I screamed for a counselor who came running. She was sympathetic, but gave both of us harsh looks for our failure to follow the rules. My axe head had caught Wendy above her left eye, drawing a lot of blood. She was transported to my old stomping grounds, Soldiers and Sailors Hospital in Penn Yan. Thank G-d, she was fine and returned to camp later that day with a large bandage which resembled a turban around her head.

I couldn't apologize enough. "Wendy," I said, sobbing through my tears, "I don't know what I would have done if I had hurt you worse than I did. I'm so very sorry!"

"Hey, Hinda," she answered with a grin. "I'm just as much to fault for this as you are." She added, smiling broadly, "Next time we'll listen harder."

The next day Wendy's father, still the Camp Director, walked up behind me and said, "Just because you cut your head open last year, did you have to do it to my daughter this year?"

I turned to look at him, to witness the huge grin I knew had to be on his face. He wasn't grinning. He scared me. I didn't answer him. What could I say? From that day on, when I was 13, I avoided him as much as possible. Years later when I told Wendy how I felt about him, she assured me it was just his bizarre sense of humor. He still frightened me.

Both of my children went to overnight camp for many summers.

Jon wanted to go to overnight camp when he was only seven. Len, the camp director, offered to meet with us, although expecting that he would have to explain to Jon why he couldn't go until the following year. When we met at the JCC, as Len began to ask Jon a few questions, my son began speaking, as if he were the one doing the interviewing.

"Do I have to eat what you serve or would I have some other choice?" he asked, learning that PB&J are always available at lunch and dinner.

Again Len attempted to speak and Jon broke in. "I heard that campers have to swim across Seneca Lake. Is that true?"

Len laughed. "No, Jon. The only campers who swim across the lake are senior campers, much older than you, and they volunteer to do it, with counselors in boats nearby in case they change their minds midway."

After that answer Jon sat back, folded his arms across his chest, and said, "Now you can ask *your* questions."

At that point Len had none. He was impressed with Jon's maturity and agreed to let him attend for two weeks.

The next year, where Jon was eight and we again sent him for two weeks, he called home a few days before he was due to come home.

"Hi, Mom and Dad," he said, "I'm not coming home."

"What do you mean?" I asked, puzzled. "You're coming home on Tuesday. We only signed you up for two weeks."

"But I decided to stay."

My husband Michael was on the other extension. "Jon, you can't just *decide* to stay. First of all, you need our permission. Then you need camp's permission. They may not have room for you."

"Oh, I already asked and they told me I could stay if you say it's okay," he blithely replied. "So it's okay, right?"

What could we do? He loved camp the way I had. He stayed.

Caralyn loved camping, too. After picking her up from the bus at one summer's end, she broke into anguished tears as we drove into our garage.

"I'm sorry, Mommy. I'm happy to be home, but…" she choked out before dissolving again.

I looked at her and saw myself as a youngster.

"Believe me, darling, I understand completely. I know that feeling. As much as you love us, camp is so special that you hate that you have to wait ten more months before you can go again, right?"

She looked up at me with a face, still tear-filled but smiling. "That's it exactly, Mommy.

THEY CALLED IT QUARANTINE

IN my mid-forties, when I was running a few miles each day, I consulted a podiatrist because my shins ached so much that I was in tears after each run. After preliminary examinations, Dr. Chase asked me to walk up and down the hallway outside his examining room a few times, viewing me from every angle.

He asked, "Did you have polio as a child?"

"No." *What a strange question.*

He was silent and thoughtful for a minute. Then he asked another unusual question:

"Did you, by any chance, ever have a disease that went undiagnosed?"

Wow. Where's he going with this? "Well, yeah, actually, I did..."

"Tell me about it."

I told him what had happened when I was nine.

He wasn't at all surprised. "Hinda," he said, "you had polio, thankfully a very mild case. Because of it you lost the use of many muscles in the front of your legs. The pain you feel from running is from the other muscles trying to compensate by doing twice as much work."

With orthotics, I was able to resume running painlessly. But I never forgot how lucky I had been.

My sister Fedg came home from college for vacations and summer breaks. On one trip to Rochester she brought along a boyfriend she had met while at college. His name was Henry Schultz, but everyone called him "Hy." Their friendship grew into love and, although they were very young, they became engaged.

Fedg and Hy's beautiful wedding was on September 16, 1948. It was a Thursday, an unusual day for a wedding, but the only date open at both our synagogue and the reception venue. It also allowed the newlyweds time to get back to Bethlehem, Pennsylvania for Hy to start his senior year at Lehigh University. The honeymoon would have to wait until after he graduated.

Lyla was maid of honor, and I, at age nine, won the role as junior brides-maid. What a thrill! I dressed in a pink silk gown, white socks with pink flowers crocheted on the sides, and white shiny MaryJanes. I carried a bouquet of tiny pink rose buds interspersed with baby's breath. Relatives came from New York, Pennsylvania and Toronto. I walked down the aisle of Beth Joseph, our syna-gogue, slowly, smiling more broadly with each "ooo," "aah," and "isn't she adorable?"

After the ceremony, festivities moved downtown to the Seneca Hotel for the reception and dinner. I had no trouble keeping myself amused at what was essentially an adult function. I moved from table to table, relishing compliments on my participation in the ceremony, on my dress and my poise. Because I was constantly on the move, I never ate dinner. I didn't care. I was eating up the compliments.

I was so happy and yet I didn't feel quite right. I wasn't going to spoil the day for my family by complaining. This was Fedg and Hy's big day. I felt way too hot and I was so tired. Were my feelings due to chit-chatting with out-of-town company, keeping late hours, or experiencing wedding excitement? Maybe. Nothing to bother anyone about.

Because the wedding was on a Thursday evening, my parents let me miss school on Friday. By Sunday when the last of the out-of-towners left, I had to confess to my parents that I hurt all over. They took my temperature, and as quick as you could say "oy vey," they called the doctor. On his advice my parents whisked me downtown by car to the old Rochester General Hospital on Main Street.

Our doctor strongly advised using the Emergency Room entrance. I knew that was a bad sign. The place was a hive of activity, lights flashing, loud public address announcements, people walking and talking very rapidly, some yelling for attention, others waiting on unmatched chairs in a room with linoleum flooring and dim lighting. I was taken into an examining room immediately.

A nurse took my temperature, asked my parents a few questions and then everything seemed to move very fast. "This girl is very sick," she said. "We're moving her immediately."

"What's going on? Where are you taking me?" I begged her to tell me as I was taken away on a gurney. Suddenly everyone was wearing a face mask. It looked as if they had huge eyes because their eyes were all I could see. *What's wrong with me?*

When my parents finally came within sight, they too were wearing masks. Worry lines appeared across their foreheads. Mummy grabbed my hand and squeezed it, trying to reassure me. Daddy put on a brave face, but I saw the worry lines across his forehead.

"What's wrong with me?" I begged them. "Tell me."

Daddy looked down instead of at me. "They don't know. They're going to keep you here until they find out."

"How long will that take? I don't want to miss any more school." I was determined to stay the top girl student at Number Eight School, keeping my edge over Audrey, Marsha and Gretchen.

Mum answered, "They don't know, but in the meantime, they're going to put you in a private room. You'll have to stay there all by yourself until they're sure you're not contagious."

I wasn't afraid to be alone. At least my parents would visit me, right?

"All right...I guess."

Mum continued, "And until they know what's wrong, we won't be able to come into your room. Will you be a brave big girl and listen to the doctors and nurses?"

"I'll try," I answered, with a catch in my voice.

Could I really do it? Maybe, but it wasn't something I was going to like very much. Before I could say anything else, I was wheeled into an isolation room.

For the first two days, no one told me anything. How much longer would I have to stay? No answer. Each person who came into my room, nurse or doctor, wore gowns and masks. The only faces I saw were those of my parents as they stood in the hall and looked at me through a glass window in the wall beside my bed. No one told me what was wrong with me. Looking through a window seeing my parents wave was not the same as having them beside me, hugging me, and telling me "it's all going to be fine."

I was thankful I could have books and puzzles to take my mind off the scariness of being isolated. Otherwise I wouldn't have had anything to do but gaze around my small room at the unadorned off-white walls, the curved metal bottom railing of my hospital bed, the tray which swung over the bed to bring me tasteless meals, and what I could see of the hallway through the small window. The place smelled funny, stuffy and medicinal, not fresh like my house or yard. The noises were peculiar, too: squeaks from food and medicine carts, muffled voices from nurses in the hall, and the public address announcing "Visiting hours are now over."

They called it quarantine; I called it jail. They even made me wear "jail" clothes: a hospital gown open all the way down in the back. I wanted my soft, homey pajamas, but they were forbidden. They didn't tell me why. This seemed like just another stupid rule to follow.

Some kids might like to be left alone, but that was never my preference. I liked to mix it up with others, play to an audience with my sense of humor, participate in group sports, and ride bicycles with my buddies. I begged for something else to do, and someone to do it with, but the nurses told me that until they figured out what was wrong with me, they had to keep me away from anyone I might infect.

After a few days the doctors finally told me and my parents that I had something called Virus X. They called it that because they had ruled out all other diseases from my symptoms. I was pretty sure that meant they didn't know any more after three days than they did when I first came in!

Even with that peculiar diagnosis, they wouldn't let me go home yet. I needed companionship, someone to chat with. When a nurse would walk into the room to take my temperature or bring food, they always asked, "And how are you doing?"

I always tried to keep the conversation going. "How long have you worked here?" "Did you always want to be a nurse? "Where did you go to school?" Anything that would keep them in my room a little longer. It never worked. They had chores to do, and none of them included keeping a little girl company. Each time one of them left the room, my heart sank a little lower.

I was bored and getting crankier by the day. I decided to break out of my jail cell.

I paid attention to the routine on the floor. I noticed regular times for meals, medications, and visitors. Late every morning, after pills were distributed, temperatures checked and breakfast trays cleared, the floor was very still. No nurses roamed the halls. This was when I chose to explore my temporary universe.

I didn't want to go too far. I had to get back before anyone knew I was missing. I didn't plan to go into any other rooms because, as they told me, maybe I was sick with something which could make others sick. But I could stand in the hall and look, couldn't I?

I crept out of my room and turned right, hearing a new noise, a soft but persistent sound coming from the room next door. It had a wheezing rhythm. I couldn't imagine what it was. I tiptoed to the doorway of my neighbor's room and looked in. The room didn't look anything like mine. In the middle of it was a large white machine shaped like a long tube. And *it* was doing the whooshing. Curiosity led me to approach. Inside the cylinder, lying on her back was a teenage girl. Only her head with just her beautiful long hair poked out. What was she doing there?

She saw me in the mirror over her head. "Hey, honey," she said quietly. "You aren't supposed to be in here."

My parents had taught me not to poke into other people's business, but I couldn't help it. The questions bubbled up. I had to know. "What's wrong with *you?*" I asked.

"I have poliomyelitis."

"What's that?"

"Some people call it infantile paralysis."

"But you aren't an infant," I replied, puzzled. When she didn't respond I continued, "So, anyway, why are you in that wheezing machine?"

"It's an iron lung. I can't breathe without it," she answered.

"How soon do you get out of it?"

She smiled sadly. I could see her expression in the mirror. "I'm not sure," she said very softly. "Now go back to your room before they catch you," She paused. "Thanks for the visit."

She didn't have to tell me a second time. I ran back to my room, breathless. I had thought I was in jail. My next door "neighbor" really was trapped, and she might be forever. I stayed in my room and obeyed all the rules until they let me go home after four more days. After all, a week between hugs from your Mum and Dad wasn't too bad when I considered the alternative. I never told anyone about that girl. But she visited me in nightmares for many years.

I had walked out of Rochester General Hospital with some damage, but I could still run. I never forgot that girl in the iron lung. Did she ever walk again? I wonder still today. As a child I never questioned my recovery or why some people got sick, some didn't, why some recovered and some didn't. After having Virus X, I never took my health for granted again.

My parents' American dream

WHILE I was growing up, Daddy co-owned Burke's, a furniture store on South Clinton Avenue. He was so strongly identified with the store that many customers called him "Mr. Burke," unaware it wasn't his name. No matter. "What's in a name?" he said. "It's the loyalty that counts." Not only did Burke's sell furniture, but it also employed a staff of craftsmen who fabricated sofas and chairs in an upstairs workshop and reupholstered them when needed.

Fedg and Hy lived in Allentown at the start of their marriage, but had come back to live in Rochester in 1949 after Hy finished his degree at Lehigh. It was wonderful to have Fedgie around again. I had missed her so much. Daddy invited Hy into the furniture store where his business education became an asset.

However, sometime toward the end of my sixth grade year, Daddy and his business partner had a serious falling out. I never learned what it was about. When they couldn't reach a peaceful resolution, lawyers were called in. Both sides were instructed to submit a bid to buy out the other one. Whoever made the higher bid would buy the business. Daddy's lawyer advised him to put in a very low bid, believing that Daddy's partner just wanted out. To their surprise, the lawyer's advice was wrong; it resulted in Daddy's share being bought out. He no longer owned the business he had co-founded.

On only one day's notice, Dad and Hy were out of their jobs. Although stunned by the suddenness of their situation, they began to plan opening a new store. All that my father knew how to do well was to make and sell furniture. His former business partner had not put a non-compete clause in the buy-out contract, so he and Hy looked around the city for a suitable location to open another furniture store, this one to be called Rotenberg's. They found a place on Gibbs Street across from Kilbourn Hall that offered two floors of retail show-rooms. Because there was no space for upholstery, Daddy reluctantly let go that part of his business.

I also had to let go of my own connections to Burke's. For all my growing-up years, as far back as I could remember, I had spent part of every Saturday afternoon upstairs in the workshop where furniture was made and remade. Daddy's upholstery workmen had taken me under their wings, teaching me how to hammer nails into leftover wood, sand pieces and apply stains. This was a wonderful part of my life. I grieved to give that up, but I knew Daddy had his own pain about leaving Burke's so I never told him about mine.

Since returning to Rochester, Fedg and Hy came to our house for Shabbat dinners every Friday night. After dinner, while Mummy and my sisters did dishes, Hy would always ask me, "Wanna take a walk?" We walked and talked though my fifth, sixth and seventh grade Friday nights. I told him about my life that week and, in return, he gave me his full attention and advice. On our weekly stroll, we'd pass a grocery store where he was usually able to persuade me to let him buy me "just a little something" from the candy department.

One November night, when I was 11, Hy and I had just returned from our walk, when Fedg joined us in the living room, smiling broadly. "What's funny?" I asked.

"We've been talking about what to get you for Chanukah this year," Hy said, smiling at me, "and we found a perfect present." He stopped and looked upset. "There's one problem."

"What's that?" I was anxious to know more. I liked presents!

"Well, we can't get it to you in time for the holiday. Would it be okay if it came a little late…like in June?"

"June! Can't it come sooner?" They broke into gales of laughter.

"Hinda," Fedgie said, taking my hand in hers, "we're going to have a baby! The present is a new niece or nephew!"

"Wow! I'm going to be an aunt! Promise me I'll be your "Number One Babysitter!"

My sisters were living lives so different from mine. Fedg and Hy were parents of a little boy. The year Mark was born they introduced Lyla to Irving Brontman, the brother of a neighbor, and, after dating for a while, Lyla and Irv were engaged. Meanwhile, I had turned 13 and was getting ready to go into eighth grade. I would go to Benjamin Franklin High, the same school my sisters had attended. It was some distance from home. I'd have to ride two city buses, traveling at least 30 minutes each way.

I assumed Burt and I were going to sign up for all the same classes. No quite.

"I'm going to take French. How about you?" he asked.

"Why would you take French? Who speaks it anymore? Take Spanish," I countered. "We live in the Western Hemisphere, and it's more popular than English." We couldn't agree and decided it was okay to have one class away from each other.

Because I was preoccupied with plans for starting high school, I wasn't paying close attention to what my parents were discussing between themselves when I was present. The money from the dissolution of Burke's had come through. I hadn't heard my parents mention what they might do with that money. Maybe if I had been listening, I wouldn't have been so shocked when, in August, as Mum, Daddy and I were eating dinner, Daddy told me, "I have great news! The deal came through. We're buying that house in Brighton."

"What are you talking about? What house?" I asked, feeling tightness in my throat.

Daddy smiled. "We found a very nice little ranch house in Brighton, and we're moving there in a few months. You'll love it when you see it," my father said, calmly.

"Love it? Move to Brighton? No!" My voice went higher in both volume and pitch. "Why are we moving at all? We're happy right here!" My voice went an octave higher. "What about me? What about Burt? I won't know anyone there. Why are you doing this to me?" I felt color rise in my face. I was shaking, sweaty and utterly spent.

It was clear from the way they responded that my parents had expected a strong reaction from me. Mummy looked at Daddy, and he got the message that he was to deal with his youngest daughter. Patiently, quietly, Daddy explained, "We can finally stop renting. We have enough money to buy a lovely house. We chose Brighton because it has the best schools. We were thinking about what was best for you"

I sulked. They smiled. I fumed. They smiled. I gave them the silent treatment. They ignored me. Hate it or love it, we had to pack ourselves up and move to the suburbs. To make matters worse, we weren't going to move until early November, smack in the middle of the first semester.

I pretended the move to Brighton wasn't going to happen. On the September day before the first day of classes, I raced inside Franklin High with all other incoming eighth graders to get a prime locker on the Hudson (St.) corridor near my friends. Our group from Number Eight School stuck together in the big building as much as we could. I put a lot of effort into my classes, especially English, which was taught by sweet Miss Corcoran, the same teacher my sisters had enjoyed years earlier. I took each day as it came, ignoring time quickly passing before I'd have to leave.

On my last day at Franklin, a Friday, I had lunch as usual with Burt and my other friends. Mummy was picking me up after lunch so we could go to Brighton High that afternoon, transfer records, and be ready for me to start there the following Monday. My gang and I didn't have much to say to one another, all well aware that this was the last time I would be there.

"I'm gonna miss you, all of you," I began to say, as lunch hour was almost over. The enormous lump in my throat stopped me from continuing. I didn't want to sit there crying, making a scene, but I was in pain.

"See you later," Audrey said, her voice quivering a little, as she left the table. She seemed in a big hurry to leave.

"Yeah, don't be a stranger," Davy muttered as he, too, sauntered away. That's all from someone who went to school with me every day and lived on Huntington Park? I was astounded he could be so casual.

One by one they walked away, finally leaving Burt and me alone at the table for the hardest goodbye of all. I sat there, not knowing what to say and not making eye contact.

Burt broke the silence. "Okay, Hinda, I have just one thing to say. In my head, I know you can't help it, but in my heart, I'm so mad at you for moving away."

"This isn't my fault…" I began to say, protesting.

Burt broke in, "I know that. But it still hurts. You're my best friend and I need you near me at Franklin, and now you won't be here. Can't I be a little angry?" He smiled a little.

"Yeah, I guess I get it. But think about me. You'll still have all the rest of our friends, and I have to start making all new ones. If you think you'll be lonesome for me, think about how much I'm going to miss you!"

We managed to smile at each other as we listened to each other's complaints and bemoaned our fates. Eventually, Burt had to get to his next class, and I had to meet Mummy. We shared a tearful good-bye hug, and promised we would always be best friends, talk to each other frequently on the phone and see each other as often as possible.

My parents had achieved their American dream, a home of their own. And, what's more, that home was in one of the best suburbs of Rochester. Although they were so happy, I couldn't join in the delight. I was still the baby of the family, the one who had to go along with decisions made by others. This move wouldn't change my sisters' lives at all; it affected only me.

When I walked into the new house for the first time, I saw why it had appealed to them. It was bright, new and well-laid out, all on one level. There were three bedrooms, a combination living room/dining room, a cozy modern kitchen, and a screened-in porch off of it. The backyard had two levels with a rock garden in-between, was fully shrubbed, and gorgeous. There was even a finished basement so, if I ever made any friends, I'd have a place to hang out with them. My bedroom, with large corner windows, was in the front of the house. I had refused to plan its décor, but Mum had chosen well. The wallpaper was a soft brown plaid and the new furniture was light wood, giving the room a rustic feel.

It took only a few days to discover that not only were there no kids my grade level on the street, there were no teenagers at all! I couldn't even ride my bike to search for others through the rest of our development, because my parents, without consulting me, had decided to donate it to a new Jewish community day school. "You don't mind, do you?" they asked me, after the fact. "You never seemed to ride anymore, and you're too old for a bicycle anyway."

I did mind. Nobody had asked me about moving, and nobody had asked me before they gave my things away. I was shocked and bitterly disappointed to learn that they had also discarded all of my play manuscripts and favorite books. Losing those vestiges of my early years compounded the pain I felt over losing my friends. The deeds already done, I never raised objections with my parents. What good would it have done? I silently moaned for all I had lost.

One bright spot was my ability to reclaim my name, to enroll at Brighton High as "Hinda." I had to bring in my original birth certificate to prove it was my actual name, but from that time onward, I had one name everywhere. It made me feel more authentic. I still had to reclaim the confidence for "Hinda" in Brighton that "Helene" had at Number Eight School.

My first weeks of school in Brighton passed slowly and painfully.

"Welcome, Hinda," said Mr. Miner on the first day I appeared in his home-room. He introduced me to the rest of the students. As I went to the desk assigned, I smiled at those who sat near me. They stared back. No smiles, no greetings. I felt that they were thinking, 'Okay, so now there's another girl here. Who cares?' Mr. Miner's greeting was the only voice I heard at school addressing me by name for more than a week. Some students looked at me in classes or in the hallways, but then looked away, talking only to their group of friends. It seemed that tight little cliques had been formed in the sixth and seventh grades. How could I break into a group? I tried to meet classmates and make friends, saying "hi" and smiling, while inside my heart sank. Everyone seemed to know everyone else, except me. Everyone had someone to eat lunch with, or walk to or from school with, except me.

I wanted to fit in. I figured out that it would help if I dressed like them, so I studied their clothes. Most of the girls at Brighton wore pleated skirts and sweater sets. Until this point, I had dressed mostly in my sisters' hand-me-downs, supplemented with inexpensive purchases from Sibley's, McCurdy's, or Forman's, but Fedgie and Lyla didn't hand-me-down anything anymore. My classmates, many of them from upper middle-class families, didn't have to worry about affording new clothes when the styles changed. Our family was able to buy a modest home in Brighton, but we couldn't afford to keep up with clothing style changes or the most popular items: cashmere sweater sets. Thank goodness for synthetic fabrics! I learned to mimic the stylish look more cheaply and carry it off with an air of nonchalance. I hoped I looked more like my classmates, but I still felt the difference inside, and it hurt.

Because our new neighborhood didn't have grocery stores or a meat market within walking distance, Mum needed a car of her own. Some days when I got home, she was gone, doing errands. I called Burt every afternoon after school, but he seemed so many miles away, and we found less and less to talk about. We didn't share teachers or classmates or even piano lessons anymore. I was the one without friends. Each day was the same. After Burt and I talked, I turned on the TV to fill the emptiness. Even hearing dumb daytime shows was better than enduring homework in a silent house.

Lyla and Irving's wedding was a reprieve. They chose to be married on New Year's Day, 1953 downtown at the Sheraton Hotel. I was the maid-of-honor, dressed in a salmon-colored velvet gown with dyed-to-match shoes. I not only felt very grown up, but looked it, too, because Lyla put makeup on me. With Daddy's encouragement, I wrote their wedding toast in rhyme, surprising them. But after the hoopla, I once again had to face the torture of the new school.

When I learned that Brighton would be closed for a few days after mid-year exams, I called Burt and made plans to visit him at Franklin. Mum drove me there and arranged to pick me up a few hours later. Burt and I were so happy to see one another. We grinned our way through his social studies class, and after that, went to lunch in the cafeteria with some of my old classmates. How exciting to be back there! I couldn't wait to talk with the rest of my old friends.

Once we got our food and sat down, I looked from Davy to Audrey to Marsha to Howie and the rest of our gang, smiling from face to face. "It's so good to see you all. You have no idea how much I missed you!" I anticipated a friendly catch-up session where I would learn everything that had gone on in my absence. No smiles were returned.

"I'm surprised you wanted to come see us now that you're a *Brighton* girl..." said Audrey, with malice in her voice.

"But I'm not!" I protested.

"Yeah, why would you come slumming with us?" said Brenda. *Did they think that Brighton was made up of snobbish people and that I had become one? I was still me. I hadn't changed.*

I was speechless. Tears glistened in my eyes. How could friends say things like that? When I recovered my powers of speech I pleaded with them, "No matter where I live, you will always be my friends. Don't you know that?"

They didn't seem to care. I had expected to return to my friends and be greeted as a returning member of the group. Instead I was met by strangers, people who had, in a few short weeks, moved on without me. With Burt as the only exception, they all turned on me. They told me that I should stay in the suburbs with my new rich friends and not come around anymore. Nothing I said to them, none of my words, reached them. I had no life in Brighton, and it seemed I had lost my old life as well. I gave up protesting. I sat silently through the rest of the meal, knowing that soon my mother would be picking me up.

In February, the second semester of eighth grade at Brighton began. Knowing I couldn't ever go back to Franklin, it was sink or swim in my new school, and I wanted to be a swimmer. My classmates talked openly about how they did on tests, quizzes and assignments. If they knew I got good grades, would that make me another kind of outsider? It might be even harder to make friends if they thought I was a brain.

When mid-year grades came out, I kept quiet about my report card, all A's. My classmates stood around comparing marks. They especially hovered around Lewis, the smartest boy in math. "What did you get?" they cried out to him.

With pride in his voice he answered, "99." Classmates offered congratulations. He acknowledged them and then turning, looked over to me and smiled. He asked, "And you? How did you do on the math exam?"

"I guess I was lucky," I said quietly. "I got 100."

There was a hush and then my classmates started whispering to each other, "Hey, that new girl is smart."

I didn't know if that was good or bad. Lewis, however, took it well that someone, for once, had outshone him in math. From then on Lew was a friend and, through him, my circle of friends grew. I had found somewhere to fit in.

Our new house was within a short walking distance of the high school. On my way home one day in late winter, I was hailed from behind. "Wait up there. I think I know you…"

I turned around to discover a short, brown-haired girl with large brown eyes and a huge smile, hurrying to catch up with me. I recognized her as Gail Mink, a girl from my homeroom. "Where are you going?" she asked.

"Just walking home. I live on Penarrow."

"Hey, I live on Fernboro, the street after that. Do you want to meet up after school and walk home together?"

"Sure!"

Within a few weeks we were also walking to school together each morning. And a few weeks after that, Gail began coming over early and sharing breakfast coffee with my mother and me. She wasn't Burt, but she was a good substitute. I felt lucky to have her in my life. She filled me in on the back-story of many of our classmates, kids she had known since kindergarten.

Eventually, I made other new friends and began to feel more comfortable in Brighton, with my classmates, neighborhood, social clubs, and after-school sports. I found myself looking forward instead of backward, excited about my current life and not missing my past one as much. With Gail I played intramural sports in every season, but the coming of spring and playing softball were our favorites. We routinely played catch in my backyard, sometimes with Hy as our coach. She and I intended to be a fearsome duo on the field in intramurals.

The first time I fired a ball back to her, she yelled, "Yowee! That hurt!"

"Well, if we're going to be a fabulous team of shortstop/first baseman, you're going to have to learn to catch what I throw no matter how hard I throw it."

"Okay, I'll do it," she agreed.

We became an unstoppable force. Once we convinced another friend, Gretchen, that we could be unbeatable if she would pitch for our team, we almost always won our games. The three of us went downtown to Sibley's, bought matching pale denim jackets and had them embroidered with our names. We thought we looked like professional ballplayers.

Changing schools was turning out better than I could have imagined, and I was more open to changes in other aspects of my life. The spring after we moved to Brighton, I wanted to go to camp with Gail instead of returning to Camp Seneca Lake.

One night at dinner I asked me parents, "How would you feel if I went to a different camp this summer? I've been thinking about the one Gail goes to in the Adirondacks. What do you think?"

"Can we afford it?" Daddy asked. "And are you sure you won't miss Seneca Lake?"

"Yeah, I might miss my friends there, but I'm ready for a change. Let's find out what it costs. If it's within reason, please may I go there?"

Going to a new camp didn't bother me in the same way that going to a new school had. My self-confidence was returning. After some phone calls and more discussion, my parents agreed to let me try Camp Eagle Cove, thinking it would help with my transition to Brighton.

Eagle Cove was a stark contrast to Seneca Lake Camp. The Adirondack cabin where Gail and I stayed was nestled on a hillside right above Fourth Lake. It had indoor toilets and showers. We had closets so we didn't have to pull clothes out of our trunks. Standing on the porch of our cabin, we could look down on rows and rows of canoes, waiting to be paddled by eager young campers like me. Daily activities, however, were similar: flag raisings, meals and song time in the mess hall, arts and crafts, lakefront swimming and boating, and basketball.

We also had Color War. For the closing event, the youngest camper on each team had to run to a specific place and hand off the baton to the next oldest. The relay progressed through the camp enrollment from youngest to oldest campers through the basketball and tennis courts, baseball fields, and on to swim races in the lake. The final leg was a solo canoe race from shoreline around a buoy and back to shore. I paddled the last leg against a girl from the Green Team and

managed to nose my canoe across the shoreline just ahead of hers. I smiled from
ear to ear for many days after that triumph.

Back at school for ninth grade, in addition to schoolwork, I filled my time
by reading at least two classic books each week. Escaping into literature became
a wonderful passion for me. I became acquainted with Dickens, Brönte, Austin,
Hawthorne, and other American and English authors. Not all of my reading was
high-brow. Like many of my classmates, I surreptitiously stood in the local five
and dime, reading about Mike Hammer's exploits in *I the Jury*, the first lurid book
I ever read.

The summer after freshman year, I returned to Eagle Cove, but under
different circumstances. Money had become a problem for our family. Daddy's
business was not thriving. When the camp director came to our house to sign me
up, Daddy was honest and blunt. "We want Hinda to have this experience, but
we can't afford to pay the fee."

Uncle Bello, which is what we campers called the director, thought for a
minute. "I'm sure there's a solution," he said. Daddy and he worked it out. I
would be a part-time camper and a part-time employee, taking on some coun-
selor-in-training duties and writing a camp newsletter. Those responsibilities
were enough to pay half of my camp expenses.

That summer of 1954 I met Neal Marsh, one of the male junior counselors,
also from Brighton High. Although he was only one grade ahead of me, I didn't
know him until I met him in the camp mess hall one day soon after camp started.
He began visiting me when I had night watch, sitting with me on the porch
of the cabin after lights-out. His attendance on those nights and his habit of
greeting me on the way into the mess hall for meals made my friends asks, "Is
he your boyfriend?" I denied it. I hardly knew him. But his attention continued,
and he acted jealous if I kidded around with the guys I played basketball against.

Neal was good looking, tall, very smart, cleverly funny, and interested, like
I, in theater and writing. I knew he liked me, but I couldn't decide if I liked him
or if I was just flattered that an older guy liked me. However, because we spent
a lot of time together, we were seen as a couple and that kept away any other
guys who might have been interested. I turned to Gail for advice, but, since she
hadn't had a boyfriend up until then, she wasn't helpful. I wrote to Wendy who
was at Camp Seneca Lake: "Holy Zee! I think I have a boyfriend! Now what do
I do?" She wrote back with advice to take it slow. This was new territory for us.

In July, I received a letter from Fedg letting me know that Hy had a great job opportunity and that they were moving at the end of the summer to his hometown of Allentown, Pennsylvania. Oh no! I was already missing them, especially Fedgie. Neal held me in his arms as I cried my eyes out about the loss. Because his older brother lived out of town, he could identify with my feelings. As summer progressed I became more comfortable with the idea that Neal and I had become a couple.

When school started that fall, Neal was a junior and I a sophomore. We saw each other before and after school, by our lockers, talked on the phone weeknights, saw a movie or went to a dance on Saturday nights and sometimes hung out at his house or mine on Sundays. We even had meals with each other's families. Our parents were comfortable with our relationship. It felt important that someone as good-looking, smart and talented as Neal wanted me to be his girlfriend. To hear a boy say he loved me was the ultimate acceptance.

We also shared some school activities. Neal was already writing for the school newspaper, *Trapezoid*, and the literary magazine, *Galaxy*. On his advice, I took the journalism course offered that year, a prerequisite to leadership positions in both the newspaper and magazine. I began to try out for high school plays and that fall won the lead role in *Years Ago*, a play written by actress Ruth Gordon about her early years in Quincy, Massachusetts.

As Neal and I spent more time together, especially alone time, I was increasingly faced with questions about sexual expectations and propriety. When Fedg and her family came to Rochester for Passover, I turned to Hy for advice. He told me that boys were all the same and that girls had to decide which type of girl they wanted to be. His exact words were, "Boys see girls in one of two ways. Either you're a good girl or you're a tramp. There's no in-between."

Neal and I had gone out steadily since the summer of 1954. Our relationship had progressed. We kissed and did a little touching. How far was I going to let this go? What was he going to expect next? I liked the idea of having a steady boyfriend, and I liked the security of always having a date. However, having a steady boyfriend also meant coming face-to-face with questions I wasn't ready to answer. The struggle between my remaining a good girl and dealing with a red-blooded teenage boy resulted in explosive fights between us. It was easier to fight with Neal than to admit that I might want him to touch me, and that I might even want to touch him.

During my high school years, being invited into a Jewish sorority was a status-booster. If you were asked as a freshman, you were considered more popular than if asked the next year. I was disappointed not to be asked to join a sorority freshman year, but then asked by two, Chi Delta and Delta Psi, at the start of my sophomore year. The popular girls joined Chi Delta, but some of those girls were also known for sharp tongues and stuck-up attitudes. Delta Psi had the sweeter girls, not as popular, but definitely kinder and gentler.

My friend Gail didn't get a bid until sophomore year either and was invited to join only Delta Psi. She and I decided we would still remain good friends no matter which sorority I chose, so I turned my attention to joining the same sorority as Wendy, my old friend from summers at Camp Seneca Lake. Wendy and I rarely saw each other because she attended Monroe High in the city. Her family belonged to a different synagogue, so we weren't in youth group together either. As comfortable as was at Brighton, I didn't want to lose touch with "little Hinda" from summers long gone. That bond from seven previous years of summer camping together was strong, and Wendy and I would be able to see each other more regularly if we joined the same sorority. Like me, Wendy didn't get a bid freshman year either.

Phone lines buzzed as we decided which bid to accept. Wendy said, "You and I have decisions to make. What do you think?"

"I'll tell you the truth." I answered. "I'm still mad at Chi Delta for not asking us last year. On the other hand, doesn't it seem that all our friends are in it?"

"Let's talk every day after school until we decide. We have to be in the same sorority no matter what!"

Finally, after a week of conversation weighing the pros and cons, we decided to join Delta Psi. I called the RSVP number for Chi Delta and left word with the mother of the Pledge Master that I wouldn't be attending the first meeting. Then I called Wendy to tell her.

"Oh my G-d, Hinda! I should have called you! I changed my mind and told Chi Delta 'yes' and Delta Psi 'no,'" she screeched. "Now what?"

Now what indeed. "Let me see if I can fix this…call you back."

I quickly dialed the Chi Delta number again and again got the mother instead of the Pledge Master. "This is Hinda again. Forget what I said. I'll be there." *No harm, no foul.*

Pledging rituals were ridiculous, but lasted only a few weeks before Wendy and I became "sisters" in Chi Delta. Then we saw each other each Wednesday night at sorority meetings. Within a few weeks I began emulating the older girls, observing their clothes, hair and makeup, and also their cigarette smoking. I began smoking myself. I thought I had kept it hidden from my parents until one night after dinner when my parents were lighting up, and my father offered me the pack. "Want one?" he asked, smiling.

"What?" I was aghast. They knew!

"I'd rather have you do something in front of me than behind my back," he said. "I'd rather you didn't smoke at all, but that's your choice."

I took a cigarette from his pack and lit up. Although my hands were shaking, I was elated that my parents were treating me like a grownup.

That year, at the end of tenth grade, I lost the only school-wide election I entered, that for Student Council secretary. The fun was in the pre-election build-up when we had poster painting parties in our basement and plastered our homemade work all over the school. Candidates had to address a school-wide assembly the morning of elections. I worked hard on my speech and rose when it was my turn with confidence. Because of having appeared in plays, I wasn't at all nervous to address the packed auditorium. In a passionate address before the assembly I delivered my speech, in it promising that, "I will be a serviceable tool of this school." I had no idea why the place erupted with laughter. I finished what I had to say, at the same time wondering, what's so funny? It was much, much later that the word "tool" was explained to me in graphic terms.

While Neal and I were never cast in the same play, we did get to work together on our school production of *Macbeth*. He played MacDuff, and I was the student director under our theatre advisor's leadership. My friend Judy Roberts won the role as Lady MacDuff, the role I had desperately wanted. Imagine being my boyfriend's wife on stage! Judy, however, had spent her sophomore year in London and came home with just the right accent for Shakespeare, so I forgave her for stealing "my" role.

Neal and I started going to bars that year, which made me feel very adult. It was something different to do besides going to movies or sitting around with friends. We didn't drink much, but we weren't really old enough to drink at all. Neal's father was a liquor distributor so most of the bar owners knew Neal and let us buy drinks. We never overindulged, just sipped rye and ginger ale drinks, heavy on the ginger ale.

The summer before my senior year, Neal and I were trying to determine what our relationship would become in the fall, when he went to Wesleyan University in Connecticut. He wanted us to remain exclusive, but I, more realistic about the separation, felt that we needed some breathing room. We fought and made up every few days over this issue. I joined his parents on the ride to Middletown to drop him off for school. We had a sweet good-bye and began our lives separate from each other for the first time in more than two years.

My senior year turned out to be a busy and happy time. In my junior year I had become editor of the op-ed commentary page of *Trapezoid*, the school news-paper, and, in my senior year, was editor-in-chief. I had the pleasure of writing a monthly column commenting on issues of the day. Two of my short stories that year were published in *Galaxy*, our school literary magazine. I appeared in a few more plays, *Twelve Angry Men* by Reginald Rose (retitled for our production as *Twelve Angry Women*) and *You Can't Take It With You*.

During high school vacation breaks, I rode the Lehigh Valley Railroad to Allentown to visit Fedg, Hy, Mark, and, after March 1955, Nancy, my first niece. For Fedg, I brought a taste of home and I was reconnected with my sister and shown how a modern family lives. I missed having Fedg close by, to talk with her and Hy about everyday things and to discuss whatever was bothering me. She was still that idealized big sister, the one I ran to as a child and now had to "train to" as a teenager. However, I began to develop a new relationship with Lyla. We weren't in competition for time or resources from our folks, and I could help her with her kids - Larry born in January of my freshman year and Patti in the fall of my junior year.

After my abrupt transfer into the school district as an eighth grader, Brighton High had become a comfortable place, full of friends, activities, stimulations and challenges. I participated in extra-curricular activities in part because they fit my interests, but also because they kept me busy and out of the house as much as possible. When I was home and my parents were there, my friends would often gather in the living room, spending time in my father's company rather than mine. I wasn't jealous; I knew my father was great company. He entertained my friends with stories he had heard from his friends or on television, and, all the while, he'd pump them for information about teenage life. Mind you, he never asked me for that information, perhaps fearing I would consider it prying. But ask my friends? Sure, that was how he found out what life was like for a teenager in the 50s.

Most evenings, however, I was the only one home, with no one to share my thoughts, activities, or ideas. My father's furniture store stayed open until 9 pm. almost every weeknight. Daddy would come home for a break at 5 pm. and then, after an early dinner, my parents would go back to the store. The good news was that there was no one there to remind me to study, to get off the phone with my friends, or catch me watching too much television. The bad news was that I was alone more than I liked. While I no longer had to compete with my sisters for attention, I still didn't get enough. I felt neglected. In my heart I knew that Daddy's business was facing challenges, and my parents had enough to worry about without worrying about me. So I showed them a happy face and shared only good news with them.

But, as I looked ahead to college, I welcomed dorm life so that I wouldn't feel so alone. I'd have roommates and classmates to keep me company and stimulate my mind.

THE GREATEST CITY IN THE WORLD

ONE Sunday afternoon in the fall of my senior year, my friend Judy and I sat in her kitchen picking at the leftover carcass of a turkey. We scraped off meat with our nails and licked our fingers, oblivious to lady-like manners. Apropos of nothing, I asked, "Have you decided where you are going to apply to college?"

She made a face, scrunching up her nose. "Well, I really want to go to Smith, but I'm also looking at Wellesley and Bryn Mawr."

"Why are you making that awful face?"

"Oh," she said, shrugging her shoulders and sighing, "My mother thinks all those schools are just so very wrong for me."

"Why?"

"She doesn't think I'll be happy going to classes with girls who've attended boarding schools. She thinks those colleges are full of those types and I, as a public school girl and a scholarship student, will feel uncomfortable."

"So where does she want you to go?" I asked, just as Mrs. Roberts strolled into the room.

"I think that since she's looking at women's colleges, Judy would be very happy at Barnard," Mrs. Roberts cut in. "It's in New York City. She'd never lack for something to do."

"Yeah," I said, "but aren't we going to have to study all the time? How much time would she get to enjoy New York?"

"Sure, college will require study, but not all the time. During free time, she'd have the Met, and Carnegie Hall, and lots of venues for dance." Her face lit up while she was talking. "No other college campus can begin to compare!"

It sounded exciting. "You know, Mrs. Roberts, I've been looking for a women's college in New York State to apply to. Maybe *I* should apply to Barnard?"

Judy lifted an eyebrow, but otherwise didn't comment. Mrs. Roberts beamed.

Choosing a college wasn't easy. Because my father's new furniture business was not doing well, and money was tight, I could consider only affordable college options. I hoped to receive offers of scholarships from colleges which accepted me, and I was also a candidate for a $350 annual Regent's Scholarship, a competitive grant offered by New York State to students who attended a college within the state. That three hundred and fifty dollars in the late 1950s would go a long way toward covering tuition, room and board. I understood that I would have to work during the school year and summers to help defray other costs. With my good grades and high SAT scores, surely I could pull this off without having to go to a local college and live at home, couldn't I?

My sisters had both gone to Beaver College, a women's school in Jenkintown, Pennsylvania. Neither of them had graduated, both marrying at 20 and choosing a "MRS" degree over a B.A. I didn't want to follow in their footsteps. The schools I found interesting were more academically challenging than Beaver. I intended to be the first in my family to have a college degree and to receive it from the most prestigious college we could afford.

Ivy League colleges like Harvard, Yale and Princeton didn't accept women at that time so I looked elsewhere - at the Seven Sisters colleges, which some considered the women's Ivy League. Besides being much esteemed, these colleges employed many more female than male professors. I would be taught by the best and brightest women in the country, role models and guides to my aspirations. The one I preferred was Vassar in Poughkeepsie, a place where I could utilize that wished-for Regent's Scholarship if I got one. Another school I considered was Connecticut College for Women in New London. While it wasn't a Seven Sister school, CCW had appeal because it was not pricey and it was right down the highway from Wesleyan College where Neal was studying. I also thought I had a good chance of being offered scholarship money there. But I needed to look for another college within the state in case Vassar didn't come through with an acceptance and a good-sized scholarship. Barnard became that school. After filling out college applications, I began the interview phase.

On one fall weekend, I visited Neal at Wesleyan and he drove me to New London for my interview at Connecticut College. The admissions officer took a look at my school record and accepted me on the spot. He couldn't tell me then the amount of scholarship money the college would offer, but he led me to believe that Connecticut College was an affordable option for my family. I felt great that I was definitely accepted at one of my choices -- not my first choice, but a decent one. I could relax. I would be going to college somewhere, and if Neal and I continued to date one another, being only 45 minutes away from one another would be a bonus.

In late January, Daddy planned on attending a furniture mart in New York City and asked me to tag along so that I could have interviews at both Barnard and Vassar. Going to New York meant flying for the first time. I couldn't believe it took less than an hour's air time to get there!

I knew one thing for certain I wanted to do in the City. Even before we got there, I asked, "Daddy, can we please see a Broadway play while we're here?"

Daddy grinned. "How about *Auntie Mame*? I think you'll love Rosalind Russell."

The only seats available when we got to the box office were in the heights of the balcony, but I didn't care. I was in a Broadway theatre for the first time, watching a legend perform! I sat on the edge of my seat, my heart beating double-time and so loudly that I thought I would disturb those sitting near me. Every so often I would turn to grin at Daddy who was grinning right back at me! I clapped so enthusiastically when the final curtain came down that my hands throbbed. I hugged my father, gushing, "Thank you, Daddy, so much. I can't think of anything I would have liked more than seeing this show with you!"

Even more exciting was what happened afterwards. Hy was also coming to New York for the furniture mart, bringing Fedg with him; they were going that night to see *Inherit the Wind*, the play about the Scopes trial. Daddy had arranged to meet them after their show outside our theatre. However, when Daddy and I walked out of our show, they weren't there.

"You know, Daddy, their play might have run a little later than ours. Maybe we should walk over to their theatre to meet them." He agreed, but once we got to their show, the performance there was over, and they weren't there. "Hmmm. If I know Fedg, she went backstage to congratulate the actors. I'll just meet her there," and with that I popped through the stage door, leaving Daddy outside in case they showed up while I was inside.

It made perfect sense to me. Fedg had appeared in many amateur shows, but also had small roles in an Equity theatre near Allentown. It would be just like her to want to go backstage to congratulate the actors on their performances.

Once inside I found myself backstage with no one in sight. As I was about to leave, a man came up to me. *Oh my goodness.* I recognized him from the posters outside the theatre. It was Paul Muni, the star of the show!

"Can I help you?" he asked, with a tilt of his head.

"Oh, Mr. Muni," I gushed. "You were so magnificent tonight. I wanted to come back to congratulate you!" I lied.

He bowed his head in appreciation.

"And, uh, Mr. Muni, have you possibly seen my sister? I'm sure she must have also come back to see you."

He shook his head. "No, young lady. You've been my only visitor tonight. Thank you for coming."

With that, I hurried out the stage door to meet my father, delighted that I had met a Broadway actor, but disappointed that my sister and brother-in-law were still among the missing. Daddy and I decided we would go to Lindy's and get a table, hoping that Fedg and Hy would show up. We ordered some of Lindy's famous cheesecake, and just as we were having our first bite, Fedg and Hy walked in.

"We knew we'd find you here" she said, laughing. "Isn't that cheesecake scrumptious?"

"Fedg!" I practically shouted. "Do I ever have a story for you!" I shared my tale of backstage delight and deceit! My sister couldn't believe my brashness in going backstage and bald-faced lying to a theatrical giant. Barnard may have been my last choice, but after experiencing Broadway up close and personally, I began to reconsider my priorities. Seeing plays would be something I could do if I came to New York; I could watch stars perform and even visit them backstage!

Sunday late morning, Neal came in by train from Connecticut, and we all went out for brunch. Neal and I spent that afternoon by ourselves, visiting the Museum of Modern Art and walking around the City, relishing every moment together. After a light dinner, Neal was on his way back to college, and I was off to bed to dream about my upcoming college interviews.

Daddy and I had breakfast at the Carnegie Deli that Monday morning before we parted, he to his furniture mart and I to my future. I wasn't ready to tackle the New York subway system yet, so I took a cab uptown to Barnard. That college hadn't been a serious choice for me when I applied, but that morning, when I left midtown for upper Broadway, I realized how great it would be to attend a New York City college. As the cab sped north along Broadway, I found it hard to believe I was still in Manhattan. Instead of seeing hotels, theater marquees and neon signs, I saw apartment buildings, groceries, cleaners, and other neighbor-hood shops. The cab continued northward and the Broadway of song and dance became an academy of knowledge. Lining both sides of it were the buildings of Columbia University, of which Barnard was a part.[12]

The campus was compact so it wasn't hard to find the admissions office on the first floor of one of the academic buildings. I saw many young men walking around, both on the Barnard campus on the west side of Broadway and on the Columbia College campus on the east side. Their presence gave me something to think about: Going to a woman's college and being amongst men were not mutually exclusive.

Probably because my interview at Connecticut College had gone so well, I hadn't prepared for this one. I tensed when I remembered that Barnard would be more select. They weren't going to take me just because I was an A student. All their applicants were A students. Would I be able to convince them I belonged there? I waited nervously in the admissions office, fidgeting and thinking about how to distinguish myself. I didn't have long to wait. A few minutes after I sat down, a tall, thin middle-aged woman in a dark blue suit called my name. When I stood up, she flashed me a broad smile, and I responded with a nervous one of my own.

"I'm Sally Mitchell, one of the admissions officers," she said. We shook hands. "Come along and we'll have a little chat."

"Glad to," I said while we moved deeper into the office complex.

Okay, Hinda. Take a deep breath, girl, and try to impress.

She led me into her office, which didn't feel private because almost all of the upper walls were glass. Through the window over her left shoulder I could see people walking along Broadway. Mrs. Mitchell called my attention back to reality by asking, "Why do you want to come to Barnard?"

This question I had anticipated. I gave what I considered to be a wholly honest answer. "Who wouldn't? I want to get an outstanding education in the greatest city in the world." My voice shook a little. I wasn't sure I said enough so I added, lamely, "Well, anyway, that's why."

Her smile and a bob of her head confirmed that she had heard that one before. I still had time to differentiate myself, not give the same old answers

---

[12] Barnard was and still is the women's undergraduate college of Columbia University; at that time Columbia College was the undergraduate college for men only.

she'd gotten from every other applicant. As the interview progressed, I began to feel a little less jittery and I managed to keep my hands still on my lap.

Mrs. Mitchell looked over my application, remarking, "I see that you're involved with theater, the school newspaper and the literary magazine. Are you planning to major in English?"

"Yes, Ma'am," I answered confidently. "I understand the English department here is outstanding." That wasn't brown-nosing. I really knew that for a fact.

She smiled. "I imagine you also like to read?"

"Oh yes. I usually read about two unassigned books a week," I bragged.

She smiled at this. "Well, in that case, what book did you last read?"

My mind went blank. *What the heck did I read?* I grasped for anything I could remember. "*Tess of the D'Urbervilles*," I managed to choke out.

She nodded and said, "Good choice." Fortunately she didn't ask me to tell her anything about it because I had read it many months ago and couldn't remember it very well.

"Why '*Tess*?' What drew you to that particular book?"

"I like Thomas Hardy and am drawn to stories about the late 19th century. I had read *Jude the Obscure*, *Return of the Native* and *Far From the Madding Crowd*. When I find authors I like, I try to read everything they've written." She nodded. Was that nod one of approval?

After a few more questions, Mrs. Mitchell asked, "Tell me, Hinda. Would you like a student to take you around the campus?" That was my clue that the interview was over. Was it successful? I couldn't tell.

"I would love that," I answered. "Thank you so for speaking with me, Mrs. Mitchell. I hope to see you again."

"You'll have our decision on your admission in the middle of May," she said as she escorted me from her office.

I swallowed hard, realizing I had to wait four more months to find out if I was accepted.

Another handshake and I was led from Mrs. Mitchell's office onto the Barnard campus by a vivacious junior. She showed me the academic buildings, the library, the dormitories, the places where commuters hung out and the tiny green space she said everyone called "The Jungle."

"If you're looking for a rolling campus, you won't find it here at Barnard, but I think you'll find we have many other attractions," she said, laughing. Aside from a few inches of lawn here and there, all the rest of the campus was filled with academic buildings and dormitories.

I spent the next two hours with her and met girls from as far away as French Indonesia and Sweden, and as close as Brooklyn and the Bronx. I loved the idea that Barnard was not only metropolitan, but cosmopolitan as well. Too soon I had to leave to take a train to Poughkeepsie. Throughout that journey upstate, all I could think about was how terrific my New York City experience had been.

Despite its being my first choice school initially, Vassar was disappointing after Barnard. The night before my interview, I slept in the dorms and listened to conversations among the girls. I was like a fly on the wall in their world. I took in everything they did and said.

"Don't you think he's absolutely so cute? I'm going to sign up for his next class just so I can continue to stare at him," one freshman said.

This is so juvenile.

"I hate Mondays. You have to wait a whole week until you can go on a date again," another said.

These are college girls?

These girls lived without men on a daily basis. None right across the street. None in their classes. Vassar had been my first choice, but it was a disappointment after Barnard. I still had stars in my eyes from New York. I craved the atmosphere of Barnard College and Columbia University even more. I don't remember my interview at Vassar because, by that time, I had soured on the whole idea of going there and just didn't focus on it. I think it went well despite my lack of enthusiasm. On the train ride back from Poughkeepsie to Rochester, I reviewed my interview at Barnard over and over again. Was it good enough to get me in?

The third Friday in May was the day applicants received their private college acceptances and rejections. Mum let me drive her car to school that morning so I could get home fast at lunchtime to discover my fate. At 12:01 pm., I stared at the envelopes Mum had stacked for me. I looked at the embossing on the front and my name neatly typed as addressee. Which should I open first? Mum looked on anxiously, ready to comfort or rejoice with me.

My hands shook as I opened the first envelope. I opened Connecticut's first because I was pretty sure it was an acceptance and a scholarship offer. It was!

The scholarship was enough that I knew my parents could afford to send me there.

"That's a yes! One down, two to go!" I shouted, although Mum was standing near me.

She smiled. "Let's see what the others have to say."

I decided to open the envelope from Vassar next. Carefully I unfolded the letter. Another acceptance! "I'm in…" I read a little further. "Oh dear. They didn't offer much of a scholarship," I told Mum.

"I'm sorry, Hinda. I know you liked Vassar a lot," Mum said. "Open the last one. Maybe it's better news."

I took a deep breath and ripped open the last envelope, the one from Barnard. I scanned the letter quickly. Then reread it to make certain it said what I thought it said. Yes! My winging-it interview and a lot of fervent praying must have worked.

"Mummy! I can't believe it! Barnard accepted me and offered a huge scholarship. Oh my, I got in everywhere and they even offered me scholarships!" I whooped. After I gave Mummy a big hug, I ran to the phone to call Fedgie in Allentown, knowing she was waiting to hear the news from me.

"Well, Sis, I guess you're going to see more of me for the next few years," I began. "I'll be in New York at Barnard!"

"Great! You can come here for weekends or holidays if going home is too long or expensive, and Hy and I go into the City all the time. Oh, Hin, I'm so happy for you, and for us, too," she concluded.

As soon as I hung up, I turned to Mummy. She looked puzzled, saying "I thought Vassar was your first choice, and they accepted you."

I sighed. "Well, Mum, the truth is I fell in love with Barnard and out of love with Vassar when I visited them for my interviews. I didn't think I had a chance at Barnard, so I kept my wishes to myself. Plus, Mum, and this is a very big plus, they offered me a huge scholarship."

Seeing me so overjoyed, she was jubilant, too. That scholarship certainly would take some pressure off the family's financial concerns.

I called Daddy and Lyla to share the good news and then walked on air back to school to compare colleges with my friends. Almost everyone was going to his or her first choice, including Judy, who was going to Smith, despite her mother's apprehensions.

I was going to my first choice school, a New York City college. I couldn't wait!

A PARALLEL UNIVERSE

B Y July, Barnard requested I choose my freshman courses and submit them so that they could create a class schedule for me. Since it was summertime, I couldn't ask my high school guidance counselors for advice. My parents and my sisters thought my choices unimportant because college was only how I would spend time until I would leave to marry. As much as I looked forward to college, I think I also bought into the idea a little bit that I might do as my sisters had done.

A freshmen English class was required, but the rest was up to me. Sometime during my four years, I had to take two science courses, one with a lab component. Lyla's husband, Irv, helped me sort things out. He told me that Zoology with a lab would be a smart choice. I added courses in Government, Philosophy and Art Appreciation.

In early August, the college sent my room assignment and the name and contact information of my roommate, Geraldine Carro from Brookline, Massachusetts. Soon we were chatting long distance about curtains, bedspreads and other paraphernalia we would be bringing to make our little room homey. We mailed each other snapshots so that when we met, we wouldn't be strangers. I was getting more and more excited about college.

Neal and I had a long serious talk before we left that fall of 1957 for our respective schools. The past year, when he went to college and I was still in high school, we had relaxed our requirements of exclusivity. If a guy asked me to go to the movies, I went, but I didn't get involved with anyone romantically. This time I wanted it to be different. I told Neal I intended to date at college and I wouldn't rule out having a romantic attachment, although I very much wanted Neal to stay in my life. He told me that he felt I was totally kicking him out of my life, but I didn't feel that way. I wanted him in my life, but not exclusively. Neal let me know it was too painful for him to think of my dating anyone else. As a result we parted ways.

In early September, because Daddy couldn't get away from business, my mother and her friend Mrs. Scott drove me to New York with a trunk full of clothes, blankets, a pillow, towels, a bedspread, curtains and other necessities. My heart leaped into my throat as soon as our car crossed the George Washington Bridge into the City, and, heading south, approached the tiny Barnard campus on Morningside Heights above the Hudson River. I was about to start my new adventure away from family and friends.

Upperclassmen from both Barnard and Columbia Colleges helped us unload, placing my possessions on a cart, rolling it to the elevators and whisking it up to my room on the eighth floor of Brooks Hall. My room was good-sized. The walls were grey, but a bright grey color, not drab. There was a large closet, two desks, two dressers and two narrow beds, both of which had fresh folded sheets on them, ready for Gerri and me to make them up. All I had to do when I arrived was to pick a bed, a dresser, a desk, and a section of the closet and I could start unpacking. Gerri hadn't arrived yet; I decided to wait for her before I made any choices. I looked up and saw my mother staring at me. She had a curious look on her face. Mrs. Scott had already gone on to the hotel.

"What's the matter?" I asked Mum.

She shrugged and smiled. "Nothing, honey. I just can't believe I'm leaving my baby at college."

I hugged her tight and didn't let go for a long time. When I let go, I said, "You know, Mum, it's not going to get any easier for you if you stick around longer. Maybe you should meet up with Mrs. Scott at your hotel. We had a long drive."

Frankly, I wasn't thinking about her well-being. I was eager to begin the adventure of college living on my own. The sooner Mum left, the sooner that journey could begin. After a few more hugs and a few more kisses, she was gone. I wasn't even ashamed that I didn't go down the elevator with her to see her off. I wanted to be where the action was.

Girls who would occupy neighboring rooms started to arrive. The roommates next door were short brunettes from Newton, Mass and Shaker Heights. Down the hall, a triple room was occupied by a girl with a pixie cut from Pasadena, a tall overweight girl from Atlantic City and a petite curly-head from Cherry Hill. A sophisticated, dark-complected girl from Newport and a droopy-eyed blonde from Deposit also arrived on our floor. Blonde and bouncy Gerri finally walked into our room with her folks. While her parents were present, we were overly polite with one another, deciding issues such as which side of the room each of us wanted. After they left, we eased into laughter, hanging Lyla's old drapes on our window and making up our beds with the sheets left for us and matching brown spreads we had chosen. Together we wandered the halls and introduced ourselves to the other girls, almost all freshmen.

Later that afternoon, we began to learn the routines of mealtimes, having visitors and signing in and out. We took a walking tour of the compact campus. The entire college campus was the equivalent of four city blocks, including the dorms, classroom buildings, a gym, the library, a theatre, and the lounge used mostly by the girls who commuted to campus. This tour was review for me because I had toured the college when I came my interview, but a few of the girls were shocked with how small the campus was. Upperclassmen would arrive the next day and the campus life would begin for the new academic year. This was going to be great!

Because I entered Barnard expecting to become an English major, I looked forward particularly to my freshman English class. I sailed into it with great anticipation. I loved to read. I loved to write. I was certain that this was going to be my most enjoyable class.

About twenty of us met at 10am on Monday, Wednesday and Friday in a small classroom on the second floor of Barnard Hall, the oldest building on campus. The floor had seen better days; there were permanent scuff marks on the beige linoleum. Our wooden desks and chairs looked like relics from before the Second World War. The overhead lights were turned on low, but bright autumn light streamed through the high windows which lined the east side of the room. Professor Miner sat, not behind his desk, but generally with one buttock on the edge of it, leaning toward us.

One Monday, about two weeks after classes started, I entered the classroom, as always, with eager anticipation. The readings so far had been stimulating. My classmates and I generally gravitated to the same desks we had sat in since classes began so I moved into the second seat from the window in the second row. Professor Miner looked as if he hadn't moved since the Friday before; he was perched on the front of his desk, one buttock down and the other in the air. Our class began to discuss a piece by Walt Whitman that he had assigned the week before. I had read the assignment and was ready to discuss it.

A classmate sitting two seats away asked, "Did Whitman intend for this part to be provocative?"

Provocative? How is she using the word and what does it mean in this context?

Before I had a chance to figure this out, everyone else in the room nodded and Professor Miner seemed pleased that she had made this observation. Another classmate answered her question and moved the conversation forward. I don't remember what was said from that point on. The class went on, but I wasn't a part of it anymore. My mind whirled. I hoped this experience was an anomaly and the next class would be better.

Before we met again on Wednesday, I read and re-read the short story assignment to be better prepared. When the class met, another classmate suggested that this author might be reflecting Homer. *Homer? Who read Homer?* It turned out that many, if not most, of my classmates had done so and had made the same connection. I was shocked. I quickly looked to my left and then to my right. My classmates seemed unfazed by the tenor of the discussion. In fact, they joined in with comments of their own. Everyone, it seemed, had read the classics and had points of reference I didn't possess. Yes, I had read much of Shakespeare, Dickens, Shaw and Hardy. But I had never been exposed to Chaucer, Ovid, Homer or Sophocles.

My head grew hot. My throat went dry. It was as if I had been punched in the stomach. Nothing in these readings had suggested to me comparisons to other writers, living or dead. What was I missing? How did my classmates know things that I didn't know? I was planning to be an English major, and I didn't understand my classmates' remarks in freshman English! How did I ever think I would fit in at Barnard? In high school, my grade point average was near the top of my class, and I scored extremely well on the SATs. Even so I was at a loss.

Why wasn't I better prepared for college? How did I wind up at Barnard? They had accepted me and even offered money. I was in over my head! Who could help me now? I was too embarrassed to tell Gerri or the girls on my floor. And I didn't yet have a close enough relationship with anyone on the Barnard faculty to admit I needed help.

Zoology was even worse than English. Our professor assumed that anyone taking Zoology was pre-med. He zoomed through our text, giving him time to add and discuss more advanced work. His lectures at 11 am Monday, Wednesday and Friday were extremely difficult to comprehend, but at least they were tolerable. Thursday afternoon's four-hour labs were difficult, dispiriting, and disgusting. The lab reeked of formaldehyde, driving me from dissecting in the lab to the bathroom across the hall to lean over a toilet bowl.

There I was at the school of my choice in the city of my dreams, and I was floundering. I couldn't keep up with all of the readings and other assignments. I didn't understand what was being asked of me. I felt as if I had been dropped into a parallel universe, one where everyone else knew the language except for me. I discovered I had never learned how to study properly. In high school, everything had come easily for me. I'd do the assigned readings, but I never reviewed them or analyzed the material. I read it; I remembered it; I was done. College assignments in all of my subjects required more diligence, but I hadn't any idea how much. I was a failure. A fraud.

Worse yet, after only a few weeks of classes, I had to adjust to a new roommate. While Gerri and I got along extremely well, the girls who roomed next door fought loudly day and night. To keep harmony on the floor, Gerri and I decided to each take one of them as a new roommate. We did so by lot and, while I stayed in my same room, my roommate was now Linda, a petite Elizabeth Taylor look-alike from Shaker Heights. She didn't seem to be having any trouble with her classes; I couldn't bring myself to admit to her that I had problems.

Thursday's weekly nausea attacks were interrupted in October when I developed a blood clot in my left leg and had to be hospitalized for a week. This had happened to me as a senior in high school so I knew the drill: bed rest with my leg elevated, out of bed only for bathroom trips until the swelling went down. I could continue reading for all of my subjects, but I couldn't attend classes and it was impossible to make up my Zoology lab.

Lying in the college infirmary at St. Luke's Hospital, I wrestled with my feelings about being at Barnard. I knew I was definitely in over my head. I was holding on by my fingernails in my course work. For the first time in my life, I felt out-of-control, jettisoned into a world of super-brilliance and I had put myself in this untenable situation. The question now was: what do I do about it? Admit failure? Unthinkable. Leave New York and go back to Rochester? Oh, no. Not that. I didn't want to leave New York, and I didn't want to admit failure and go home.

One of the reasons that Barnard had originally appealed to me was because Allentown was only a short bus ride away. Fedg and Hy would also come into New York from time to time. I would meet them for dinner beforehand or for breakfast the next day before they went home. Hy also came to town alone for business and took me to fabulous restaurants I would otherwise have been unable to enjoy. He would listen to me go on and on about my life and rein me in when he thought my ideas were off-base or too ivory-tower. He'd try to lighten my concerns and give me pep talks about how I was just as smart as the other girls and it would all turn out just fine. I wanted to believe him.

Except for problems with school, I loved everything about New York City. I attended concerts at Carnegie Hall for 99c on certain Saturdays. I took the subway to the Village and heard extraordinary jazz played by Thelonius Monk, Sonny Rollins, John Coltrane and Max Roach. For a very low ticket price, I saw dress rehearsal previews of American Ballet Theatre's season. If a snow storm hit the East Coast, Fedgie's friends from Allentown would call to give me the seat numbers on their Broadway play tickets. Then, with a friend, I would go to the theater and explain why I didn't have the actual tickets. After everyone else was seated and the usher saw that those seats were still empty, we were allowed to enjoy the finest Broadway plays, all for free. I just couldn't give up this rich cultural life!

I thought to myself that maybe I should just tough it out, adopt an air of nonchalance, still try to do the best I could, take a lighter load and fake it until, perhaps, I'd begin to make it. That was a strategy I could live with. Maybe in the end, it would turn out, as Hy said, "just fine."

One day when I was still in the hospital, a young guy walked into my room looking as if he had stepped out of a poster advertising an early 20th century carnival. He was wearing a red-and-white striped jacket, a jaunty straw boater hat, and an enormous from-the-heart smile. My spirits lifted instantly! Ricky was a Columbia College sophomore who was volunteering at St. Luke's as part of his fraternity's social action requirement. He came by every day to see me. We talked about everything, sharing thoughts, goals, interests and ideas. I confessed to him my academic problems and he recalled his own tough freshman experiences. When I was released a week later, we began to date.

Ricky was bright and serious about his education, but he was entertaining, too. One evening when I was cramming for an upcoming exam, I refused to see him because I had to study. He begged me to come down from my dorm room for "just a minute" to see him. He promised he wouldn't keep me from my books for long. Reluctantly, I went down. He looked strange. His chest was twice the size it usually was. He grabbed me by the hand and led me outside onto the front porch of my dorm, without saying a word.

"What's so important?" I spat out impatiently. "You know how scared I am to take this test…" I stopped. He had taken off his jacket, revealing a beautiful velvet vest over a long-sleeved pink shirt, strange attire for a weekday. He said nothing. "Ricky?"

He remained silent, but was now smiling. He slowly unbuttoned his vest and cast it on the ground. He was still wearing a vest, but this one had blue and white stripes.

"What's going on?" My voice reflected my puzzlement.

Without acknowledging that he heard me, he unbuttoned that vest and threw it on top of the other one. He was now wearing a bright yellow vest! The striptease show went on for a long time. I must have counted 17 different vests! By the time he was down to his plain pink shirt, I was laughing hysterically.

Ricky grinned at me and said, picking up his clothes and departing, "Now you can study. I think you may be a little more relaxed."

"You bet! Thanks so much for the laugh break, Ricky." I went back to my studies with renewed enthusiasm.

By the end of first semester, I may not have learned enough to test well in my courses, but a little bit of New York had rubbed off on me. When I returned home for Christmas break, high school friends, especially those who had gone to colleges in small towns, oohed and aahed: "Hinda's gone beat!" Jack Kerouac's *On the Road* was all the rage and his female followers wore lots of sooty black eye shadow, no lipstick and all black clothes with black tights. I had the look, just not the sophistication to accompany it.

In fact, I was so unsophisticated when I started at Barnard that I was shocked by what I saw in the dorms. Girls drank a lot and not just beer. They drank hard liquor. Some girls even smoked marijuana. Girls had sex, not only with boys, but with each other! When I was home for Christmas break I shared some of my bewilderment with Mum, but I asked her not to tell Daddy. I knew he'd worry too much.

As we ate breakfast together on my last morning home before returning to New York. Daddy said, "So, Hinda, you've been exposed to some 'loose' women!" A small smile flittered over his lips,

"Arggh." I shot a glare at Mummy. "Uh, Daddy, I didn't want you to know about that. I asked Mum not to tell you!"

"But your mother and I have no secrets from each other, my dear."

I thought for a moment. "Let me ask you something, Daddy. Now that you know about the girls who might be bad influences on me, well, why are you letting me go back there?"

"Hinda, my daughter dear, I have had 18 years to teach you right from wrong. Wherever you go, I have to believe that you learned those lessons, and that you will make the right choices." And then, as if everything that needed to be said on the subject had been said, he continued, "Now, let's get a move on and get you to the airport!"

As I suspected, when first semester marks came out, I was in trouble. I managed to get Bs in everything, even English and the classroom portion of Zoology. However, I had failed the lab portion. This combination resulted in a D in Zoology and was enough to send me into academic probation for second semester, a secret I kept from my family. I knew they would try to persuade me to transfer out of Barnard, perhaps to the University of Rochester, where I could save some money by living at home. I begged my class advisor to allow me to drop the lab part of Zoology for second semester. I needed to take one science course with a lab to meet graduation requirements, but I promised to take a lab science the following year. She allowed the changes. Anything for Geology lab would be hands-down better than dissections!

By sophomore year, I had decided that it wasn't such a mistake to come to Barnard after all. I discovered other places to learn, such as the United Nations. Through a friend of a friend, I met an amazing man named A.C. Thompson, an American who worked there as a liaison to some African countries unrepresented as member nations. His job was to assure that they would receive financial support serving their health and education needs, especially for children. If I went to the U.N. on a free afternoon, I could use his name to get myself a special pass to the Delegates' Lounge where he would meet me and we could mingle with representatives from all over the world. I couldn't believe that I sat among international decision-makers. After all, I was just a young girl from Upstate New York and they were world leaders.

On one of her trips into the City, I decided to take Fedgie there. "Say, Fedg, let's head over to the United Nations. Have you ever been there?"

She said that was a good idea and that she'd never been there and had always wanted to go. I didn't tell her where we were headed within the building. As we walked into the U.N., she craned her neck to take in the unfamiliar surroundings.

I was delighted to be the leader for a change, the one guiding my older sister to a new experience.

When we approached the front desk, I smiled at the receptionist. "Hi," I said, "we're guests of A.C. Thompson. Will you please provide passes for the Delegates' Lounge where we're meeting him?" Fedg raised her eyebrows at the words "Delegates' Lounge." I was thrilled with her surprise. In a minute, passes in hand, we swept past security guards and ascended the escalator to the second floor.

"Are you sure you know where you're going?" Fedg asked as she followed along with me, flabbergasted at our easy entry.

"Oh, I've been here a time or two," I answered. When we got off the escalator, I turned sharply to the left and said, "We're almost there." We entered a large room filled with sofas, loveseats and chairs of various sizes and colors. The windows were floor-to-ceiling and had views of the East River and, beyond it, the borough of Queens.

"We can sit anywhere. A.C. will be here in a little while, depending on what else he's doing. Just make yourself at home," I said casually, knowing she didn't feel at home at all.

Her eyes grew wider when we sat down among people from all over the world, dressed in their indigenous clothes and speaking various languages. When my friend A.C. finally joined us and offered us dessert and coffee, Fedg could hardly eat or drink. She sat speechless, looking around the room, apparently shocked that her baby sister had access to such a throne of power! That U.N. association sparked my interest in learning more about how governments work, about giving a voice to the littlest among us, the children, and to how individuals could devote themselves to making the world a better place.

My social life was busy. I knew almost every girl who lived in the dorms, probably 600 of us. The rest of the college was made up of commuters, and I knew many of them because I sometimes made up the fourth for bridge between classes in the commuters' lounge. The summer before my girlfriends from Brighton High and I left for college, my friend Ellyn's mother insisted we all learn to play bridge. At Barnard, however, most of the girls who lived in the dorms played chess, not bridge. Playing bridge with the New Yorkers allowed me to expand my friendship circle.

Although Ricky and I no longer dated, I saw a number of different guys, one from Harvard, one from Cornell Med, and another from Columbia. But social life was not my prime consideration. I still needed to find a way for me to achieve at Barnard. Although I was doing better in my classes and pulling steady Bs, I decided success might lie in extracurricular activities.

Every year, freshman and sophomore classes competed in an event called Greek Games, and I was elected chairman of the whole shebang my sophomore year. While the actual competition took only four hours on a Saturday afternoon in March, planning took many months. Our committee chose Aphrodite as our theme and created dances, songs, poems and costumes to reflect various myths about her. We sewed replica costumes of ancient attire, not only for the athletes and dancers, but also for the girls who would pretend to be the horses pulling the chariots. The classes competed against each other in chariot racing, discus, and other ancient sports. It was fun as well as creative, and I was very proud when our class won. I got to ride around the auditorium in our chariot, pulled by other sophomores, yelling "Nike! Nike!"[13] at the conclusion of the day.

I had to work at school because money was tight at home. I was proud that I wasn't a financial drain on my parents. I joined the wait staff for formal dinners at the college. It was easy work and a good source of income until I was given the honor of serving the head table for a special dinner. I approached Mrs. MacIntosh, our college president, and the guest speaker invited to address the college, to serve coffee. Intent on being charming to the guest, I didn't pay attention to the coffee pot as I was pouring. Instead of just filling their cups, I overfilled them, spilling coffee on the tablecloth and the floor. I was mortified.

Mrs. MacIntosh was sweet, but firm. "Hinda," she said, placing her hand over mine, "perhaps you should think about changing to another campus job."

So I switched from waitressing to working the old-fashioned dorm switchboard every Sunday morning from 8 am to noon. It was fun to pull plugs from one place (callers) and line them up with other plugs (receivers). Hardly anyone called during those hours. I took my pillow with me and often slept between the calls. The neat part was that the father of one of my classmates was a journalist for the Associated Press on permanent assignment in Moscow. His weekly calls to his daughter came in two parts. First, the Russian operator would call and tell me that a call from Moscow was expected to come through in fifteen minutes. I would call Irina to alert her so that she could come downstairs to take the call in the privacy of the Residence Director's office. Then, when Moscow called back,

---

[13] Victory

I was again connected to the other side of the Iron Curtain. I tried to engage the Russian operator in conversation, but she was all business. My mind raced with scenarios to explain her reluctance to speak with me. Was she being watched? Were we being recorded? We were in a Cold War after all.

My best-paying job for one semester was with Columbia's Bureau of Applied Social Research, which was conducting a national survey of all Protestant clergy. The Bureau needed people to code answers from the surveys into a number system that could then be transferred into a computer. They paid coders based on an estimate of the number of surveys they believed would be completed in an hour. I thought I was doing well, but the graduate student in charge told me that I was working so fast that the Bureau would run out of surveys before they ran out of their grant money. He and I worked out a system where I worked at my pace, but they paid me by the batch I completed. Good for them. Good for me.

My preferred job was babysitting. I got to spend time in comfortable New York apartments and play with youngsters while getting paid for it. Once the little ones went to bed, I could do homework or watch TV, a luxury for me in those years. The only television set in the dorms was in a first floor dorm lounge and there were strict rules about its operation, mostly not allowing it turned on during evenings when we were supposed to be doing homework.

Babysitting jobs were initially secured through the Barnard Employment Office, but after a few assignments, most parents called me directly. At one home, I babysat for a five-year-old girl on Central Park West who had dark curls and amazingly round eyes. We had a lot of fun together, usually playing games and singing Broadway tunes. I was amazed that she knew every word of every song.

When I mentioned this to her mother, she laughed.

"Chlöe comes by her entertainment talent naturally. It's all in the family," she said. I didn't ask her what she meant, but I noticed she had a sly little smile as she spoke. It took me until my third visit to the apartment to notice the photograph of Chlöe's maternal grandfather, the entertainer Eddie Cantor, from whom she had obviously inherited her musical talents and banjo eyes.

My favorite babysitting assignment was for the literary critic, Alfred Kazin and his then-wife, writer Anne Berstein. The first time I went to their bright apartment on Riverside Drive, I thought Mr. Kazin looked familiar. Before I went back a second time, I noticed his picture on the flyleaf of a book I had just read, *A Walker in the City*. When I asked him to sign my copy, he looked both honored and uncomfortable. I later learned that *Walker* was his least favorite book. After it was published he felt that it was too revealing, too personal. He preferred his later books of literary criticism.

I adored their little Katie and loved playing with her, but after she went to bed, I was transfixed by their library, from which I was free to borrow. The Kazins treated me as an adult, not a college student, and encouraged me as a potential writer. When they invited me to one of their parties where I would get to meet their friends, Philip Roth, Saul Bellow and Bernard Malamud, I told them I couldn't come because I had to study. I wasn't confident enough to mingle with literary giants.

Even with all of my jobs, money was tight. I didn't travel much, even to go home, unless I could get a ride. I bought almost no clothing or shoes. I found used books when I could. I couldn't ask my parents for money. I had to rely on myself.

I began regaining more confidence by my junior year. I was still, as I had intended from the very start, an English major. At Barnard, the English Department was so large that a student was required to choose a specialty within the department, in literature, speech, drama or writing. As a sophomore, I had chosen writing as my specialty. The next year, however, I had a run-in with Mr. Parker, the professor who taught the core introductory writing course.

On the first day of classes, he looked around the room and announced he was not going to grade papers for so large a group. He insisted on reducing his class size and asked for volunteers to drop out. A few girls did. When I objected to his methods because he had not limited his class before enrollment, Mr. Parker snidely asked me to leave. I ran to Inez Nelbach, my wonderful class advisor, in tears. She knew that I wanted to take that class as a prerequisite for any future writing classes. G-d bless her. Miss Nelbach got me into a play-writing class without the prerequisite and suggested I switch my specialty to drama. I did.

I loved being able to participate in writing workshops, especially play-writing. My teacher was a professional playwright and adjunct professor named Howard Teichman, a creature of Broadway rather than of academia. He had co-written the hit play, *The Solid Gold Cadillac* with George S. Kaufman. Mr. Teichman was funny and supportive. Our major assignment, aside from the critiquing of plays, was to write an original one-act play.

I used members of my family as the characters and imagined a scenario not far removed from actual events. My play, *Far above Rubies*, centered on the role of the mother, my mother, in a situation where she stood behind her husband after he made a disastrous business decision, one which made no sense at all, but was based on emotion alone. She did it, as I dramatized her, because she believed it was her destiny as a Jewish wife to support her husband always and forever, whatever happened. When I began the play, I had no idea where it would go. I sat at my typewriter, letting the dialogue flow from my fingers. I was utterly spent when I typed the last words. It seemed as if the characters themselves had written the ending. I got an A on it, but the greater satisfaction came from having written my first serious play since grade school.

Later that year I wrote our junior class play, a musical based on the works of Lewis Carroll, called *T'was Brillig*. I also played a small part in it. I was thrilled that the play was performed on campus for three nights in the Minor Latham Theatre, considered an off-Broadway venue. While no one from *The N.Y. Times* or *Village Voice* came to review it, I knew deep inside that my play had an off-Broadway run.

During my junior year, Fedg started coming into New York weekly for acting lessons from a world-famous theatrical couple. I knew the husband, Herbert Berghof, because he taught a directing workshop at Barnard. One of my friends had roped me into participating in a one-act play she was directing as her course-work for Mr. Berghof's class. He critiqued her work and ours, the three of us actors, after a rehearsal and again after the final performance.

When Fedg and I met for dinner one week after her lesson and before her bus back to Allentown, she was confused about her most recent acting assignment and wanted to talk it out with me.

"Mr. B. wanted me to try to play a character very unlike myself. He said I'm always so 'sweetness and light' and I should try to find other emotions."

"That's good, isn't it?"

"Yes, but..." she shook her head slightly. "It's a part that's very hard for me to do. It's not even from a play, you see. Mr. B. had seen someone act this part and thought of me in the role. He said I reminded him of that actress. The dialogue comes from a short story about these two women..."

Oh my G-d! This is too great a coincidence! "Who wrote it?" I demanded.

"I think it was J.D. Salinger."

"*Uncle Wiggley in Connecticut?*"

"Yes, but how did you know that?"

Unbelievable! "Fedg, this is really important. Which role did he want you to play? Was it the woman who drinks?"

She stared at me, shocked. "Yes, that was the role, but ... what's going on here?"

I looked at her with a huge smile. "Oh my G-d, Fedg. *I'm* the woman Mr. B was referring to. One of my friends at Barnard took his directing workshops and had to stage a play. She picked '*Uncle Wiggley*' and needed actors. I helped her out and did that part for him twice. You reminded him of *me!*"

I was gleeful. Without knowing it, someone had recognized our sisterhood. We didn't look alike, we weren't built alike, our voices were entirely different. But there was something recognizable that we shared. We both *kvelled*[14] in that moment of sisterhood.

As much as I enjoyed most of my classes, all was not well between the English Department and me. In the first semester of my junior year, I enrolled in a course called "Drama." This was right up my alley. But the professor, Lucille Hook, taught the class solely as dramatic literature, expecting us to analyze a play from its words alone.

I knew that she and I might disagree, but I felt that I had to express my opinion. "Miss Hook," I said confidently in a class a week or so after the course began, "a play is so much more than just the words."

She didn't seem surprised by my words. Her tired tone in response indicated that she had heard them before. "This is how I have always taught this course, and this is how I will continue to teach."

I just couldn't accept that as the last word on the subject. I was a playwright, so words were important to me, but they were just the start of what made a play. "But, Miss Hook," I persisted. "What about the director? What about his or her interpretation? What about the actors, the set designer, the costumes? Don't they count?"

"Not in my class they don't!" And that was her final word on the subject.

I was frustrated. If I stayed in the English department with a concentration

---

[14] rejoiced

in drama, I was going to have to take additional classes from Miss Hook. That prospect didn't appeal to me, and I was pretty certain she wasn't looking forward to having an argumentative girl like me in her future classes. I went to see Miss Nelbach, my understanding advisor, to ask her what to do.

She listened to my dilemma and smiled. "You know, Hinda, you don't have to stay in the English department. You have quite enough credits in Government to change majors. How about getting the heck out of English before you get into another dispute?"

This sounded like good advice, something I could live with. I had many credits in Government because my visits to the United Nations had spurred my interest in government service as a career. By changing majors, I could avoid the conflict with Miss Hook and be allowed to take some of my upper level classes on the Columbia University side of Broadway, classes which were open to both colleges. My menu of available courses had just doubled.

One of the courses I chose for the next semester at Columbia was Modern Hebrew. I had always wanted to go to Israel, but I couldn't speak the language. The Hebrew I had learned at my synagogue from age eight until I was 13 was liturgical, not conversational Hebrew. Jewish children like me were taught ancient Hebrew using the Bible as textbook. What I had learned was useful for praying, but not for conversing.

Not knowing Modern Hebrew hadn't bothered me when I was a kid, but a long-distance phone call to my parents the previous summer had changed my thinking. The call came from was a woman speaking half in Yiddish, half in Polish. At first my parents were confused by what she was saying, and then they understood. The call was a voice from the past, a voice once thought silenced by the Holocaust. It was Daddy's niece Malka, thought to have gone to Treblinka with the rest of Daddy's family. She called to say she would soon be coming to see us all the way from Tel Aviv, Israel!

Malka was three years old when Daddy left Poland as a young man in 1920. Until her call, he hadn't known she had survived. But he remembered her, a little red-haired toddler, his half-brother Zechariah's youngest daughter. Malka became determined to discover if she had any relatives still living. It took her 15 years to locate Daddy and her cousins in Toronto. She and her fifteen-year-old son Benjamin (Yumi) came to Canada and the United States during the summer of 1959 to meet relatives lost to her so long ago.

I'll never forget the day Malka came to see us. One of our cousins from Toronto drove her and Yumi to Rochester. All morning we kept looking out the window, as if watching for her would make her arrive sooner. Finally, in the early afternoon, we heard a car pull into the driveway and, looking out, saw it had Ontario license plates. Mum, Lyla and I all looked at Daddy, who was ashen-faced, his feet seemingly frozen to the floor. He didn't even blink. When the doorbell rang, someone, maybe Mum, opened it up. In walked a well-dressed petite woman with prematurely graying red hair. Her facial expression appeared solemn until you saw that her eyes were sparkling. Malka nodded at Mum as she passed by her, not ignoring her, but keeping her eyes boring straight ahead as they locked with those of Daddy. They stood there and stared at each other for what seemed like forever, but was probably just a moment or two. I don't remember who made the first move, but at some point, Daddy and his long-lost niece threw their arms around each other, neither one of them able to let go, Malka's head just reaching Daddy's shoulder, Daddy's head bent over hers. They just stood there together and sobbed. Daddy groaned and gasped deep breaths, making mournful noises I'd never heard before and haven't since. Yumi and our Toronto cousin stood with us and watched this scene, no one able to speak.

When they let go of each other for a moment, Daddy croaked out, "I remember you. You were just a little girl, but I remember your red hair. You were always smiling…"

"Uncle, uncle," Malka kept saying. "Mine uncle."

They embraced again, perhaps even tighter than before. We were silent, weeping with them and for them as we all thought of all those who were not in the room, the rest of the large family who had been annihilated.

The two of them were all that was left of the Rotenberg family from Ivansk. Those of us who witnessed their reunion stood silently, respectfully, under-standing the power of their emotions. Tears streamed down our faces. It took a while - maybe fifteen minutes - until Daddy and Malka were able to let go of one another. Mum offered coffee, tea, some cake, but no one accepted the offer. What we were hungry for was Malka's story.

She was able to speak only a little broken English, so she spoke mainly in Yiddish which Mum later translated for Lyla and me. As a teenager in Poland, Malka had dated a young man named Meir Kohn who was active in a Poland Zionist organization helping Jews leave Europe for Palestine. They married in the spring of 1938. Meir left almost immediately for Palestine with a group of Jews, promising to come back for her. He returned a year later to save her. They left for Palestine a few weeks before the Nazis overran Poland, effectively closing the door on future escapes.

As best as she could in English, Malka talked to me about her daughter Sarah who was my age. Since Sarah was studying English, Malka suggested that Sarah and I should correspond. Within a few weeks, Sarah and I began writing to one another but, because of my limited Hebrew, we wrote in English only. Being able to take Modern Hebrew at Columbia in my junior year would be a gift.

Word by word my Modern Hebrew vocabulary grew. I was able to take only one year of Hebrew so the verbs I learned were all in the present tense. But I could make myself understood, albeit just barely.

When I learned that Sarah was planning to visit North America, I looked forward to trying my Hebrew with her in person. In the spring of 1960, she visited first her father's relatives in Montreal and then our mutual relatives in Toronto. On Spring break, I convinced my parents to let me drive to Toronto to stay with relatives and meet my pen pal for the first time. Although we had exchanged photos and had written letters sharing our thoughts and dreams for the future, when we met, we met awkwardly, as strangers. We sat silently and then both of us started to say something at the same time. That made us laugh, and the laughter allowed us to be more comfortable with one another. After our initial shyness passed, Sarah and I became friends. It was hard to let go of her when my break ended, but I had to go back to school. She was staying in Canada through the summer and flying home through New York, so I made her promise that before she left, she would visit me at Barnard.

That fall of my senior year was exciting for a number of reasons. One important one was that I voted for the first time. Jack Kennedy was my choice for President. The dorm advisors suspended the television rules election night as a crowded roomful of us waited up for results. We were exhausted the next day, but oh, so happy!

Two weeks later, Sarah came to stay with me in my dorm room. Wanting to make a good impression on her, I made my friends promise to be on good behavior. We were angels for all of two days.

On the third morning, the hall telephone rang at 7:30 am. One of the girls whose room was closest to the phone banged open her door and went to answer it, yelling every curse word in her extensive vocabulary at the top of her lungs.

I sat up in bed suddenly and looked at Sarah who also sat upright in her cot. I shrugged my shoulders and gulped, "Oops."

She giggled. "I was wondering when you would all start acting like real American college girls."

Sarah came to my classes, went to concerts and museums with me, and generally enjoyed New York. Together we visited the latest phenomenon in the City: Israeli coffee houses. For some reason that I never discovered, Sarah wouldn't admit to Israelis that she, too, was a *sabra*, a native born Israeli. She would, however, give herself away when she'd blush over some remarks about us made in colloquial Hebrew by young Israeli guys at the next table. We had so much fun together that it was hard to say *l'hitraot*[15] when she left for the airport. We were committed to developing our relationship through long-distance correspondence.

I returned to Rochester each summer a little more sophisticated on the outside, but a little more frightened inside. The sophistication came naturally from living among New Yorkers in the most forward-looking city in the world. The fear came from the realization that, at some point, I would graduate, and I would have to do something with myself.

During the summer between my junior and senior year, I was working in downtown Rochester at a well-paying, boring secretarial job when I was introduced to a tall, amiable, young man named Tom. He was a few years older than I, entering his third year at Albany Law School. We dated almost exclusively for the six or seven remaining weeks of summer before we returned to our schools. He was nominally Jewish, but not Jewishly educated. He was eager to learn more about Judaism, and I was eager to teach him. I liked him. He loved me. When we returned to our respective schools, we wrote and spoke long distance about once a week. Every five or six weeks, he'd come to New York City for a weekend, staying with friends who worked or went to school in Manhattan.

When Thanksgiving break came, I took the train to Albany, and Tom and I drove to Rochester together. That weekend he took me to dinner at his home, and I met his parents for the first time. They lived in an elegant house in an affluent part of the city. His father was a doctor with an office adjacent to the house. His mother was well-read and seemed interested in art, ballet, theatre. I warmed to them immediately.

---

[15] (Leh-hit-rah-ot) Good-bye, until we meet again

After dinner, Tom's mother took me on a tour of the downstairs and made special mention of her china and silver. "Tom is an only child," she remarked.

I nodded, wondering why she mentioned this.

She turned to me and continued, "All of my things will go to him and his wife including my jewelry, and I have a lot of really nice pieces!"

I didn't know how to respond to this so I only nodded and remained silent. *What had Tom told her about us?* I asked him in the car on the way home, but he just smiled and led me to believe that this was his mother's way of letting me know she liked me.

During Christmas vacation, it became apparent that his answer at Thanksgiving had not been the full story. Tom proposed. I had some niggling doubts about my feelings. On the other hand, the future seemed to have fallen into place: We would both graduate from our schools in the spring and move back home with our parents. I would get a job in city government. Tom would take the New York State Bar exam and join a law firm by the time we married in the fall or winter. It seemed ideal. I accepted him.

Tom planned to come to New York for a weekend before Valentine's Day so that we could go to the Diamond Exchange district to pick out my engagement ring. I began to panic. I adored this sweet, bright man, but I knew I didn't love him. How could I marry him?

During my senior year, I was President of the dorms and, as a result, became close with Miss Stevens, our dorm advisor. I popped into her office to ask for her help. For the past three and a half years, she and I had had numerous conversations about school, family, my social life, and concerns about the future, but she could sense that this time I wanted more than talk. I needed answers. Miss Stevens had always maintained an open door policy, but, at my request, she closed the door.

"What should I do? Tom's so nice and so dear, but I just don't love him."

Miss Stevens looked me straight in the eye and said, "Hinda dear, if you don't love him, why in the world would you marry him?"

Why indeed. I nodded, truly sorry that I had let things between Tom and me go so far. When I didn't say anything, Miss Stevens could see from my body language that I knew what I had to do.

"Remember," she said as we parted, "the longer you let this go on, the worse it will be for both of you."

I left her office still not saying anything. I'm not even sure I thanked her for her help.

I thought over my situation and resolved to do the right thing. I didn't want to marry Tom and it was wrong to let him think otherwise. I called him. After chit-chatting about nothing of importance, I blurted out, "Tom, I don't want you to come to New York to buy a ring because I don't want to marry you." I caught my breath after this outburst. There was silence at the other end. "Tom? Are you there?"

His voice was low and shaky. "Hinda, you're just getting upset because I've rushed you, right? Let's give it some more time. We don't have to get formally engaged yet. We can wait until..."

"No, Tom, I mean it," I broke in. "I've thought this over and over again. I don't have the feelings for you that I should have for a future husband. Please accept what I'm saying. I never meant to hurt you, but...I just can't."

Finally, he accepted my decision, and we hung up. I felt terrible about breaking his heart, but so relieved that I had broken up with him.

It didn't take long before my parents called. Although they were both on extensions, Daddy did most of the talking. "What have you done? You've embarrassed us. What's the matter with Tom? He'd be a fine husband."

"Daddy, I'm sorry that you're embarrassed, but the truth is I don't want a fine husband. I want one I can love, and I don't love Tom."

Mum suggested, "You could always grow to love him..."

"Mummy, while you're growing to love someone, you still have to go to bed with him. I don't want to go to bed with him."

End of discussion.

So there I was. Spring semester of my senior year loomed, and I had no idea what I would do after graduation. I thought about taking the LSATs, the entrance exams for law school, but three things stopped me: even if I scored well, my undergraduate marks probably wouldn't make me an attractive candidate to any school I might want to attend. I also was coming out of Barnard with a little debt and couldn't imagine how I would pay for law school, and, most of all, I thought that if I did get into a good school and managed to find the money to pay for it, I was still taking a man's slot at that school. Even after almost four years at a woman's college, I still couldn't think of myself as a career woman.

I would have to jump into adulthood without a parachute.

For weeks after I broke up with Tom, I couldn't fall asleep until well after midnight, and when I finally slept, I couldn't get myself up in time for my classes. Questions about the future beset me. What would I do after graduation? What did I *want* to do? Where would I live? Where would I work? Would I be able to find a job? What would happen to my college friendships after we all split up after graduation? I slept through weekends, hardly studying at all. Every now and then one of my friends would drag me to the Cloisters or down to Riverside Park for a picnic, just to get me into the fresh spring air. While I was out with them, I felt good. When I returned to my dorm room, the same questions hovered over me.

My roommate didn't help much. Although I had been living with Gennie since our sophomore year, we frequently went our separate ways. She was committed to her studies, hoping to go home to Newport to teach, save enough money, and, hopefully, be accepted at the Sorbonne in Paris for a Master's degree in French. She focused on herself and her studies, and she let me do, or not do, my thing. Her only suggestion was, "Go see Dr. Nelson at the college health center and tell her what's going on." Not knowing what else to do, I followed her advice.

Dr. Nelson listened as I told her what was going on with my upside down life and handled me some pill bottles, saying, "Take one of these pills every morning and one of these other ones every night. You'll be fine."

"How do I know which is which?" I asked.

"The green ones are 'go' for when you get up, and the red ones are 'stop' for when you want to go to sleep. Simple."

That was her entire advice. She didn't ask me to come back to see her. There was no suggestion of counseling. I did what she had advised. The red ones knocked me out so deeply that, no matter how early I took one, most of the time I still awoke too late for morning classes. When I did manage to get up, the green pill made me jumpy and unable to concentrate all day. I was never hungry and often slept through mealtimes. I lost 10 to12 pounds in a few weeks. After about a month, I stopped taking the pills; they weren't helping me straighten out my life.

With my bizarre sleep/wake schedule, I was fortunate to pass most of my courses. I managed to do extensive research for my required senior thesis. I delved into the organization of the Jewish Agency, the quasi-government of the Jewish part of Palestine under the British Mandate which had divided the land between Arabs and Jews. I developed theories about how those areas became fully operational Cabinet departments of government, once Israel was created on May 14, 1948. In the end, my advisor wasn't impressed with the scholarship of my research or my writing, which disappointed me, but I was relieved that my thesis was at least accepted. Unfortunately, with all my absences, I failed Spanish and Economics, leaving me a few credits short for graduation. I would have to go to summer school to receive my degree.

I had to let my parents know that I wouldn't be graduating on time. I waited three days before I made the call. Mum answered and I plunged in, "I have something to tell you. Maybe ask Daddy to get on the extension so I can tell both of you at the same time." Before he picked up the other phone, I was already crying.

When I heard that they were both listening, with sniffling punctuating my words, I said, "I messed up and failed two courses." I paused to swallow the lump in my throat. Neither of them said a word. "I'm so ashamed. My advisor tells me I can make up the credits this summer. If you come to graduation it will look just the same, honestly, with me getting something from the college president, only it will be a conditional certificate not a diploma. I'm sorry to disappoint you. I'm so sorry."

I waited for someone to say something on the other end. Silence. Finally, Daddy said, "Well, I can't say I'm happy, but we'll come for the graduation. We'll talk about it when we're together."

Mum and Daddy came to graduation exercises and their fake smiles mixed with long faces let me know that they were terribly disappointed in me, but trying to make the best of it. We went out to dinner and celebrated as if I had actually graduated, but we all knew I had not. I would have felt better if we had talked about it, but I could see by their faces that the subject was closed. Daddy suggested that I return to Rochester to take my remaining credits at the University of Rochester. If there was anything I knew, it was that I wasn't ready to go home. I was desperate to stay in New York, to be able to enjoy everything the City had to offer. I told them that if I couldn't arrange a summer job and classes in New York, I would come home.

Luckily I was offered a part-time job working in the Barnard dorms over the summer. It came with room and board as well as enough of a stipend that I could support myself while I took two morning classes at Columbia University

to complete my degree. The decision about what I was going to do after graduation was thus postponed from May to August.

SCRAPPING BY

WHEN my summer job in the dorms ended, I found an inexpensive rooming house near Barnard offering a bedroom and the use of a shared bathroom and kitchen until I was settled with a job and a roommate. I called Wendy Phillips, my red-headed friend since we were seven years old at Camp Seneca Lake and my high school sorority sister. She and I had agreed that if we were both still single after college graduation, we would work and live together in New York. By August we put that plan into action.

Wendy moved into the rooming house with me and we began searching for jobs. As a graduate of Syracuse University in communications, she looked into broadcasting and soon found employment with a public radio station uptown from our temporary home.

As a government major, I considered employment with either federal, state or city government. I put in applications with the City of New York and the State of New York, and signed up to take civil service exams. I was disheartened to learn that, if I didn't get a very high score on a civil service exam, I would qualify for only the same ones that any high school graduate could get.

I was truly on my own for the first time. Because I wasn't going to my real home, I decided to try to recreate some semblance of family for myself in New York. Living with an old friend like Wendy was one step. Perhaps working for a Jewish organization, hopefully with other young Jewish people, could be another. I asked the Barnard employment office for help.

One of the places they sent me for an interview was to the Jewish Theological Seminary (JTS). Mrs. Rose, head of personnel there, spent a lot of time with me and asked a lot of questions about my background, education and interests. Was she considering me for an administrative position?

Then she casually asked, "Can you come back tomorrow for a typing test?"

I was appalled. Since when did a Barnard graduate need to type to get a job? I nodded, too shocked to speak, but I vowed that was the last they'd see of me!

I returned to the Barnard employment office a few days later to get more leads. Suzie, the counselor who worked with me, mentioned JTS. "They really like you, Hinda. They called here because they wanted to offer you a job, but you didn't go back. What happened?"

I debated with myself whether I wanted to confess the reason. "Suzie, they wanted me to take a typing test!"

"And?"

Her reaction surprised me. I thought she would immediately understand how insulted I would be. "I would hope employers would want me for my brains, not for my secretarial skills."

She laughed. "Is that all?"

Didn't she get it? I plowed on. "Well, I might have to do some typing on a job, but I type with only a few of my fingers, and I look weird doing it." I paused. "I'm actually pretty fast and accurate though."

Suzie smiled. "Go back and see Mrs. Rose. I think she has something in mind for you that will require you to type, but will predominantly use your brain. And I don't think they'll care how many fingers you use."

I went back and was hired to work for JTS temporarily as secretary to Dr. Simon Greenberg, the Vice-Chancellor of the Seminary. A six-week job was better than no job, so I accepted the offer. In addition to his administrative and teaching schedule at JTS, Dr. Greenberg was the President of the University of Judaism in Los Angeles. I was to be laid off when he left for California.

A week before his departure, I asked him for a few hours off the following morning so that I could go to a promising job interview with the U. S. Housing and Home Finance Agency. "Oh no," he said, with finality in his voice, "I'm not letting you go anywhere."

I frowned and didn't try to hide it. He was being selfish. After all, I was going to be out of a job in another week!

Then, with an impish smile and a teasing tone, he asked, "What if I can arrange for you to continue working for me, even when I'm not here? Would you stay?" He told me that I was the best assistant he'd ever had, the only one who could maintain his erratic schedule, understand his scribbled notes, decipher his dictated sermons and maintain contact with his students, especially when he was unavailable.

Whew! "I'd love to stay, Dr. Greenberg. I really like it here." I enjoyed working in an academic environment, expanding my Jewish knowledge, and flirting with rabbinical students. Dr. Greenberg arranged for me, in his absence to work as a research assistant with the American Jewish History Center.

A few weeks later, entering the cafeteria line for lunch at the Seminary, I had an unexpected reunion. I had to look twice at the man in line in front of me, but then I was sure.

"Burt? Is that you?" I peered into the familiar yet unfamiliar face of Burton Kolko.

He turned at the sound of my voice and stared at me. It took him a few seconds to speak. "Hinda?"

"Yeah, it's me. What brings you here?"

He chuckled. "Kosher food, of course. And you?"

"I work here. Let's catch up over lunch unless you're meeting someone else…"

We sat down across from each other and chatted while we ate. He caught me up on his life, from college at University of Pennsylvania, marriage to Naomi, his college sweetheart, and enrollment at Columbia Law School. I told him about graduating from Barnard, now working in New York and living with Wendy who he remembered from camp. Although talk flowed easily between us, there was no spark in our being together. It was as if we had never been best friends. Burt ate his lunch quickly and I had the sense he was rushing to get away from me. There was no talk of getting together, of introducing me to his wife, of exchanging phone numbers. It had just been too long a time since we were children and too wide a gap had formed. Although I was sad that we couldn't rekindle the spark of our friendship, I was content knowing that he was happy.

Now that Wendy and I had good secure jobs, we scanned the ads for a permanent apartment in our price range. After looking at many places on the upper West Side, our preferred location, we walked into a fourth-floor walk-up on West 88th Street between West End Avenue and Riverside Drive. We were immediately struck by the brightness of the place, with huge almost floor-to-ceiling windows in both the living room and the bedroom. Another nice touch was a fireplace which, we were told, was non-working, but it still gave the living room some pizzazz. The bathroom was so tiny that the only way we could be in there at the same time was if one of us was in the shower. The main room worked well as both a living and dining room with a compact kitchen at one end: a counter with a sink, a drop-in stove, and a half-size refrigerator below. Above were shelves for dishes, pots, pans and silverware. Best of all, we could afford the rent. We took it.

After we signed the lease and got the key, we dedicated a Sunday to readying our new home before the formal move-in. We laughed and scrubbed almost the whole morning until we heard a knock at the front door. We opened it to discover a young, slightly built black woman, holding a mop in one hand and a bucket in the other.

She smiled at us. "I thought you might need some help."

Wendy and I looked at each other, not knowing how to respond. My first thought was 'how the heck did she know we were in here cleaning?' My second was that we had no funds to pay a cleaning lady. I turned to Wendy, who looked as confused as I.

"Gosh, thanks," she said. "We're just about done here." I was grateful she stepped in.

We were just about to close the door when the woman spoke again, still smiling. "Well, if you need anything, just knock on the door of the next apartment. I'm Lee Beasley. My husband Red and I are your neighbors. See you soon I hope."

Oh my. After we closed the door, Wendy and I turned to each other, embarrassed. We hadn't considered Lee might be a neighbor. We had assumed that she was a cleaning woman as soon as we saw her complexion. We may have been college graduates, but we certainly had a lot to learn. Over time Lee, Red and their baby Donna became a part of our lives. As neighbors, we shared meals, penetrating conversations, music preferences, and sports talk. When there was something on television worth seeing, they invited us into their apartment for the show. When they wanted to kick back and listen to music, we shared our stereo with them.

Wendy's aunt and uncle were downsizing as we were moving into our place and donated a kitchen table and some kitchen gear to us. The best donation coming from them was a bird cage. We bought a parakeet and named him Lollypop. We bought inexpensive couches, chairs and a rug, and asked our landlords if they could supply bedroom furniture. They could and did!

Because we had little room to store fresh food, one of us stopped at the corner market after work every day. Money was tight. We each got paid every two weeks, and when we did, we each put $20 in a "food cup." We generally ate well-balanced meals the first week and squeezed out leftovers or ate pasta the second.

I had stayed in New York City so that I could have more time to enjoy all the plays, concerts, performances, museums, and galleries with no competition from schoolwork. Now I had the time to do these things, but not enough money to pay for them!

One Sunday, for example, Wendy and I wanted to see a double-feature at the local art film house, but we weren't sure we could afford it.

"How much is in the food cup?" I asked.

Wendy checked. "Counting change, we have $5.04."

"I think I have at least a dollar in my wallet. How about you?" We began checking our wallets and looking for loose change in the bottom of our purses. We came up with a little more.

Wendy said, "We'll need $3.00 apiece for the movie and 55 cents apiece to get to work tomorrow. That's $7.10. We have that and a few cents to spare."

"Wait a minute. How about having money for lunch tomorrow and then getting back home?" I asked.

Wendy smiled. "I get paid tomorrow. I'll cash my check at noon, and you can walk over, and we'll have lunch together. Then we'll have bus fare to get home and to work the next day when you get paid."

We enjoyed that double feature, but we couldn't afford any popcorn.

Wendy and I had many friends in the City, people we knew from college, colleagues from work, friends of friends. We hosted a few BYO parties at the apartment, providing snacks and desserts, and invited everyone we knew. We both dated some terrific guys, but developed no relationships that became serious.

Fedg still came into the City from time to time and we generally met for lunch. One Monday in December we arranged that she would meet me at the Seminary and have lunch with me there. When she arrived, she seemed distracted.

"What's wrong, Fedg?" I asked as soon as we finished eating.

"Gee, Hinda, I hate to tell you this, but Bubbie died over the weekend."

I was shocked. Mum and Daddy hadn't told me. "So why are we here in New York and not with the family in Rochester?"

Fedg explained that Aunt Min was gravely ill and Mum, Daddy and Aunt Min's husband, Uncle Joe, wanted to bury Bubbie as soon as possible so that there would be less strain on Aunt Min. They didn't want to have to wait until Fedg and I could arrive from out-of-town.

"Well, we still have to go to Rochester as soon as we can anyway. Mum and Aunt Min need us there to comfort them." She agreed. She was able to get to Rochester during the week and I spent the next weekend there. It was the last time I saw my aunt alive. She died less than four months later and Mum was left with no members of her nuclear family. When we were in Rochester for Aunt Min's funeral and *shiva*[16], my sisters and I arranged for a professional photographer to take our portrait so that we could give it to Mum as a surprise for Mother's Day. We were her family now.

During this time in New York and at the Seminary, I was happy, but not at peace. I felt that something was undone and I wouldn't be really happy until it, whatever it was, was completed. Was it a love interest? A job that would lead to a career? Something else? I wasn't sure.

The more I worked at the Seminary and the more I became steeped in Jewish learning, the more desperately I wanted to visit Israel. I had thought about going since 1948 when the State was created. How wonderful that there was some place on earth where Jews could be Jews, and no one could make us leave or kill us if we stayed.

I wanted to visit Sarah, but after paying the rent, the utilities, the phone bill, and still have money for food, an occasional movie and bus fare, I just couldn't seem to save anything. Also, Barnard required scholarship grantees to take part of their senior year grant as a loan, so I had that expense as well. To keep my connection with all things Israeli, I continued to frequent Israeli coffee houses in my neighborhood, learned all of the newest Hebrew songs recorded by popular groups and kept current on Israeli politics.

At the Jewish Theological Seminary, it seemed that almost everyone had been to Israel at least once. Israel and Israeli life were part of the Seminary's social life, conversations, billboard advertisements, and concerts. Even the food in the cafeteria mimicked Israeli food vendors, with offerings such as *chumus*, *t'cheenah*, *falafel* and *pita*.[17] The desire for Israel grew within me daily.

In August of 1962, I called home to discuss my dilemma with my parents. After listening to me, Daddy asked, "Are you ready to come home?"

---

[16] Seven day period of mourning during which mourners are visited by friends

[17] Middle eastern foods

"What are you proposing?" I asked, knowing and not knowing at the same time.

Daddy continued, "If you're serious about saving for Israel, here's what I'm suggesting. Come back to Rochester to work, and live with us. That way you won't have to pay room and board, and you can put that money away for your Israel trip."

Daddy had found a great solution for me, but I had someone else to think about. I couldn't accept Daddy's offer until I had talked it over with Wendy. "Thanks, Daddy. Let me call you in a few days and let you know my decision."

After talking with my parents, I told Wendy about their offer and asked what it would mean to her if I left. Our lease would be up the next month, so we had no obligation to stay in the apartment.

Wendy smiled. "It's funny that this is coming up right now. Some girls from work are looking for an additional roommate to live with them nearby on West End Avenue. I told them I wasn't available, but now I can tell them I'll be their roommate." She gave me her blessings.

I went home.

TIME TRAVEL

COMING home to live with my parents was comforting, but not really comfortable. While I was at college, my parents had moved from our three bedroom house to a two bedroom apartment. They had turned the second bedroom into their television room. Every night I had to open up the sofa and remake it as a bed. Each morning I had to do the reverse. I felt like a guest in my own home and that wasn't the worst of it.

Alas, they had relapsed into being "The Parents" and nothing I did or said could forestall their questions. I heard: "When will you be home? Where are you going? Who are you going with?" All were questions I had successfully avoided for five years. Now I couldn't dodge them so I kept my eye on my goal, going to Israel and saving enough to get me there.

Initially I sought employment with Jewish organizations because I had the experience of working in that environment at Jewish Theological Seminary. There was little available. I interviewed for a secretarial position at a Reform temple. Rabbi Bronstein was impressed with my background and knowledge, but wouldn't hire me. "Hinda, you need a job to challenge you. This isn't it," he said. I kind of agreed with him, but I wanted a job so much that I took his turn-down hard.

Within weeks I found a secretarial job with the Department of Urban Renewal, part of Rochester's city government. Technically, I wasn't allowed to work for the city because I lived in a suburb, but I was told by others who had government jobs that applicants sometimes fudged their addresses. So I did it too; I really wanted the job.

Our department had many simultaneous projects in the pipeline and a great deal of federal money was flowing into the city for renovation and renewal in the Genesee Crossroads area, the Third Ward, and at the Liberty Pole. My boss, William Denne, and I had great rapport. He trusted me with non-secretarial responsibilities on a few projects, such as making all arrangements for and hosting the jury during the Liberty Pole design competition. I was the only staff member to work with the judges, all out-of-towners, and the first to know which design they ultimately chose. I was also the only secretary in the department with a college education, and the others turned to me frequently for assistance and assurance. Maybe I was only a secretary, but the people I worked with and the assignments they gave me made me feel important.

In many ways, this year in Rochester could have been a wasteland for me. My life had been in New York for the past five years. There I had friends, college or work, a bustling city, and opportunities for cultural enrichment. In Rochester I had almost none of those things, at least at first. Fortunately, within a month of coming home, I reconnected with Tala Hoffman, a friend I had known back in grade school. She and I attended every dance and party we could get ourselves invited to. When neither one of us had a date, we went together to movies, plays and dance performances. I couldn't believe that Rochester had so many excellent cultural venues such as the Rochester Philharmonic Orchestra, the Memorial Art Gallery and the Nazareth Arts Center. I started to miss New York City's arts life less and less.

I eventually met guys through mutual friends, and dated a few. No one seemed interesting enough to warrant a long run. My mother would say, "Go out with him anyway if he asks. You never know who you'll meet while you're out." I saw it differently. I felt that if I were seen with one of the geeky guys, a really nice guy might consider me less interesting and pass me by. My goal was singular at that time anyway: Make money to go to Israel.

After a year of saving, I had earned enough to afford a trip to Israel for three weeks. I would be the first in my family to make this pilgrimage. Even before I booked my tickets, I had done research, planned where I would travel and what in particular I wanted to see. On the morning of my overseas flight, I arrived in New York six hours early to run last minute errands and to meet Fedg, who had taken a bus into the City to spend the day with me. She was almost as excited as I was that I would soon fly off to Tel Aviv.

The day in New York was blazingly sunny and hot for September. Fedgie and I walked around, talking nonstop about Mum and Daddy, Lyla and her family, and what was happening with her bunch in Allentown. "Anyone interesting in your life?" she asked, smiling widely.

"No, sister dear. There's no one special – yet!" I filled her in on my job, and we shared what we were reading, seeing at the movies and doing for fun.

I had sent bi-monthly checks for my Israel trip to a savings account at the

New York branch of Bank Leumi L'Yisrael. One of my errands that day was to go to there to withdraw cash and turn some of it into traveler's checks or Israeli *shekels*. After lunch, we stopped at a shoe store to buy me a pair of sandals and then to a drug store for last minute necessities. Fedg and I exchanged a warm hug as she left me in the late afternoon. With my head already in the clouds, I taxied to the airport.

I flew on El Al, Israel's national airline, the only airline serving Israel from the United States in the 1960s. Fortunately for me the plane wasn't full, and I had all three seats in my row to myself. As I sat there I thought about that day back in 1948 when Israel was founded and Burt and I pledged to go there together. He could have been sitting in one of those seats near me, but he was now a married law student and seemed, from our last meeting, not eager to maintain our once-precious friendship. I was on my own. The stewardess told me to make myself comfortable for the ten and a half hour flight. I did so in a flash. Up and out of the way went the armrests and, after dinner, down I went to a peaceful sleep.

Sun in my face woke me. I looked at my watch confused. The sun was shining, and it was 2 o'clock in the morning! It was my first time flying so far east, and I hadn't accounted for the time changes. That's when it hit me, how distant a journey in miles, time and history I was undertaking. I would see a brand new country, only 15 years old, and at the same time, a civilization thousands of years old. That dichotomy stayed with me through the trip.

Sarah and her father Meir welcomed me at the airport, saying both "Shalom," the universal greeting in Hebrew, and added "welcome home" in English. I was a jumble of emotions: excitement, wonder, nervousness, astonishment. I couldn't believe I had accomplished my dream. What would I see, hear, taste and feel?

In the car on the way to their apartment, I looked out the window, marveling at everything I saw, even if it was only construction workers. Sarah turned to me and said. "Yes, they're Jewish."

"Pardon me?"

"I saw you staring out the window at the workers paving the roads. Americans are always surprised to see Jews doing this kind of work. But in Israel they do."

Frankly I hadn't been thinking about the road workers at all, but now that she mentioned it, I had to ask, "Jewish people do other kinds of work here? *Every* kind of work?"

She laughed. "Yes, Hinda, in addition to being doctors, lawyers, teachers and business owners, we have Israeli gangsters as well as policemen and prostitutes as well as those who go to the prostitutes. Israel is a mix of people. The only difference is that most of us are Jews."

In America, Jews usually chose occupations which put them into the middle class, like teaching, law, medicine, social work. American Jews were almost never laborers or, G-d forbid, criminals! Actually being in Israel was already so different from my research and planning.

With its beaches and brightly colored buildings, Tel Aviv could have been any modern Mediterranean city, except for the neon signs in Hebrew. Sarah, her parents Malka and Meir, and her brother Yumi lived in an apartment on Rembrandt Street, far away from downtown. I shared Sarah's small bedroom with her and quickly adapted to the family's routines. The most radical departure from my routine was the Israeli breakfast. Familiar items such as coffee, juice, eggs and toast were offered, but they were accompanied by cucumbers, tomatoes, onions and savory cheeses. Other meals more closely resembled what I was accustomed to at home, except that the mid-day meal tended to be a little heavier and the evening meal a little lighter.

I learned another difference when I went to take a shower. Sarah sat down with me in our room beforehand and explained what I had to do. "You see, Hinda, in Israel we don't have much water and every drop we waste means less available for agriculture. So we don't take showers here; we take baths. And we don't wait for the water to warm up before we put the plug in. If your bath is a little less hot than you're used to in Rochester, well, the good news is that you're taking your bath in Israel," she said, smiling. She spoke with a light tone, but I knew that underneath her words was a reality of this young country's situation. I was happy to comply, feeling patriotic doing so.

It took me very little time to become acclimated to their neighborhood and the city itself. Within days, I felt very much at home. Sometimes Sarah, who tutored adults in English, could not accompany me on my journeys around the city. With my rudimentary Hebrew, I was able to travel in Tel Aviv on my own. Sometimes passengers waiting for busses asked me questions, assuming I was Israeli.

(In Hebrew) "Which bus goes to Dizengoff?" I would answer, "*Ani lo m'dabaret Ivrit* (I don't speak Hebrew).

Most shrugged and asked someone else. One woman didn't let me get away with that answer. She challenged me, also in Hebrew, "But you just spoke Hebrew!"

Pushy, aren't you? I replied, "*Ani m'dabaret Ivrit raq kitzat* (I speak only a little Hebrew)." With a smug but satisfied smile, she finally let me be.

The days sped by with something different to do almost every day: visiting the museum where in 1948 the State of Israel was declared, walking around art galleries and museums, and strolling through Independence Park on the Mediterranean. Together Sarah and I took a day bus trip to Jerusalem, about an hour away. At that time, Jerusalem was divided into Israeli and Palestinian areas, and Jews were not allowed to visit the holy places of Jewish history such as the Western Wall of Solomon's Temple or the historic Jewish Quarter. Sarah and I stood silently, me in tears, at the dividing point of the city, the Mandelbaum Gate, the closest any Jew could get to the Old City. Sarah had shed her tears on previous visits, but for me, the pain of witnessing the breach in the city of Zion was brand new.

Sarah took me to the office of a travel agency which arranged for overnight bus travel around the country. Because of her tutoring commitments, she could not accompany me, but assured me that even if there were no English-speaking tourists aboard my bus, all tour guides spoke English. I chose two different trips, one northern and another southern, which would allow me to see pretty much the whole country.

The first trip was three days going first north to the Sea of Galilee, then to the Lebanon border, south to Caesarea and Haifa on the Mediterranean and back to Tel Aviv. The most significant place of Jewish history on the trip was the ancient city of Safed (S'fat). Jewish mystics lived there in the 15th and 16th centuries and, while there, wrote many important tracts on Judaism. Many more of the places we visited were of historical and religious significance to Christians, such as Cana, Capernaum, Nazareth, the Sea itself, and the Mount of the Beatitudes. As it turned out, I was one of only two English-speaking passengers on that tour. The other one, a student at Fordham University, and I were given semi-private lessons by our multi-lingual bus driver on what Jesus did and said at each place. The driver brought history alive for us and it was thrilling to be in the places where miracles was purported to have happened. True, what I learned didn't come from my religious tradition, but it was important and interesting nonetheless.

When we visited the small *kibbutz* settlement at the south end of the Sea of Galilee, one of the oldest in Israel, I began to understand how geography might influence political decision-making. As we stood at this *kibbutz,* we looked across

the Sea to threateningly tall mountains on the other side known as the Golan
Heights. That high ground on other side was Syria. I had no doubt that gun
emplacements were perched in those hills with this *kibbutz* and its fields in their
target sights. I began to understand the threat under which these settlers lived
every day and shivered in fear for them.

The second bus trip, a week later, was south to the desert, the Negev. The
first stop our band of tourists made was in Beersheba, which was hot, sandy and
barren. The town square was a large and open, dusty area. Bedouins and their
camels rested wherever they liked, and our bus driver had to negotiate around
them. For many hours after that stop, we drove south, seeing only mountains,
desert shrubs, cacti, and flowers. I wondered to myself whether my current
surroundings were unique to this part of the world or if parts of southwestern
United States looked the same. The road was barely drivable. My mind was filled
with Bible stories of Moses and the Children of Israel wandering through this
area or something just like it. Was this what they had seen? I wondered how
much it could have changed in the centuries between then and now. There was
no construction, no cities, no manufacturing, just desert as far as you could see
in all directions. The only changes would have come via the wind. I was on a 20th
century tour bus connecting with ancient history and in awe.

Hours later, after a stop at an unimpressive place reputed to be King
Solomon's mines, we arrived at Eilat, a resort town on the banks of the Red Sea.
The temperature was 105°F! The water invited us and almost all of us accepted
the invitation.

Once we cooled off, we ate dinner. The younger passengers went out dancing
at a bar called, "The End of the World." We were so far from any metropolitan
area that it *did* seem a bit like the end of the world. Eilat was as far south as a
person could go in Israel. Looking south from its shore, you could see Egypt to
the right and Jordan to the left.

During the time I was visiting my Israeli family, we celebrated Judaism's
major holidays, Rosh Hashanah and Yom Kippur. I accompanied my cousins to
synagogue and, because theirs was an orthodox synagogue with separate seating
for men and women, Malka, Sarah and I sat upstairs in the women's gallery. I was
familiar with the prayer book and able to follow the service easily. However, what
seemed strange to me was that many of the Israeli women couldn't find their
places in the prayer book. They knew Modern Hebrew, but were totally unfamiliar with the ancient Hebrew of prayer. I likened their frustration to knowing

how to speak English, but having difficulty reading *The Canterbury Tales*. When they saw that I was saying the right prayers at the right time and keeping pace with the service, they turned to me with questioning looks. I didn't understand their words, but I could interpret their needs. There was irony in the fact that I, a non-traditional American Jew, could be of liturgical assistance to Orthodox Israeli women. I would turn the pages of their prayer books to the correct places and point to where we were in the service. They nodded and smiled in appreciation, but soon after, they lost the page again or another woman needed me to find where we were.

One *Shabbat* I bravely went off on my own to a beach south of Tel Aviv to join people I had met on my trip to the Galilee. Israel is a secular country, but the Orthodox factions have strong leverage in government. As a result, public transportation in Israel cannot run on the Sabbath. Instead, communal taxi cabs called *sherutim* drive along bus routes and take passengers, for a higher fee than bus fare, to their destinations. I had no trouble finding my new friends on the beach at Bat Yam and spent the afternoon enjoying their company.

When I was about to leave to catch a *sherut* back to Tel Aviv, one of my new friends had a suggestion. "Alex came on his motorcycle and he's going back to Tel Aviv. He can drive you." I was introduced to Alex and it seemed a good solution so I accompanied the handsome, well-built young man to his bike. We were on the road north to Tel Aviv, when he leaned over his shoulder and said something to me in Hebrew.

"I speak only a little Hebrew," I protested.

He tried another language.

Although I knew it was French, I didn't understand a word of what he said. "You'll have to communicate with me in English."

And that's when we discovered we had a major problem. Alex, a refugee from Egypt, didn't speak any English! And I didn't speak any of the three languages he spoke. Fortunately I knew the way back to Sarah's apartment and with a combination of hand signals and the Hebrew words for right and left, which I knew, Alex somehow got me back home. Whew!

Sarah and I took long walks most evenings, just the two of us. We shared our hopes and dreams for the future. Both of us in our early 20s, we speculated about when we would meet the men of our dreams, settle down in marriage, and have children. Sarah and I had found much in common the more time we spent together and it surprised us. She had roots there, born in the Land even before the country was founded. For me, Israel was something to dream about. I lived in a country with a much more diverse population, where Jews were a small minority. She lived where Jews were not only the majority, but also those who ran the government, businesses, the media and the universities. My country was almost 200 years old; hers was just 15. But we shared the love of study, of reading and of travel. We mused that someday, perhaps, we and our future husbands might travel together in Europe. I knew in my heart that the man I married would have to be committed, not only to Judaism, but to the State of Israel as well. Time did not stand still for us. It was all too soon time for me to leave. Sarah and I parted again with the phrase "*l'hitraot.*"

While I was making travel plans for Israel, I had also arranged to stop in Paris for a few days on my way back home. My college roommate, Gennie, had received her advanced degree at the Sorbonne and had married a Frenchman whom she had met when he was doing graduate work in the U.S. Now newly-weds living in Paris, they hosted me for three days and nights and showed me the most beautiful city I had ever seen. Included in my tour was a ballet perfor-mance, the Louvre, the Left Bank, Montmartre, Sainte Chapelle, and a French synagogue for a Sabbath service. It was wonderful to be there and experience Parisian life, but not difficult to say *au revoir.* After my experience of Israel, I wanted to get home to share it with everyone.

Once back in Rochester, I must have talked nonstop: whoever would listen, whoever asked a polite question about my trip, those I worked with or joined for lunch, heard about my trip to Israel. Thank goodness my friends and colleagues were tolerant of me.

I had accomplished what I had wanted to do when I first came home to Rochester. Now that I had made it to Israel, I found myself without new goals although I did have some ideas of possibilities. Although my work in the City's Department of Urban Renewal was not compelling enough to be called a career, working there led me to reconsider government service as a calling. It made sense since I had majored in Government at Barnard. I thought of various options: What about the Peace Corps? Or what if I stayed in urban renewal, but sought work at the federal level overseeing projects throughout the country? These ideas seemed like the start of a plan. I applied to both agencies and prepared to sit for entrance exams for each in January 1964.

Meanwhile, I had something else to worry about besides a career. The new sandals purchased on the eve of my departure for Israel had proven problematic. Over the course of the three weeks in the warm, humid atmosphere of Tel Aviv, the cool northern country and then the hot, dry Negev, both feet had developed sores on the inside arches of both, sores which simply would not heal. I saw doctor after doctor, but nothing prescribed was working. I couldn't wear normal shoes because they pressed on the sores so I wore a variety of slippers, all color-coordinated to match my outfits. Until those sores healed and I was released from treatment, those feet would keep me in Rochester.

One day in November 1963, I sat eating lunch alone at a downtown café, thinking about my options for the future. Suddenly my waitress appeared, distraught, and told me there had been a shooting in Texas and President Kennedy was wounded. I flew out the door of the restaurant. Did I pay for my food? Leave a tip? I don't know. I literally ran the two blocks to my office. Someone had brought it a television set and we stood together watching and listening until Walter Cronkite told us what we didn't want to hear. Like most Americans alive at the time, I will never forget that moment. This wasn't the same experience as when I was a little girl hearing on the radio about the death of President Roosevelt. This leader was young, energetic and offered so much promise. He was the one I had cast my first vote for. And he died, not from a disease, but at the hands of a fellow countryman. He had urged us to "ask not," but all we could do was ask "why?"

When I was recuperating from my foot sores, Rabbi Bronstein reappeared in my life, inviting me to join a singles' group he was forming. He and his wife hosted an organizational meeting at their home on a Sunday afternoon in late December.

When I arrived, a little late, I took the last seat in the circle of chairs in the living room. About two dozen young men and women were there. I knew all of them except one dark-haired guy with glasses and a knock-out smile.

Turning to a friend seated next to me I whispered, "Hey, Jeff, who's the guy sitting next to Murray?"

Jeff looked where I was indicating and then back at me as if I had asked something stupid. He whispered back, "Don't you know him? That's Mike Miller."

"New to Rochester?" I pursued.

"Don't you know his sister Joan?"

I thought back to day camp long ago. Joanie Miller had been my favorite counselor. "Joanie Miller who married Allan Wolk?"

Jeff nodded.

"Joanie has a brother?"

Jeff nodded again.

I love that smile. I want to get to know him.

JUST A REALLY NICE GUY

DURING the rest of the meeting at the Rabbi's house, I thought about Joan Miller, the junior counselor I adored at JY summer day camp. What I remembered most about her, aside from her gentle nature, was the warmth of her smile. I could see that Michael had that smile as well, one which invited you into his circle, which promised to listen to whatever you had to say.

As the meeting continued, Michael volunteered to lead efforts to interest other young Jewish singles in joining our group. When the meeting broke up, I got up to help the Rabbi's wife serve refreshments. As I did so, I passed nearby Michael and Murray and stopped to talk.

"Hi, Murray. It's nice to see you again." I turned to Michael and introduced myself. "I'm Hinda Rotenberg. Be sure to let me know if I can help you in any way on your committee." Michael said he would call. Murray, our mutual friend, stood there beaming.

In subsequent weeks, Michael called me to work on the membership committee. That work mainly consisted of telephone calls back and forth to discuss ideas to attract new members. Since we both worked downtown, we would occasionally run into each other during lunchtime.

The first time we ran into one another when I was lunching with Tala, I introduced them. After he left she asked, "Someone you're interested in?"

"Oh, no," I answered. "He's someone I met through Rabbi Bronstein's young adult group. He seems like a really nice guy, but not my type." Romance definitely wasn't on my mind.

I was thinking, rather, about my future. On successive Saturdays in January I took the Federal Civil Service exam and then the Peace Corps examination. I was getting ready to move on.

About a month after Michael and I met, as we talked on the phone about the young adult group, I casually asked him what he had planned for that weekend. He told me he was going to the movies with Murray and asked me what I was doing. I told him I was going to a singles dance organized by Peter, one of the guys in our singles group.

"A dance?" he asked, sounding interested. "Where is it? Who are you going with?"

I laughed. "This week's dance is in Greece at a hotel. Do you know Peter Bloom? Well, he organizes these parties all the time, making arrangements for a ballroom, a band or disc jockey and a cash bar. He charges an admission fee to cover his expenses and I guess he makes a little money on it, too. I'm going with my friend Jane."

"Have a good time."

"Have fun yourself!" We wished each other a good weekend and said good-bye. I thought nothing more about our conversation..

Friday evening I picked up Jane and we drove to the dance in the hotel across town. The event was well-attended and there were lots of new faces in the crowd. The music was terrific, a good mix of oldies and early rock and roll. She and I chatted about our jobs while we stood around, sipping wine until someone would come up to ask one of us to dance. The other one would hold the extra glass until the dancer returned. After we'd been there for about a half-hour, Michael and Murray showed up and joined us. I was surprised to see them, but didn't ask why they had changed their plans. We stood there creating a little circle, chatting. Neither Michael nor Murray asked us to dance so, when someone else stuck his head around my shoulder and asked me to, I went off with him. After the second time I went to dance with someone, I came back to find Jane standing alone.

"Where are the guys?"

She shrugged. "They stormed out of here as soon as you left to dance with that guy. Michael looked very angry."

"I wonder why." I was puzzled.

Jane and I stayed at the party for a few more hours, having fun, chatting together and dancing. When I got home that night, however, I thought about Michael's behavior. His potential friendship was too important to me for me not to understand his abrupt departure. On the Sunday night of that same weekend, our Temple's Young Singles group held a bowling party. I hoped Michael would be there so we could straighten out whatever had gone awry.

Entering Clover Lanes, I saw him sitting in the bar area sipping a beer.

When he caught sight of me, he crossed his arms and began to scowl. His body language was not going to stop me from approaching him.

With a wide smile on my face, I stood before him. "Somebody owes somebody an apology or an explanation," I said.

"Okay, go ahead." he said, not cracking a smile. "I'll accept your apology,"

What? I sat down quickly. He was supposed to do the explaining! I was stunned. I was expecting at least a hint of a smile from him. "Michael, what's going on? What do you think I did that was so unforgiveable?"

He didn't have to stop to consider what he wanted to say. It came out in a rush. He ticked them off on his fingers: "First, you invited me to meet you somewhere and then, you left me standing there while you danced with other guys. How was that supposed to make me feel?" He looked hurt and his eyes wouldn't meet mine.

I sat there, trying to digest what I heard. *What I say now and how I say it will determine if we can ever be friends.*

Speaking slowly and deliberately I began, "Michael, I did NOT ask you to meet me. I TOLD you I was going there with Jane. And YOU said you were going to the movies. If I had expected to go with you, I would have expected you to pick me up." I paused to let that sink in. "I'm sorry we got our signals mixed."

He raised his eyes to meet mine, but paused just long enough to make me nervous. "Okay," he said slowly. "I can see how you could have said one thing, and I heard another." He stopped and then added, "It's okay now."

I wasn't completely sure it was okay, but I was going to make sure it was. I took a deep breath and said, "Michael, you and Murray were going to see a movie Friday night. What movie was it?"

Looking surprised at the question, he answered, "*The Cardinal.*"

"Did you go?"

He shook his head. "By the time we left the dance, the last show had already started."

"Okay, to make this all fair and square between us and have a fresh start, let me take you to see that movie, okay?"

I barely got the words out when he said, "Sure," and began to smile.

"When do you want to go?"

"Saturday night?"

I usually reserved Saturday as a date night, but why not? I could give up one date to cement a friendship. I owed it to the guy. "Great. Let's make it next Saturday."

My instincts told me that Michael wouldn't let me go up to the box office and pay when we got to the movie house so I went there that Saturday afternoon to buy tickets.

Michael picked me up late because he got lost finding the apartment, and we drove to the movie, parking on a side street. As we walked from the car, I handed him the tickets I had bought.

"What's this?" he said, looking surprised.

I smiled up at him. "Well, I was pretty sure you wouldn't let me pay, so I came here earlier to get tickets."

He flashed a smile even bigger than mine. "So what do you suppose I'm going to do with these?" he said pulling out a matching set from his wallet. We laughed that we had both done the same thing, trying to save each other from potential embarrassment. Funny we had that in common. We were already on the way to becoming great friends.

After the movie, we went to a bar on West Henrietta Road and ordered drinks. Michael started the conversation with words that were magic to me: "I heard you just visited Israel. Tell me about it." I started telling him about what I did, what I saw and what I thought about all of it. About an hour later I came up for air. He had nodded at all the appropriate times, smiled at the funny things, asked follow-up questions and let me entertain him with my favorite topic. What a good listener he was.

Finally, I recovered my manners and began asking him about himself. "Tell me where you went to college."

"I went to Syracuse, following my family tradition. My sister Joan was an upperclassman there and my father had gone to Syracuse for both undergraduate and law school. Plus my friend Dan was going there and we could be roommates."

"Danny Fybush?" I asked. I knew Dan and his twin sister Judy because their parents' fabric store was a few steps from my father's furniture store on Gibbs Street.

"Yes! You know Dan?" The rest of the time we spent at that bar we talked about many other people we both knew as well as favorite books, movies and sports. We found that both of us had majored in government, shared a deep interest in Democratic politics and loved baseball. We talked about our sorrow at President Kennedy's assassination. I kept thinking that I had finally found a really good friend, someone with whom I would never run out of things to talk about. I felt he took me home much too soon, although it was well past one.

"Thanks for a wonderful time," I said at the door of my parents' apartment.

"My pleasure," he said. "Maybe we can do it again sometime."

"I'd like that." I hated to see the evening end.

Our conversations continued on the phone during the next week and then into our next Saturday night date and the next and the next.

At the end of February our young adult group planned a Sunday day trip skiing at Song Mountain. I didn't ski, but that didn't stop me from accepting an invitation from David, one of the other guys I was dating, to drive with him to Song Mountain and join the group. A few days after I said "yes" to David, Michael asked me if I wanted to go with him.

"I'm sorry, Michael. I've already made plans," I said, truly disappointed that he hadn't asked me first.

That Sunday David and I drove to Song Mountain, he ready for the slopes and me happy to hang out in the ski lodge to drink hot chocolate and chat with the other non-skiers, like my friends Wendy Williams and Morley Gwirtzman who were dating. Within a few minutes of David ascending the t-bar, Michael showed up. We joined Wendy and Morley in casual conversation for thirty or forty minutes until Michael decided to get himself some food. Just as he left my side, David showed up fresh from the slopes, checking up on me and making sure all was well. As he left to return to skiing, Michael reappeared. This happened two more times! They never encountered one another and I was never without one of them as a companion. Morley and Wendy were witnesses to this appearing/disappearing act and were hysterical every time it magically happened! As funny as it seemed, I had some time to think about what had happened while David drove me back home to Rochester. Whose company did I prefer? It was becoming obvious to me that David wasn't the one.

The last week in February, Michael told me he was going to be out of town the next weekend, or at least that's what I heard him say. Other guys called for dates, guys I went out with sometimes on a Friday or a Sunday night, but I turned them down.

"Are you going out with Michael again?" asked Mum.

"No, he's going out of town."

She was curious. "So who are you going out with? I heard you turn down David and Brian when they called," she asked.

"Well, I don't have a date for this Saturday. I just don't feel like seeing those guys anymore." Mum smiled, but didn't let on what she suspected, that I had met The One.

When Michael called on Thursday night to ask what we were doing that Saturday, I was surprised. "But you told me you were going out of town!"

"Oh, I am. During the day I'll be in Utica, but I'll be home by evening." And then in a rush he blurted out, "You don't have another date, do you?"

Whew. I was thrilled to say I didn't. Why was I so thrilled? I still didn't know what I was feeling about him, but I knew it was probably more than friendship. The man hadn't even kissed me yet, but somehow it felt just right to see him every Saturday night.

That Saturday night was different from the preceding four. Perhaps it was because he realized I might not have been available that week or maybe he just wanted to move our relationship to a new level. That night ended with our first kiss at the door of my apartment. I was hoping he'd finally do so and when he did, I was more than ready. It started out sweetly, but the weeks of waiting must have built up in us because it was passionate by its conclusion. We were both breathless. We grinned at each other as I opened the door and said good night. Michael was more than just a friend; he was definitely my boyfriend.

Every date with Michael I learned new things about him, some of them surprising. In early March, he asked me to go out to dinner with him for the first time. He chose Grinnell's, a popular local restaurant, but he had neglected to make reservations. He then grew impatient waiting at the bar for a table.

"Let's go. I can't stand here waiting anymore," he barked. Before I could agree or protest, he helped me into my coat, and took me out of there. I suppose I might have thought less of him because of his actions; on the contrary, I was amused by them. Since he'd promised me dinner, we ended up at The Brighton and had a snack there instead.

A week later he took me to a movie for the first time since our first date. The movie was *The Unsinkable Molly Brown* and it was pretty awful. I would have sat through it, but was actually relieved when, after 20 minutes, he stood up and, without a word, grabbed my hand to leave. "I couldn't stand another minute of that, could you?" he asked.

On the night of his 25th birthday, we sat in a booth at The Brighton, which had become our favorite haunt. He was morose and kept groaning, "I'm a quarter of a century old," as if that were a bad thing. He shared with me his fears that he didn't believe he was a good lawyer and how sad that was because he hadn't even wanted to become one in the first place. He had always wanted to become a teacher and his sister was the one who aspired to be a lawyer. Their parents saw things differently: the boy should be the lawyer and the girl should be the teacher. We talked long into that night about how he was trying to model himself after his father, trying to become the type of lawyer Mr. Miller was. I suggested to him that he might have more success becoming his own kind of attorney with his own special area of practice rather than modeling himself after his father. Because of his honesty about his situation, I was able to share with him questions about my future, trying to figure out what to do professionally as well as whether to remain in Rochester.

My parents, of course, had met Michael when he came to pick me up for dates. After we were seeing each other for six weeks or so, Mum and Daddy decided it was time to invite Michael for a formal Friday night dinner. She served chicken noodle soup, roast chicken, potatoes, broccoli and salad, followed by a fruit dessert.

Before we sat down to eat, we said the Sabbath blessings. Oops! I spilled my glass of kosher wine all over Mum's beautiful white tablecloth. I was embarrassed, but my parents were calm and made jokes about it. As I tried to clean up the table, and to diffuse the tension, I asked Michael, "What would you like to drink with dinner?"

"Milk would be great," he answered.

Milk would NOT be great. The laws of *Kashrut*[18] restrict milk being served with any meat meal and we were eating chicken. His request alerted my parents to what they might have considered a serious flaw: This young man's family, while Jewish, didn't keep kosher. I looked at them for a reaction, but they didn't bat an eye.

As I stuttered, trying to find the right words to explain why he wouldn't be getting milk, Daddy laughed, put his hand over Michael's, and with a big grin, said, "Well, young man, in this house we don't serve milk with meat. Will water or ginger ale be all right?" I was grateful for Dad's light touch. I let out my breath, breath that I didn't even realized I was holding.

Conversation was free and easy, comfortable and current, with lighthearted

---

[18] Rules for keeping kosher

chatter about books, movies, and education. Daddy shared Michael's interest in Democratic politics, and they discussed the new Johnson administration, as well as Michael's own aspirations.

When Michael and I began to date his parents were wintering in Florida. He told them about me in his phone calls south and they were anxious to meet me when they returned to Rochester. Through Michael they invited me to their home for a Friday night dinner. My beloved counselor from day camp, Michael's sister Joan, and her husband Allan were also invited. They arrived just as we drove up to the house. I watched as Allan went around their car to open Joanie's door, which I thought was so courteous. As we caught up with them on the walkway into the house, he muttered to me under his breath, "She wouldn't get out of the car until I opened the door. I think she wants to impress you." He shrugged and grinned. I liked him already.

Before dinner we congregated in the den for drinks and appetizers. As we sat there, I looked around at a beautifully appointed room, with its stark color scheme of black and white. I realized that someone had spent a lot of time, effort and money making it look like something from a magazine and yet so livable at the same time. My usual self-confidence deserted me. I was feeling the strain of getting to know Michael's family and having them get to know, and hopefully, to like me. After what he had told me about how they had such definite ideas of what he should and shouldn't become, I wondered: Would they like me? Would they approve of me? Michael's parents, especially his mother, seemed to be doing all the asking and I was doing all the answering.

"Michael tells us you grew up in Brighton. Did you know each other in high school?"

"No, we didn't," I answered, smiling and turning my glance from face to face, addressing my remarks to everyone, "but we had many friends in common."

"Who, for instance?"

"Well, Danny Fybush for one. Our family has known his since they moved to Rochester."

There was more "ask and tell" to follow. It felt investigative, but not terribly intrusive. Internally I was listing the differences between Michael's family and mine, the large house as opposed to the apartment, the shrimp cocktail I was eating as opposed to kosher meals at my home. The tension I felt actually eased when I inadvertently spilled cocktail sauce all over my dress. Gasps and sudden silence. While everyone sat silently, I laughed out loud. "Okay, Michael, you can

relax now. I spilled something so you don't have to hold your breath all evening."
Everyone laughed. Any tension between his family and me had been broken.

After I cleaned up my dress as best I could, Mrs. Miller approached me with
something in her hands that she had taken off one of the shelves in the den. It
was a small silver cup.

I knew what it was as soon as I saw the cup's size and shape. I held up my
hand to stop her from bringing it any closer to me. "Mrs. Miller, would you look
at the side of the cup and tell me if it says JEA 1952?"

Mrs. Miller looked surprised at my request, and then checking the cup, said,
"Why yes, it does say that and it has Michael's name engraved on it. He won it
for being the best student in the Temple B'rith Kodesh religious school that
year." Michael must have told her that I was a committed Jew and she wanted to
impress me with her son's Jewish background.

How could it be? I didn't respond immediately because I was so moved. When
I was able to speak, I said, "This may be hard to believe, but I have the identical
cup with *my* name engraved on it. Michael and I won those awards the same year
and received them the same night at the same ceremony." None of us could
believe the coincidence. Michael and I both remembered that night and what
was discussed by the grownups there, but we had no memory of each other.

The rest of the dinner went well. I liked these people and felt well-liked in
return. After dessert, we began discussing to an upcoming formal charity event
chaired by Mr. Miller's primary client. Michael had invited me to go with him and
I mentioned that I wasn't sure if I had anything suitable to wear.

Joanie and Mrs. Miller both jumped up from their chairs. Mrs. Miller said,
"Don't worry about that, Hinda. Come with us." Joanie grabbed me by the hand,
pulling me down the hall into her former bedroom. She opened her former
closet and showed me an array of formal gowns. In less than five minutes, I was
standing there in my underwear trying on gowns she had worn for proms and
fancy balls. As they zipped up each one, I went into the living room to model it
for Michael, Mr. Miller and Allan until we found the "winner." The Millers really
got to know me that night – down to my skin!

Michael let me know the next day that I had made a positive impression on
his parents, sister and brother-in-law. They certainly had won places in my heart.

Soon after that evening I received a letter from Sergeant Shriver asking me
to join the Peace Corps in Peru starting later that summer. I was in a quandary.
I was honored to be invited to do this important work, but what about Michael

— where were we going? I asked the Peace Corps to defer my admission until the fall.

THE BEST LAID PLANS

A month after meeting his parents, Michael kissed me goodnight and casually said, "You know, one of these days we're going to have to get married." I parried with, "Sure, when we grow up." I didn't exactly believe that this was a proposal, but I didn't exactly believe that it wasn't. I hoped he was serious; I know I was. In anticipation of an engagement ring, I even stopped biting my nails, a childhood habit I could never before kick,

One night afterwards, when he and I came home after midnight from a date' I invited Michael into the apartment. We sat on the living room couch. Since it was late and the door to my parents' bedroom was closed, we assumed they had already gone to bed. We began kissing, at first vertically and then horizontally, on the couch. All of a sudden we heard the front door to the apartment open and my mother's gasp. We jumped up quickly and disengaged. I don't know which of the four of us was most embarrassed. Nothing was said except abrupt "good nights" all around. My parents went to their room and Michael left.

The next morning when I came out of my room, Mum was waiting for me. "Well," she said, "after what your father and I saw last night, I certainly hope Michael plans to marry you!"

In one of the few times I used this title, I said, "Mu-*ther*! We weren't doing anything except kissing."

She smiled. "But what if we hadn't come in when we did? What then?"

I just walked away, shaking my head. I was 25 years old, but Mum still needed to mother me.

Not long after that, one afternoon on the phone, Michael suggested that I take my mother and go someplace that evening for an hour or more. He said he had some "things" to talk over with Daddy and said they were "private." I suspected that he was going to ask Daddy for my hand and I was impressed that he wanted to do this "by the book," the "book" being Emily Post on etiquette.

Mom and I, having been kicked out, left with no agenda in mind. She and I walked around Pittsford Plaza for a while, stopping into a toy store to buy a

Monopoly game. When we returned home about an hour later, we found Michael looking quizzical and Daddy beaming.

"What do you think I should tell this young man?" Daddy asked me as soon as we walked in the door.

I grinned. "I'm hoping you told him that it's okay with you if it's okay with me."

"Is it? Is it okay with you?"

"You bet it is!" I answered. We all toasted the informal engagement and Michael and I left the apartment for our favorite haunt, The Brighton, to talk by ourselves.

Once we ordered drinks, I couldn't hold back my curiosity any longer. "Michael, tell me everything you said and Daddy said, from the beginning."

Michael told me that Daddy, of course, knew why he was coming to see him. "Apparently, he wanted to put me somewhat at ease, so he began talking about current events."

The most significant local event that summer was the outbreak of riots in the Joseph Avenue area of Rochester. Michael continued, "I kept trying to turn the subject around to marrying you, but your father wasn't making it easy. Finally, apropos of nothing we were discussing, I jumped in: 'Mr. Rotenberg, I'd like to marry Hinda.' And your father came back with, 'Can you support her?' "

Uh oh.

"I told him that I was just starting out, and I hoped to build my law practice, but that you were going to have to work for a while. He didn't say anything after that because that was when you and your mother came home."

That explained the puzzled look on Michael's face when we walked in.

Well, Michael must have assumed that Daddy's answer would have been "yes" because, on August 18th, as he arrived to pick me up for a date, he was shaking all over.

"Are we alone?" he asked, with a quiver in his voice.

"Yes. My parents are at Lyla's house. What's going on? Are you all right?" I was worried. I had never seen him in this state.

"I, uh, I, uh, have something for you," and he fumbled in his suit jacket.

Oh my goodness! This is it!

"Just hold onto me for a minute, will you?" I asked as I snuggled up to him. I wanted to savor the moment with his arms wrapped around me. When he relaxed and let me go, he offered me a small white box. I opened it to find the most perfect pear-shaped diamond ring. After a bit of fumbling, Michael silently slid it on my left ring finger. We were officially engaged!

As happy as we were in the moment, we believed we had a potential problem. We were absolutely certain that we didn't want a big wedding. Because we were each the youngest child of our respective families, we were convinced that our parents would want to stage a huge event. We wanted to avoid what we thought would be a circus.

We had an idea. Michael's law school roommate and his wife, Lester and Carol Mittleman, lived in Adelphi, Maryland and, as it turned out, we were driving down to visit them the following week. We had heard somewhere that Maryland had a very short waiting period between getting a license and getting married. We decided we could avoid a big wedding by getting married while visiting our friends. The only hang-up was that we really wanted to be married by a rabbi, not a justice of the peace.

We decided to ask my rabbi for help. A few days later when we met with him, we asked Rabbi Karp if he could recommend a rabbi in the Beltway area.

"Why do you need a rabbi down there?" he asked. We didn't really want to share our plans with him, but how else to get the name?

"Rabbi," I began, "we really don't want a big wedding. We believe our mothers will plan a big extravaganza and all we want is to be married. We figured we could elope, still be married by a rabbi, and save ourselves all that hoopla."

Rabbi Karp wasn't shocked. He actually looked amused.

"Hinda, Michael," he said, turning from one to the other, "both your families have had tough times, no? Deaths? Sicknesses?" We nodded. "And what happened at those times? The families came together, right? This wedding, your wedding, whatever your parents plan, is for them to invite people to come together for a joyful occasion. Please don't deny your families this pleasure. If all you want is to be married, then look at it this way: Whatever they plan, I'll be there and you'll be there and I promise I'll get you married."

We listened to Rabbi Karp's wise advice. As we left for our Maryland mini-vacation, we designated Mum to work out our wedding date. We gave her just one instruction: we wanted a winter wedding so we would have time to find and furnish an apartment, and allow whoever wanted to throw parties in our honor to do so. We would also get away from Rochester during the brutal winter weather by honeymooning in a southern site.

Many Jewish weddings in Rochester at that time depended on the availability on the same day of the chosen site (my synagogue), a caterer (kosher required in our case), and the best dance band of that time, Len Hawley's orchestra. By the time we returned from our weekend in Maryland, my mother was able to announce the convergence of those three factors: We would get married Saturday night, January 9, 1965.

In the months that followed our engagement, relatives, friends of my parents and future in-laws as well as some of mine threw lovely bridal showers. I made choices about china, crystal and silver with a little input from Michael. Our mothers made choices about guest lists, menus and flowers. I made only four decisions about the wedding: I chose an A-line long-sleeved white-on-white brocade wedding dress with a simple pillbox headpiece and veil. I met with the wedding organist and selected every piece of music to be played before, during and after the ceremony in the order it was to be played. I picked out the engraved invitation, complete with the "half after seven" formal language. And my favorite Jewish morsel, stuffed sweet and sour cabbage, had to be part of the menu. Michael and I added friends to the already huge guest list, but we knew that many out-of-town invitees wouldn't actually accept the invitation, not wanting to come to Rochester in the winter.

On the Sabbath before one's wedding, it is Jewish custom to invite the prospective groom to recite blessings when the Torah is opened and read. So the Saturday morning of our wedding day, Michael and I went with our families to Temple Beth El, the same Conservative synagogue where we would be married ten hours later by Rabbi Karp and Michael's rabbi, Phillip Bernstein, from the Reform synagogue where his family belonged. Michael was given the honor of being called to the Torah and, quite loudly, chanted the blessings. When I asked him later why he was so loud, he said, "I wanted everyone there to know that, even if I come from a Reform temple, I still know how to say the prayers correctly!"

As we were leaving Beth El after services, everyone seemed to have some-place to go except Michael and me. We looked at each other, at a loss for what to do next.

"Want to come home for lunch?" I asked.

"Sure, I think my mother is going to the hairdresser."

At my parents' apartment I made scrambled eggs and toast, a little coffee, and a dish of fruit compote. We conversed easily, comfortably, as if it were any old day. As he was leaving, Michael said, "Well, I'll see you later."

"Yeah, see you later."

We both realized as we said it that the next time we would see one another was going to be under the *chuppah*, the wedding canopy. The word "later" took on dramatic connotations.

I had asked Fedgie to be my matron-of-honor, completing the circle that had Lyla standing for her and my standing for Lyla. Michael asked his brother-in-law Allan to be his best man and an assortment of cousins and friends as groomsmen. As Fedg and I stood in line together outside the doors leading into the sanctuary, we watched our parents and then the ushers walk down the aisle. I think she was more nervous than I because she kept commenting on this and that. Finally I said, "Look, Fedg, I love you to pieces, and I'm thrilled to have you at my side tonight, but I'd rather not talk to you right now. I spent one entire afternoon picking out all this music and I'd like to hear it."

She shook her head and laughed. "Okay, I'll shut up," she said with a big grin. I grabbed her hand and held onto it. Together we silently listened to the music until it was her turn to walk down the aisle and then Daddy came to claim me and march me towards my groom.

Even with all the responses citing weather as a reason for not attending, almost three hundred people came to our wedding. It was festive and fabulous. Our one problem was that, with so many people coming up to us to extend their good wishes, we never had a chance to eat anything, including the stuffed cabbage! At the end of the evening, after we changed into our going-away outfits and thanked our parents, we were starved. As we drove away from Temple, my stomach growled.

"Husband of mine, I'll go off with you to the ends of the earth, but first you have to feed me!" After all the beautiful wedding food, our dinner that night was burgers in the car from a fast-food restaurant on Mt. Hope Avenue.

While we let our parents make all wedding plans, we concentrated on honeymoon planning down to the last detail. Since we were getting married on a Saturday night, we planned to stay overnight at the hotel where we had drinks on our first date. The next day, Sunday, we would fly to Puerto Rico and stay a night at the San Juan Hilton. Monday morning we would fly to St. Thomas in the American Virgin Islands and take a launch over to St. John's to stay four nights at the quiet and beautiful Caneel Bay Plantation recommended by my co-workers. Then Friday we would double back to St. Thomas and fly to Miami Beach, staying at the Carillon Hotel right on the ocean. By the next Monday we'd fly home.

Almost none of that plan was implemented. This was a January wedding and January in the Northeast isn't kind to air travelers.

Saturday night went as planned. On Sunday morning, when we got to the Rochester-Monroe County airport to fly out, we were met by our families and some of our wedding guests to see us off. Michael went to park the car and I went to check us in, waiting behind a man also checking in. When I heard the airline clerk say to him, "Sir, there are no flights today," I rudely interrupted.

"What did you say? We're going to San Juan today. We can still get there, right?"

The answer was no. While Rochester was sunny and storm-free, a major snowstorm had closed every airport on the east coast. When I spotted Michael, I gestured for him to join me in line and hurriedly explained the situation.

He suggested an alternative plan: "Maybe we could stay tonight at our apartment and leave tomorrow instead..."

That wasn't going to work either. The airline clerk explained that because there was a backup from Sunday's cancelled flights, we couldn't get out of New York City on Monday either. Maybe we were going to honeymoon at home. We were disappointed, but not devastated. We'd still be together.

Our friends from Maryland provided another answer. Lester offered this choice: "Ask if they can rebook you to fly out of Baltimore tomorrow. If so, you can drive home with us, stay overnight at our place, and get your plane south from there tomorrow."

Honeymoon revision #1: To fill the time before Les and Carol were going to leave Rochester, we dropped in on Danny and the rest of the Fybush family. They had all been at the wedding and were shocked to see us that morning, but nonetheless made us a great breakfast and again wished us well. In the afternoon we drove home with Les and Carol, staying overnight in their apartment. We took a cab the next morning to what was then Friendship Airport[19]. We decided that we wouldn't let on that we were honeymooners; we didn't want people to fuss over us as they sometimes do over newlyweds.

As we stood waiting to check in, I smiled and said hello to a tall blonde women ahead of us in line, her male companion a few steps away.

---

[19] now Baltimore Washington International Airport

She asked, "Where are you going?"

"St. Thomas. And you?"

"We're going there ourselves."

We were standing there waiting to board for what seemed a long time so we kept talking.

"Where are you from?" she inquired.

"Rochester, New York. And you?"

"Emmaus, Pennsylvania. It's a small town…"

"Oh, I know. Near Allentown, right?" I knew this because, through Fedg and Hy, I was familiar with the whole area. I then noticed she had the Allentown Call Chronicle in the bundle of things she was holding

Light suddenly seemed to dawn on her face. With a huge grin on her face she began shrieking. "Oh, my stars! You're the couple who got married two days ago in Rochester, right? I read all about it in this morning's paper!"

It seems my sister Fedgie had put the announcement of our marriage in the Allentown newspaper. So much for our secret that we were newlyweds. Once we got to St. John, I wrote Hy and Fedg a postcard, letting them know of meeting Pat and George in the Baltimore airport.

Honeymoon revision #2: St. Thomas wasn't on our original itinerary, but since we couldn't get all the way to St. John that Monday, we found a place to stay for one night. On Tuesday we took a cab to the launch and motored over to St. John for the remaining three nights of our reservation. I'd never seen such a beautiful place. We had a little house, like a beach hut, to ourselves, and the paths from place to place were surrounded by magnificent plantings. We could be solitary if we wanted to, or we could do things with couples we met in the dining room. We noticed that what we had been told by the friends who had recommended the resort was true: most guests fell into one of two categories, either the newly-wed or the nearly dead!

One of the older guests at Caneel Bay Plantation had gone deep-sea fishing one day and reeled in a large fish that he offered to the kitchen to cook and serve. After we ate it, we went over to his table to thank him. He asked where we were off to next and, when we told him we were going to Miami, he asked if we liked horse races. Once we answered "yes," he wrote out a note and told us that if we were still in the Miami area the following Wednesday, we could use his note to sit in the owners' box at Hialeah because he had a horse running and he wouldn't be there to use it. Nice gesture. We tried to extend our stay at this wonderful St.

John resort because we arrived a day late, but, because they were over booked, we'd have to sleep in the infirmary. No thanks. We had loved St. Thomas even with that one-night stay and decided, if we could get lodgings, we would stay in the V.I. before going on to Miami.

Honeymoon revision #3: We had passed an interesting looking hotel, with beach huts shaped like overturned half-pineapples a few days before on our ride to the launch. On a whim we asked our taxi driver to stop there after the launch docked backed on St. Thomas and were fortunate to book a three-night accommodation at the Pineapple Beach Club. As well as relaxing on the beach, we also sight-saw through the town of Charlotte Amalie and souvenir shopped as well.

On Monday we flew into Miami and almost immediately hated it. It was much colder than the Islands had been, overcast, and required clothing that was too formal for our tastes. We had lived in bathing suits all day every day in the Virgin Islands. To "dress up" there we had worn shorts for dinner. In Miami it was too chilly to spend time at the pool, and anything else we wanted to do required that Michael wear long pants and a shirt, me a dress or skirt and top. We had to go out for all meals, something which had come with our room in the Islands. We weren't ready to go home, but we definitely didn't want to stay in Florida.

Honeymoon revision #4: We spent Wednesday afternoon at Hialeah race track in the owners' box, coming out way ahead on our bets. Late that afternoon we flew to Nassau in the Bahamas, again without reservations. We begged the Nassau Beach Hotel to let us stay, but we had to promise to leave after one night because they were booked. We spent three additional nights in Nassau at a smaller hotel. Somehow, although the weather wasn't much better than Florida, it was more fun to be in the Bahamas. We loved the English-style policemen in colorful uniforms and the Bahamian accents, a mix of Island and British. We danced the nights away to ska bands and loved the food, culture and weather.

On the Saturday two weeks after our wedding, we flew from Nassau to Miami and then on to Newark, exhausted and broke. Once again winter weather interfered. No air traffic was available to Rochester. We appealed to United Airlines. "Please, we're broke. Can't you help us?" Bless them; they were willing to pay for a hotel room.

Honeymoon revision #5: I had a thought. "Wait a minute, Michael. We're so close to Allentown. Why don't we go there instead of getting a room here and surprise Fedg and Hy?"

United Airlines was willing to give us the cash equivalent instead paying for a hotel room. We called Allentown and kept getting a busy signal, so we rented a car and drove there with no advance warning of our arrival. We walked in the back door just as they were making dinner. "Surprise!" We loved the shocked looks on their faces.

After we ate, Hy smirked as he asked, "So, you met Pat and George. Did you get to know them well?"

"Not really. We had a few drinks with them between planes in Puerto Rico," I answered. "They were very nice about telling us to leave our boots and heavy coats in an airport locker and not dragging them to the Islands." Michael was quiet. "Michael, weren't they nice?"

He looked down. "Well, Pat was nice, but George was a bit strange." I couldn't imagine what had happened for Michael to say this.

Hy started to laugh. "Okay," he asked, without the slightest bit of surprise, "What did he do?"

"I didn't want to tell you this, Hinda," he said, looking right at me, "because I knew you would be upset and they said they were friends of Fedg and Hy…"

"Well, what happened?" My voice rose an octave.

Michael told us that, when Pat and I went to the ladies' room at the airport and he and George were alone, that George proposed that the two men go bar-hopping that night in Charlotte Amalie, the major area of St. Thomas.

"I reminded him that I was on my honeymoon, but he just laughed and said I'd have the rest of my life to f--- you and he could show me the best pussy in the Islands."

Hy began to laugh uncontrollably. Fedg and I gasped, but then we laughed, too. Michael turned colors in embarrassment.

Was he really was going to keep this from me?

When Hy finally regained control of himself, he asked, "Did they tell you how they happened to take this trip, what they were celebrating?"

Michael and I looked at each other and then shook our heads. Neither of us remembered a celebration being mentioned.

Hy continued, "They were both recently released from federal prison where they spent time for sending pornographic films through the mail, movies they took of swinging parties in their home!"

Holy cow! Thank goodness we never saw them again after we left the airport!

The rest of that night and the next morning at breakfast we enjoyed this unexpected reunion with Fedg and Hy. We left them with smiles and hugs to drive back to Newark Airport and fly home to begin married life in our own apartment. The honeymoon, planned for a little over a week, had expanded to two weeks, but now it was over.

Reality set in early the next morning when I walked into the kitchen to find Michael sitting at the table reading the morning paper.

"Honey," I asked gently, "what are you doing?"

"Why, I'm waiting for my breakfast," he answered, looking surprised.

"Well, my darling husband, this is the way things are now. You and I are both walking out of here for work at the same time. Your mother isn't here to make breakfast and clean up afterward. It's all going to go so much faster if you help."

Later that week, I taught him about using a hamper for his dirty clothes and hanging up his clean ones. I kept using the line, "Mother isn't here, honey."

The honeymoon was over.

THE STORK

BEING married wasn't anything like I thought it would be. I didn't have a clear idea of marriage, but I was sure it was nothing of the life I was living. I never knew of the squabbling that we were experiencing in the marriages of, my sisters, friends, even my parents. Somehow, in a few short weeks, I had metamorphosed from a bustling blushing bride into some kind of shrew, a down-and-out bitch. I found fault everywhere, about everything, mostly with Michael. Fortunately, either he had a high tolerance for pain or he was too ashamed to admit he'd obviously married the wrong woman and I, the wrong man.

What was wrong with me? I was so irritable. I thought it might be the pressure of holding a full-time job, and, simultaneously, trying to be the perfect wife for a professional man, maintaining the proper attire, makeup and attitude to blend well with the ladies at the country club, and still have time to be a dutiful daughter and daughter-in-law. Maybe that was part of it, but it was probably also the challenge of learning to live with a husband, even as dear a husband as Michael, the "forever-ness" of it all. There was no escape, no leaving this "roommate" for another apartment, another city. Michael and I both felt the pressure of making our marriage work. We had just allowed my parents to throw a large, elaborate wedding. We experienced an expensive extended honeymoon. How could we tell anyone we might have made a mistake?

Michael and I finally sat down and talked about what to do about our seemingly unsuccessful union. We decided to give it some time before giving up on us. Time, as they say, is a healer, and, with patience and practice, our life together became harmonious.

Before we had married, we had sought an apartment within the city limits, but had fallen in love with and rented an apartment in a brand new development in Brighton. Unfortunately, in March of 1966, the new manager of the City of Rochester decided to enforce an existing requirement that all employees live within the city's borders. As a result, I lost my job with the city's Department of

Urban Renewal. Fortunately, by the time of my layoff, Michael's law practice was doing well and we were able to meet our bills on his income alone.

But I was bored. I read a few books every week, played bridge with young married women friends, bowled in two leagues, played golf, substitute bowled in Lyla's league, and even found some pick-up secretarial work with my old friend Rabbi Bronstein.

Michael and I had stopped using birth control long before I lost my job, hoping to start our family early. We started talking about buying a house, and, without too much effort, found a brand new four bedroom home in an established Brighton neighborhood. Our apartment furniture fit beautifully in the new place, but the house seemed empty. Who would fill the other bedrooms? When would they arrive? And what about that old saying: New House, New Baby? It was abundantly clear that, after trying to conceive for more than two years, we were not going to have children without outside help.

Despite our happiness with one other, Michael and I wanted more. We wanted to be parents. Through our nieces and nephews we experienced the ups and downs of parenting and were realistic, we thought, about midnight feedings, poopy diapers, ear infections and defiant behavior. The arrival of each of my periods, just irregular enough to make us hopeful, crushed us.

Years of tests, medications, prayers and love-making on a schedule went by. We experienced month after month of disappointment. My OB/GYN advised us to try artificial insemination using Michael's sperm. We tried, hopeful, but it didn't work. Dr. Law then suggested that we should try insemination again, but this time using Michael's sperm mixed with that of an anonymous donor. The up side was that it usually resulted in a pregnancy. The down side was that we wouldn't know if the resulting baby was Michael's or that of a stranger. We asked the doctor for time to think about it. If we went ahead with it, and it was successful, our family and friends would assume this would be our child 100%. But we wouldn't be sure.

Michael and I lay in our king-sized bed one night, staring at the ceiling, sleepless. Earlier that day, we had received a phone call from friends. Elaine and Joel, who married a year after us, told us that Elaine was pregnant. Of course we were happy for them, but as soon as we got off the phone, I dissolved into wrenching tears. *Why them? Why not us?* That sleepless night resulted in this middle-of-the-night conversation, full of thoughts each of us had bottled up for a long time.

It was good that it was dark in our bedroom that night. I didn't want to see

Michael's face and I didn't want him to see mine. It was easier to be honest when I wouldn't have to respond to whatever reactions his face would show. We had been waltzing around this issue, trying to be understanding of the science and gentle with each other.

Michael finally asked, "What do you think about Dr. Law's idea that we try artificial insemination using a donor?"

I had given the idea a lot of thought since the doctor proposed it. Lying there that night, I looked up at our plain white ceiling, searching inside myself for an honest answer. I sighed. "We tried it with your sperm and even that felt artificial. I don't think I could live a lifetime not being sure of our child's fatherhood." The firmness of my reply left no doubt that, as far as I was concerned, this subject was closed. Michael didn't try to convince me otherwise. I think he was relieved.

We lay there holding hands. The house was dark and quiet. There were no street noises. The only illumination came from the clock on Michael's nightstand. The only sound was that of our breathing.

I spoke first. "So, if that's not the answer, what are we going to do?"

Michael answered, "I don't know."

We lay in silence again. After a few moments, I ventured an option. "We could adopt..." We knew that babies were being born to women who couldn't care for them. It seemed so unfair that we couldn't reproduce and those we considered the "wrong people" got pregnant. They didn't intend to have a baby, but it was all we thought about. In 1967, abortion was illegal in New York State. Many unwed mothers bravely decided to carry babies to term and then surrender them. Social service agencies investigated potential parents and made placements. True, an adopted child wouldn't be genetically ours, but in that case, unlike the earlier scenario, we would be on equal footing, and there would be no secrets from our friends and family.

"Let's think about this for a while," Michael suggested. "I think it may be our answer, but it's an idea that takes some getting used to."

There was irony in our situation. Years before, during the months we were engaged, I read an article in *Glamour* magazine about topics you should discuss before marriage. Over lunch one day at The Dickens, I had raised some of these with Michael. We had easily agreed on a few of the issues such as moving to another city if an appealing job arose (no), religion (we were both committed Jews), and money (a lot would be nice, but enough was just fine.)

Hesitantly that day at lunch I had ventured the question, "What would you want us to do if we couldn't have kids?"

Back like a shot Michael had answered, "Why, we'd adopt, I suppose."

On that night of reflection almost three years later, lying there in our bed, we discussed another alternative. The thought had lingered in the air until Michael finally posed it: "What if we decided not to have children?"

I thought about it a bit, and then suggested what it might mean. "We could have careers without conflicts with childcare, school activities or croup. If we didn't have to save for college tuitions, we would be able to afford glamorous vacations and for other indulgences."

Michael had another suggestion. "We could live anywhere we liked, regardless of the school district."

We both agreed that we'd still get any kid pleasure we needed from our nieces and nephews.

For the first time that night, as we talked about the childless option, we turned to face each other. We held each other close and remained silent. I felt the tension in myself and in his body as well. I clung to him tightly, feeling his arms tighten around me, his breath on my shoulders and back. It was almost in unison that we said, "No! That's not us!"

Michael and I knew we were meant to be parents. No Caribbean, European or Asian adventures could replace a trip to the zoo with a child; no fancy, carefully kept home would replace messy art projects; no sky-rocketing careers could ever take the place of sticky fingers, wet kisses and high-pitched giggles. We were parents; we just didn't have children yet.

Not too long after that sleepless night, we decided that adoption was our choice. I phoned Jewish Family Service to make an appointment with their adoption specialist

"When were you married?" inquired the woman who answered my call.

"January 9, 1965."

"We don't see anyone for adoptions until they have been married at least three years," she replied firmly.

"Our anniversary is very soon. Can we make an appointment now for after our anniversary?"

"No. Call back." Click.

How rude. How heartless. We were already feeling persecuted by science and now we were being maltreated by some dumb rule. Given no other choice, we waited until the day of our third anniversary to call again. This time I reached either the different secretary or the same one in a more accommodating mood.

"Let me tell you what to expect," the woman said. "The social worker assigned to your case will want to see both of you at first. Then she'll meet with each of you individually until your case file is complete. Then you'll wait for a placement. We have no idea how long that will be." She sounded as if she were reading from a prepared script. Maybe she was.

We scheduled an appointment and were on the road to parenthood. Jewish Family Service sent us a stack of forms to complete before our appointment two weeks later.

We were prompt in getting to the first meeting, sitting and nervously waiting to meet the person we considered the arbiter of our fate. Our adoption specialist turned out to be Mrs. Thomas, a woman maybe ten or fifteen years older than we, short, squat, and serious-looking. She greeted us with a smile, but her body language told us this was consequential business.

She invited us into her neat cubicle of an office and, after small talk, began asking penetrating questions: "Are you both really sure you want children?"

Michael and I smiled at each other. He nodded to me that I could take that question. "We've discussed parenthood's ups and downs at length and are very sure."

"Are you sure you want to adopt?"

I again answered, "We have discussed our various options. Our very good friends had a great experience adopting two children happily through Jewish Family Service, and we know that this was what we both want."

"Have you had any experience with children?"

"We have seven nieces and nephews, three of whom we took care of when their parents spent ten days in South America." Michael said and laughed. "That was some on-the-job training!"

Other questions followed, such as did we have a preference for a boy or a girl? No. Just a healthy baby-- please.

We gave details of our attempts to get pregnant. Mrs. Thomas listened to us closely, which was both disconcerting and flattering. She had our future in her hands and seemed to want to help us. She directed some questions to Michael, others to me, and some to both of us. Before the appointment ended, we scheduled appointments with her over the next few months. After that day, we would meet with her one at a time. She was all business, no longer the smiling woman we had first met.

On the days when one of us met with Mrs. Thomas, we could hardly wait until dinnertime to talk about the experience.

"What did she ask you today?" I inquired at dinner on his first solo appointment day.

"Oh, today she was interested in how I felt when you didn't get pregnant," Michael replied.

"And what did you say?"

"You know, how disappointed I was, for me, for you, for us…"

Another day, after I'd had an appointment, he asked, "What did two you talk about?"

"Why I wanted to have a child. What I thought parenting would involve. What 'expectations' I might have from a child."

"Expectations?"

"Yeah. I told her I didn't expect anything from our child except to *be* our child. That my 'expectations' were more about me, about wanting to be a good mother."

Much of the time, Mrs. Thomas was interested in hearing how we were raised and if we would want to do the same for our children. Michael and I were comfortable with each other's answers. It felt as if we were making progress towards becoming a family.

However, at one appointment, Mrs. Thomas shocked me by saying, "I don't think Mr. Miller wants to adopt as much as you do."

I was bewildered. "Where on earth would you ever get such an idea?"

She paused, perhaps considering how to word her answer. "He seems, I don't know, less convinced, unsure…"And then she said, "Maybe you don't know your husband as well as you think you do."

Without considering the ramifications, I shot back, "And maybe YOU don't know my husband as well as YOU think you do. I know Michael. He has always been uncomfortable in any new situation. He may want something, but, at the same time, he's nervous about it." *Am I really speaking this way to my social worker?*

I lowered my voice. "Mrs. Thomas, please understand this. Michael very much wants to adopt children, but also questions what kind of father he'll be. He's not at all unsure about adoption."

She sat there stunned by my outburst. I sat there stunned that I had talked back to the woman who had my life in her hands. We both smiled nervously.

She finally broke the silence. "Well, Mrs. Miller, I guess you do know your husband pretty well. And if he has any uncertainty, I'm sure you will help him through it." She extended her hand. "Go home. I don't have to see either of you again. The next time you hear from me, I'll be bringing you news of the baby you've been waiting for. You aren't the first couple on the waiting list, but I hope it won't be too long."

"Thank you, thank you, thank you," I gushed as I left the office.

The waiting had begun. It was late March. I kept myself busy. One way I passed the time was through volunteer work. Every Tuesday morning I volunteered at Strong Memorial Hospital with a friend, pushing the Coffee Cart to bring coffee and tea to patients confined to their rooms.

One Tuesday in April, as I entered a room on the Maternity Wing, I saw Mrs. Thomas visiting a young woman. I didn't know for sure, but I suspected she was visiting an unwed mother, perhaps getting a legal surrender for the baby. I didn't acknowledge that I knew Mrs. Thomas and was in and out of the room as fast as possible.

I was sure she would call me later in the day to discuss what had happened, but she didn't. So, I called the agency to speak with her. "Seeing you at Strong was a shock. Do you think I should stop visiting the maternity floor?"

Mrs. Thomas had obviously also given it some thought. "I knew you volunteered there, but I never realized you came into rooms. It would be best if you had someone else deliver coffee to the rooms on Maternity from now on." I never again set foot on that floor.

About a month later, on a Friday morning in mid-May, the phone rang. It was Mrs. Thomas. *Oh my G-d! This is it!* I could barely hear what she was saying over the joyful buzz in my head. I was finally able to decipher her words.

"Mrs. Miller, I know I told you that you and Mr. Miller were not first on the list of waiting adoptive parents, but we have a special situation we want to tell you about. "

Oh, was I listening hard! "Yes?"

"A baby girl was born six weeks ago. Her biological parents were very intelligent and highly educated. They and we want to be sure that whoever raised her would be able to recognize her intellectual needs and also be in a financial position to meet them. Do you follow me so far?"

"Go on, please."

"Of all parents waiting for a child, you and Mr. Miller are the only couple who fit the description. Incidentally, she was not born at Strong Memorial. What do you think? Are you ready for a baby?"

The only question I could think to ask was, "How soon can she be here?" The answer was "Monday afternoon," a scant three days away.

After I recaptured the breath that this call had taken from me, but before my heart stopped racing like cars on the Indianapolis Speedway, I called Michael to come home from work so I could tell him face-to-face. I waltzed around the house, looking at every corner she would take over, spending most of the time in what would become her room.

When Michael walked in the door and looked at my face, he knew what I was going to tell him. We just hugged. I told him the details. Michael asked, "When is our baby coming?" *Our baby. Wow.* Grinning as happy tears poured down my face, I answered, "Mrs. Thomas said she'd deliver her Monday afternoon."

He panicked. "How can we get ready? It's too soon. We won't be ready."

"Oh yes, we will," I said calmly. "What does a baby need? A place to sleep, which we can borrow from someone until we get a crib of our own, some diapers which we can buy, bottles, and a few outfits, which I'll get tomorrow. We can't buy formula until we find out what she's on and then you'll just run out and get it. We'll be ready. And I'll bet by Monday, you'll wish she were here already!" My serenity calmed Michael.

Before the baby came, we had people to inform that we were "expecting." Up until then we hadn't told anyone we were considering adoption and we didn't know how our news would be received. That Friday night, before Shabbat dinner with my parents, we told them of the impending arrival of their granddaughter. They were thrilled, not only for us, but for themselves as well. They were already Poppy and Nonny to my sisters' five kids; one more sounded wonderful!

After dessert we went immediately to my in-laws to share the good news with them. Michael's mother's first words weren't "Why didn't you tell us before?" but "What do you think of the name Caroline?" I knew then my mother-in-law was very accepting of our decision and hoping we would name the baby for her late mother, whose Hebrew name was Chaya, meaning "life." I, on the other hand, had expected, if I ever had a daughter, to name her after my mother's sister, my Aunt Min. We were amazed that both sets of parents were so accepting to the way our family was being created.

When we got home we phoned other close family and our friends to share our joy.

We heard a lot of "Why didn't you tell us?" and "*mazal tov*" and "What can we do to help?" Later that night, thrilled, excited and brimming with showers of love from friends and families, we began to talk seriously about a name for the baby. I liked my mother in law's suggestion of Caroline, but I preferred it pronounced "Care-o-lynn", not "line." Having grown up with an unusual name myself, I also wanted our daughter to have, if not an unusual name, then at least an unusual spelling of her name. And a middle name? My aunt's name, "Minnie," meant "loving benediction" so we looked for names that also meant "loving." Amy was the best choice.

One of our friends, a young mother herself, offered to take me shopping for the necessities. Although we had known for some time that Jewish Family Service would be placing a baby with us, we hadn't gotten a nursery ready. Jewish families are superstitious; even if I had been pregnant, no baby clothes or things would have come into the house until after the baby was born. With my friend as advisor, I bought baby clothes, towels and wash cloths, cloth diapers for burp cloths, bottles, a food warmer, baby-safe detergent, and Pampers. I carefully washed and folded every bit of clothing and bedding that would touch our daughter. Our friends, Les and Carol, whose son was six months old, loaned us their bassinet until we could get a crib.

Monday morning was the longest morning of my life. We knew Mrs. Thomas wasn't coming with our baby until the early afternoon. Fortunately Daddy got me out of the house, taking me to a baby furniture store to purchase a crib, dresser, bassinet and rocking chair to be delivered later that week. My parents and in-laws had arranged to split the cost of furnishing the baby's room. On the way home we listened to the radio. The song playing was "The Look of Love." Over and over I heard the words, "I can hardly wait to hold you, feel my arms around you, how long I have waited, waited just to hold you, now that I have found you, don't ever go…" I sniffled and smiled all the way home. (To this day, whenever I hear that song, I consider it a love song for my daughter.)

We asked our parents, family and friends to allow us to meet our daughter by ourselves. At the appointed time, not a minute early or late, the doorbell rang. Mrs. Thomas, aka The Stork, walked into the house with an armful of baby. As if we had done so each and every day of our lives, Michael and I reached out to greet our daughter. Mrs. Thomas placed our baby girl in my arms and Michael put his arms around both of us.

Caralyn Amy Miller had come home.

SPECIAL DELIVERIES

OUR wish had been granted. We were finally parents. We had an adorable baby girl whom we loved a little bit more each day. Life was turning out as we had hoped. Michael was a young practicing attorney, and I was a stay-at-home mother. It was mostly a joyous time. Caralyn was a delight, fascinated with everything and everybody. I would sing to her a lot, especially when I changed her diapers and, beginning when she was just over a year, she would sing along with me to the "bob-bob-bobbin'" part of the "Red Red Robin."

But it wasn't all joyous. Sometimes I was just plain bored. Being a homemaker and mother did not engage enough of my mind. Caralyn was so independent, so self-sustaining. She slept through the night from six weeks old, something most parents would have seen as a blessing, but to me it meant she needed us too little. If she could have managed to change her own diapers, she might not have needed me at all! She was a baby for so short a time before she seemed to turn into a little person. This wasn't what I had thought motherhood was all about. Where was the challenge? I was happy-ish, but bored silly.

Every weeknight evening Michael would come home, exhausted from a day in the office. All he wanted to do was to read the newspaper, open the mail, and generally unwind from his day. I would pounce on him. "What's new downtown?" and "Who did you see today?" and "What did you talk about?"

I craved attention, dialogue, stimulation. Michael had been in the "real world" all day and I was jealous. I had been in the kitchen, the family room, the baby's room, and sometimes to the supermarket or drug store. I knew I was very lucky to have this lovely little girl to love and care for, but I also felt cheated. I was blessed to be the one experiencing the joy of Caralyn's presence and her first "everythings," but I wanted and needed more. I needed intellectual stimulation.

Much of my adult companionship came through the telephone. My intellectual stimulation came from the books I read and game shows I watched. The latter activity turned out to be a bonus. My favorite game show was "Concentration" on weekdays from 10:30 to 11:00am. coinciding with Caralyn's morning nap time. I watched it almost every day and became good at solving the puzzles.

"Concentration" was played by two rival contestants who looked at a large numbered checkerboard. One at a time a contestant called out two numbers, each of which was turned around to reveal a prize. If the prizes matched, that prize was awarded to the contestant and the squares revolved around one more time, revealing pieces of a rebus[20] puzzle, usually a well-known quotation, person, or place. The first contestant to solve the puzzle was awarded all of the prizes he or she had accumulated. If your opponent solved the puzzle before you did, you lost and had to leave with the consolation prize, usually American Tourister luggage.

At home, I was a whiz. I didn't need very many pieces revealed to solve a puzzle. That was good and bad; good because I might be able to win easily and bad because, if I won, I wouldn't have collected many prizes.

When Caralyn was about 16 months old, I was watching when the announcer said, as if speaking directly to me, "If you'd like to play this game with us, come to New York and try out!" He mentioned that tryouts for the show were the next week and, coincidentally, Michael and I were already going to New York then, and had engaged someone to babysit Caralyn. Without really thinking about it, I called NBC right then and scheduled myself for a tryout. When I told Michael, he was enthusiastic. He didn't often see me so energized.

We flew to New York and, while Michael went to a pre-arranged meeting, I took a cab to Rockefeller Center. As I entered this majestic building, I thought to myself, are you nuts? I quickly assured myself that I wasn't nuts; I was brave. I had nothing to lose by trying.

After an elevator ride to the 14th floor, I entered the offices of Norman Blumenthal, the producer of "Concentration," and was led into a room with about a dozen and a half potential contestants. We were escorted into a classroom and told to sit at a desk for a test. We were given a closed notebook, a pen and a sheet of lined paper. After the woman in charge said "You may start now," we opened the notebook to find a series of partially revealed rebus puzzles. Our test was to solve as many of them as we could within a half-hour limit. Six or seven minutes later I was done. I looked up to get the attention of the woman in charge. She came over.

---

[20] A puzzle made up of pictures and symbols

"Is something wrong?" she whispered.

"What do I do next?" I whispered back.

"You mean you've solved them already?" she asked.

"Yeah. I just did what you asked," I answered, thinking I had done something wrong.

She picked up my notebook and the paper on which I had written my answers. "Come with me." I followed her to her office. She checked my answers against the answer sheet, looked at me and smiled from ear to ear. "How soon can you come back to tape a show?"

"That's it? I'm going to be on the program?" I was astounded.

"You sure are."

I thought quickly. "I'll have to make arrangements for a babysitter for my daughter. Would two weeks from now be okay?" We agreed that it would. I couldn't wait to tell Michael.

We were able to get Mrs. Baldwin, our babysitter, to return so two weeks later, Michael and I again flew to New York. Shows were taped, not live. Future contestants were required to sit through a full day's taping, usually three shows, before they would appear. The tapings I and my fellow contestants sat through went rapidly, with some contestants solving puzzles rapidly. As a result, although I wasn't supposed to appear until the next day, I was introduced at the end of the third taping of the first day. That meant I would start the following morning opposite the then-reigning champion.

I appeared for professional make-up before the taping, a little nervous, but a lot excited. I wore my favorite yellow knit dress and, at my neckline, I wore an antique pin Fedg had given me framing a picture of Caralyn. Michael was a calming influence. "Think of it this way: The worst thing that will happen is that we'll walk out of there with some new luggage."

I was nervous at first, but as soon as I began playing the game, I relaxed and enjoyed being there. I forgot about the spotlight, the cameras, that there was a live audience. I focused on playing the game, just as I did when I was playing it in my family room at home. Answers to the puzzles came to me easily and before I knew it, I had won a trip to the Rose Bowl and I was the champ! During the commercial break I looked at the audience. Michael smiled and mouthed the words, "Will you take me with you?" I had to laugh. The next game sped by, and I was still champion, having won a brand new convertible! By the lunch break I had also won a grandfather clock, champagne, a set of five bicycles, women's clothing, men's shirts, dining room furniture, and Reed and Barton silverware in a pattern of my choice.

We went back to our hotel during the lunch break and called Rochester, begging our babysitter to save time for us in late December so Michael and I could go to California. She promised she would. Then I called my sister Lyla.

"Hi Hin, how are you doing?"

"Pretty good," I said modestly

"You said you'd call only if you won a car… Oh, Hin honey, did you *really* win a car?" she shrieked.

"Oh, I did, and let me tell you what else!" We laughed together long distance, as I confirmed the good news, and I asked her to tell Mum and Daddy. Until we got back to Rochester, no one else knew what I had won. We returned to the studio for the next taping.

The afternoon taping began. In the first game, I won a mink jacket, silver candlesticks, a home bar and many other items. Then I couldn't make a match during the second game, and even though I knew the puzzle's answer, I didn't get a chance to solve it. My opponent beat me to it and my adventure was over. Although I was done with the show, I was delighted. I came home satisfied that my intellect was intact, and I hadn't become just a housewife and mother.

After we came home, I made a list of everything I won and divided it into three lists: what we wanted to keep, what we wanted to sell, and what we would give to charities. We wanted to keep the sterling flatware, a future gift for my daughter, and some of the household items such as a recliner, the grandfather clock and kitchen carpeting. We planned to sell the car which, as a small convertible, wasn't practical for our young family. Other items we couldn't use, like the bikes and some furniture items which duplicated ones we already had, we would sell. We accepted other prizes knowing we would donate them to charities, such as a home bar which we gave to St. John's Home for their new residence recreation room, the mink jacket which we gave to our public broadcasting station for their annual auction, and the silver tea set and candelabras to the synagogue.

Being on television, winning great prizes, traveling to California and receiving publicity in our local newspaper was great, but I had another longing these couldn't satisfy. I had been wishing to have another child. I had even thought I was pregnant the previous June and was devastated when my period came. I couldn't stop crying. Michael was stunned. "I didn't know it was so important to you to give birth to a child."

"Oh, Michael. It's not that at all. I just want a baby."

"We have a baby. Her name is Caralyn."

I shook my head. "Caralyn isn't a baby anymore and hasn't been for a long time. I know she's only 18 months old, but she's so independent, so sure of herself. She's been that way almost since Day One. I want an infant. Can we please, please, please go back to Jewish Family Service and try to adopt a sibling for her?"

He grinned as he said, "Whatever you want."

We went to the agency after we came back from the second New York trip. The procedure was much faster this time. Our new "Stork," Mrs. Richardson, assured us it wouldn't be as long a wait.

My appearances on Concentration aired in late December, about six weeks after the taping. Michael played hooky from work, and we watched the shows together in our family room. As much as I enjoyed watching myself on television, I had an even better time watching Caralyn watching me. She'd walk over to the T.V. and point to me and then come over to me and point again with the funniest expression on her face, a sort of "What's going on here? Which Mommy is the real Mommy?"

The last show I appeared on aired the morning Michael and I flew to the west coast.

California was fun. Our hotel was terrific and well-located. We rented a bright orange Pinto to take us to tourist sites. The first morning we were there, I went to the hotel gift shop to buy postcards. The proprietor was watching "Concentration" on television, and became very excited upon seeing me. "I know you! You were on the show yesterday!" He called out to anyone nearby to tell them who I was and how I'd won the trip to California and to that hotel.

Because Michael and I had no idea when we would ever get back to California, we took in as many of the sights as we could. We spent a day at San Pedro, another at Disneyland and a third at Universal Studios. For the Rose Bowl parade we sat right behind three astronauts who were the Grand Marshalls, but also had prime seats for the Rose Bowl game. We were having such a good time away from the Rochester winter that, after checking with our babysitter, we spent a few days in San Francisco, and then Las Vegas, before flying home.

After the trip was over, the prizes started arriving. Every few days the UPS man rang the doorbell. After a while, we became friends, and each time he came with something new, I invited him in to see what we had unwrapped from his last visit: one day a recliner, another a case of kosher food, a third day kitchen carpeting.

In the midst of this prize spree, Mrs. Richardson called to ask if Caralyn would like a little brother. I didn't know how she felt, and I sure wasn't going to ask! I almost shouted, "Bring him on!" The next day at noon, Jonathan Adam Miller was delivered by Mrs. Richardson. He was only three days old and uncircumcised. We were going to be able to celebrate a *Brit Milah*, a ritual Jewish circumcision on his eighth day of life, a tradition in the Jewish faith. It took us that whole week to decide on his name, calling him many variations before we found just the right one.

When the UPS man made his next delivery, he took one look at our son in my arms and asked, "Where did *he* come from?"

I answered, "Sometimes the most special things come from G-d, not UPS."

THE GOOD, THE BAD AND LIFE GOES ON

TWO young children in the house meant a lot of grocery shopping, preparing meals, washing clothes, cleaning house, as well as play times at home and with friends. Most of my friends were also mothers of young children. We toted our kids everywhere with the stated reason that they would have someone to play with. The real reason was that we would have a grownup to converse with, someone who had read a book, seen a movie, and didn't spit up while eating. While I may not have loved every single minute of every single day during those years, mostly I was a happy camper.

We had planned to send Caralyn to an excellent traditional nursery school two or three mornings a week when she was three. Instead, on the advice of my sister-in-law, who sent her children there, we enrolled her in a Montessori school which met every weekday morning. It turned out to be just the right choice. Classrooms were mixed ages, three to five. Caralyn loved being in an environment where she could choose what to do and when to do it, such as working with Cuisenaire Rods, colored rods to teach concepts of math. She was happy to stand at a special table measuring water or sand and reading primary books. In her second year she was showing the older children how to do many of the tasks. We couldn't keep up with her thirst for something new to read and got her a library card in her own name when she was four. Her Montessori teachers suggested we have her tested for school readiness. When we heard the results, we entered her into first grade at age five, a year early. Based on our experience, with Caralyn, a few years later we enrolled Jonathan in Montessori school as well.

Something I enjoyed doing outside the house was bowling once a week with a league organized through a Jewish women's organization dedicated to teaching the trades to immigrant Israelis. I was aware of the organization's mission, but frankly, I was a member just because I liked getting together with women who were also stay-at-home mothers – and I liked to bowl. In the summer of 1972, I heard that the organization was holding an international conference in Israel, and there were especially low rates to encourage participation. I was anxious to return to Israel and, at lowered rates, Michael could join me. I became totally on board with the mission!

Michael and I talked about the possibility of taking this journey together. Because we met one another only a few months after I returned from my first trip, we had spent a large part of our first date talking about Israel. We decided we'd go. I was going to be able to realize two dreams, returning to the country I loved so much and sharing it with the man I loved. I was thrilled to write Sarah that we were coming. Once again Michael and I hired Mrs. Baldwin, our reliable babysitter, to come stay with the kids, and in late October, off we flew El Al to Israel.

This was not the Israel I had visited nine years earlier. The country I experienced in 1963 was in its first flush, only 15 years old, and compact in land mass. One area north of Tel Aviv stretched only 15 miles from the Mediterranean Sea on the west to the country of Jordan on the east. This more modern Israel that we would experience had suffered the Six-Day War of 1967 but, as a result, had greatly expanded its borders to the north, east and south.

After our plane landed, Michael and I taxied from the airport into Jerusalem. As tired as I was from the flight, I kept swiveling in my seat, trying to take in all I was seeing. "Oh, my G-d," I whispered. "The walls, the walls…" I was too choked up to explain to Michael what I was feeling. We were driving along the ancient walls of Jerusalem, walls that when Sarah and I had stood at the gate dividing Jerusalem years before, had been too distant for us to see. Yes, Michael and I were touring Israel together this time, but we were sometimes having very different experiences. He was seeing everything for the first time and I was comparing and contrasting the sights and sounds with those of my previous visit.

Experiencing Jerusalem was the most thrilling part of this trip for me. We stood at the Western Wall of what was once King Solomon's Temple, we visited the Dome of the Rock, one of Islam's holiest sites, and we walked the Via Dolorosa past the Stations of the Cross and then to the Church of the Holy Sepulcher, viewing significant sites of the world's three great monotheistic religions within blocks of one another. This couldn't happen anywhere else in the world. We went to art galleries and important sites from Israel's history, saw the Dead Sea Scrolls, and, most difficult of all, spent time at Yad Vashem, the memorial to the Holocaust. As we stood in the final hallway of Yad Vashem, seeing memorial candles flickering over plaques with the names of the towns and villages from which Jews had been transported to their death, I heard someone saying the *Kaddish*, the memorial prayer for the dead. I looked around to see who it was. It was me.

As participants of the conference, we were invited to the Knesset, Israel's Parliament. The building itself was awe-inspiring and the artwork within it breathtaking, transforming a utilitarian structure into something of beauty. Every floor was inlaid with mosaics based on Biblical themes though modern in their rendering. Above us were fantastic huge tapestries designed by Marc Chagall.

We were greeted by General Yigdal Allon, then Deputy Prime Minister. We were forewarned by our guides that Israelis were very informal and instructed not to dress up for the occasion. However, when we went through the receiving line to shake hands with the Minister, we noticed that he was wearing a tie.

"Forgive me, Mr. Allon," Michael said, shaking his hand. "I didn't wear a tie because I was told you were informal, and I wanted you to feel comfortable."

Allon didn't miss a beat as he smiled at us. "And to make you feel more comfortable, I *did* wear one!" As we laughed together, I realized that I couldn't imagine a similar scenario with the Vice President of the United States.

During the next week we toured the country north to south. One of our first stops was on the Golan Heights, where we looked down from former Syrian battlements over the Sea of Galilee to an Israeli kibbutz in the sights of Syrian guns. This kibbutz was the same settlement I had visited on my first trip to Israel. I remembered looking up at the Syrian hills nine years earlier and shuddering. As we traveled frrom the former Syrian town of Kuneitra, we heard and then saw planes with the insignias of the Israeli Air Force roaring overhead. Our buses reversed direction and took us west to an Israeli village. We never learned if the planes were responding to an actual emergency or on a training exercise, but we were grateful our drivers had been cautious.

We visited scenes from the Bible, going to Jericho where Joshua and the early Israelites won a decisive battle, and to Hebron to visit the Tomb of the Patriarchs and Matriarchs beginning with Abraham and Sarah. We spent time in Bethlehem at King Solomon's Pool and Rachel's Tomb before going farther east to the banks of Dead Sea.

Later that week we flew south, to Eilat, the farthest south I had been when I was in Israel nine years earlier, but this time we caught another small plane and traveled over the Sinai desert further south to Sharm El-Sheikh, part of the territory conquered from Egypt in the Six-Day War. After we landed we drove along horrible roads to a Bedouin campsite where we turned down invitations to ride incredibly filthy camels. One site in particular gave me chills: a former Egyptian stronghold and fortification guarding the Straits of Tiran. That little piece of land had precipitated two major Arab-Israeli wars. We briefly visited the new town of Ophira, a new Israeli settlement on the Red Sea, which was offering incentives for Israelis to settle there. 130 degrees in the summer? No way would I make that move! But it did offer the most beautiful unspoiled beach in the world and crystal clear Red Sea waters where we enjoyed snorkeling while multi-colored fish kept us company.

While many sites in Israel provoked memories of Biblical passages and stories from the Jewish past, probably the most stirring was our visit to Masada, the 2,000 year-old fortress built originally by King Herod. After the Roman Empire conquered the Land and burned the Temple in Jerusalem in 70 C.E., taking control of the country, this fortress was defended by the Zealots against the power of Rome for four additional years. Nowhere else in Israel did I feel that strong a connection to Israel's history as I did there. Perhaps I was roman- ticizing the past, perhaps because Masada recalled for me echoes of the brave fighters in the Warsaw Ghetto. For whatever reason, Masada was my most emotional experience.

Finally we went to Tel-Aviv, a city which, by comparison to everywhere else we had been, was so modern I felt it lacked any personality. But the city was just a setting for a highlight of the trip, a reunion with Sarah and her husband Raphi with whom we stayed for the weekend. I couldn't believe it had been nine years since she and I had seen one another, but then, looking at our husbands and enjoying her children, daughter Rona and son Itzhar, we had no choice but to accept the passage of time. Raphi was a delight, someone who seemed almost like an Israeli Michael. They were both tall, dark, soft-spoken, gentle, warm men. We enjoyed a restful Shabbat with them, happy not to be on a schedule and loving the home-made food prepared in our honor. As a gift, they presented us with a drawing by Shmuel Katz, a famous Israeli artist. Coincidentally, we had purchased a work by that same artist in an art gallery we had visited in Caesaria! We left them reluctantly to tour some more, but managed to spend our last evening in Israel with just Sarah and Raphi, double-dating, so to speak. It was lovely, but it was too brief. Saying *lihitraot* was difficult. We had no idea when we would see each other again. The trip had been everything we would have wished it to be, but we were looking forward to getting home to the kids.

Mom and Dad Miller had continued to vacation in Florida for at least a month every winter. In 1973 they decided to spend more time away from the cold and rented a two-bedroom apartment in Bal Harbour, a small community on the ocean south of Hollywood, Florida. When they weren't using their place, they let us. Michael and I would drive the Millers' car to Florida in the fall, spend a week or ten days there and fly home, leaving the car for them to use while they vacationed. Then, in the spring, we would fly down there with our children, spend another week or ten days and take the auto train partway home, driving the rest of the way.

Despite our continual correspondence about every part of our lives, I was stunned when Sarah wrote in early 1974 that Raphi's employer wanted him, already a pediatrician, to complete an additional residency in neurology and that they were coming to the United States for three years. For the first two years of his program, the family, which now included another son, Omer, lived in Coral Gables, Florida. This was wonderful for at least three reasons: they had all the appropriate clothing for a warm-weather location in the United States, my parents' apartment was only 25 minutes away, and we would be able to visit them when we went to Florida for vacations. For two years we enjoyed each others' company twice each year, and our children became acquainted with one another.

They chose to spend Raphi's third and last year of residency in Minneapolis so that the children could experience an American winter. When his program ended, they traveled through much of the United States before spending their last week with us in Rochester. Each time together, each visit, we had grown closer, but once again we had to part.

Since before we were married, Michael and I had been active with the Monroe County Democratic Committee, doing whatever we could to get our candidates elected. In the spring of 1973, the Brighton Democratic Committee asked Michael to run for the Brighton Town Council. We almost laughed. Brighton voters had always overwhelmingly elected only Republicans to local office. But the demographics of the town were changing. There was a slim chance of winning if he ran a full-press campaign, walking all of the neighborhoods of the Town, ringing every doorbell, introducing himself to the voters and listening to them as well, and attending every public event from June to November. It was an ambitious goal, made more challenging because he would be leaving me at home with two small children while he was out politicking.

When Michael asked me, "What do you think I should do?"

I made only one request of him. "Honey, I can handle the stuff at home, but if you do this, give it all you've got."

So, from August until Election Day, he walked door to door after work, four nights a week, and four hours at least Saturdays and Sundays through every neighborhood of the Town. He came home when the street lights came on. He spoke at every community event and debated the other candidates at forums. He gave it all he had.

Election night was more than exciting; it was electric. For the first time in the more than 150-year history of the Town of Brighton, a Democrat, Michael Miller, was elected to Town office. Two months later we held a wonderful New Year's Day party at Town Hall to celebrate his landmark installation. When Jon, then age 3 ½, saw his father stride out on stage for the official swearing-in ceremony, he ran up to him, grabbed him by the ankles, and wouldn't let go. Caralyn didn't want to be left out so she joined them a few minutes later. Michael took the oath of office with both kids holding on to his pant legs. He went on to win three more times, serving 16 years as Town Councilman.

As the seventies passed, life brought sorrow along with it. Fedgie required a complete hysterectomy one year, and then painful back surgery and rehabilitation a few years later. In 1977, Lyla discovered a lump in her breast and had a mastectomy. Her doctor was confident that he removed all of the malignancy and she wouldn't require further treatment. She seemed so certain that she would be well that I wasn't frightened for her. I did, however, begin getting mammograms as a precaution for my own health.

The next summer, during one of our usual catch-up phone calls, Fedg told me that she had discovered lumps in both of her breasts.

Aghast, I asked, "What are you doing about them?"

"Nothing right now."

I was incredulous, but my primary emotion was fear. Lyla and I called her every few days, leaning on Fedg to be more proactive in her health care. Nothing could convince her to have them biopsied. She continued to delay. She made excuses. She was scared to death.

During one phone call, I resorted to begging. "Just do it, Fedg. If there's nothing, there's nothing. But if they find something there, you can get lumpectomies. You'll be relieved."

"You don't understand, Hin. They're huge. If I take them out, I'll need breast implants."

That revelation made me even more frightened. "All the more reason to get rid of them as soon as possible. Please!"

She made no promises.

Meanwhile, that fall of 1978 Michael, in his second term as Brighton Town Councilman, got the Democratic nomination to run for Monroe County Family Court Judge. He was looking forward to ending his law practice and taking on the challenge of a new aspect of his professional life. He was endorsed by almost every organization, association and newspaper in Monroe County. But despite these recommendations and the highest ratings from the Monroe County Bar Association, he lost the election.

A few days after the loss, we went to his parents' apartment in Florida to lick our wounds and heal. I tried to keep our vacation upbeat, but in the back of my mind I knew we would return to the same old daily life.

When we were in Florida, Michael told me a story about something that happened one day when he had taken Jon to the office with him. He gave Jon some paper and colored pencils to keep him busy while he attended to business. As they went to leave, Jon turned to him and said, "Well, Dad, now I know what you do at the office."

Michael hadn't thought Jon was paying attention to what was going on so he asked, "And what is it I do?"

Jon looked up at him and said, "You talk on the phone and get aggravated."

Exactly. Because he lost the election, Michael would have to continue his aggravating law practice, a prospect he didn't especially relish.

Our ten days away in Florida gave us respite from the intense feelings of that loss. Thanksgiving would be in four days after our return and we had much else to be thankful for.

Within an hour of our homecoming, Lyla called and, without asking if it would be okay, told us that she and Irv were coming over. They entered our house, unsmiling and not making eye contact. Without preamble, Lyla told us to sit down in the living room and once we did, began by saying, "We have some very bad news."

I sent the kids into the family room so we adults could have privacy. I held my breath, waiting for her to continue.

"Fedg is in the hospital," Lyla said. "They finally did the biopsy of her breasts and found cancer in both. She is having a double mastectomy tomorrow and will need further treatment."

As I sat there absorbing this news, I focused on the words "biopsy", "cancer" and "mastectomy." I had heard them all the year before. Then the final word registered: treatment. Lyla had not required any further treatment after her mastectomy.

I stared at Lyla. "Treatment?" Lyla looked back at me and nodded. "As in radiation? Chemo?" I held my breath.

"I'm afraid so."

In the background, I could hear Caralyn and Jon playing, the television set blaring a detergent jingle.

I was alert to fight this terror hanging over our heads. First things first: "Do Mum and Daddy know?"

"Yes. Hy told them about the surgery and they spoke with Fedg, too"

"How much do they know? Are they aware she'll need chemo?"

"Not yet."

"Okay. What can you and I do?"

Lyla had a ready answer. "If you can work it out, I'd like the two of us to drive to Allentown this Friday. Fedg will still be in the hospital, but maybe we can cheer her up. She's so frightened."

"Of course we'll go." I didn't have to ask Michael if it was okay with him. Family was always a first for us. "Fedg will be thrilled to see us, especially you, Ly, 'cause of what you've been through and your complete recovery."

I smiled and thanked them for coming over to fill us in. Once they left I let the fear take over my body. This was new territory and a severe test for my usual Pollyanna-ish philosophy about life's uncertainties: Don't worry too soon; if something is really wrong, you'll have time enough to worry later.

Thanksgiving Day was subdued. As was our custom, we attended the annual Interfaith Service at a local church sponsored by our synagogue and neighboring churches since 1863. We shared turkey and fixings at our house with my in-laws. It was hard to keep smiling and behaving as we usually did whenever we celebrated a holiday together. When Michael and I were alone however, our conversation centered on Fedgie and our hopes for her well-being.

Friday morning, Lyla picked me up early and we were off to Allentown, a five-hour drive. We had little conversation in the car or during the stop we made for lunch. We were both tense. It didn't help that snow began falling gently and then more densely the farther south we drove. We didn't bother checking into our motel, just continued to the hospital to see Fedg as soon as possible.

We could tell she had prepared herself for our arrival. We found her sitting up in bed, hair done, makeup perfect, wearing a pink fluffy bed jacket and an enormous smile. However, we could still see her bandages and the drains coming from the sides of her body.

"I want hugs and kisses!" she called out to us by way of greeting. "Only don't hug too hard because the dratted drains are still in," she exclaimed. It was so like Fedg to say "dratted" instead of "effing." We obliged happily.

She looked wonderful. She didn't look as if she had had surgery or was in any pain. But Fedgie had been a consummate actress her whole life, even gaining her Equity card years earlier when she worked in summer stock. She was now playing the part of someone we weren't supposed to worry about. "I'll be fine, you'll see!" she told us. And we went along with her because it was what we wished for in our hearts.

After some time together, we could see that Fedg was getting tired. We pleaded fatigue from our long drive and told her we would see her in the morning. More hugs and kisses, and we departed. That night in Allentown, Lyla and I couldn't stop talking about Fedg, her attitude and her prognosis. She looked great and her spirits were high. Lyla and I felt lucky to live in Rochester, with an outstanding health care system, and hoped that Allentown's matched up. We had every confidence in her health care professionals and, even with some trepidation, felt that this cancer had been caught in time.

When Lyla and I got to the hospital the next day, we talked about this and that, nothing important, just chitter-chattering to fill the time. Lyla and I ached to be useful.

"Do you need anything?" Lyla asked.

"Do you want something to read?" I inquired.

"Can I make you more comfortable?" (Lyla again)

"Can I can get anything?" (me again)

Fedg smiled and assured us she was just fine and thanked us over and over again for coming to Allentown.

We three did a lot of reminiscing, about Mum and Daddy, Huntington Park neighbors, Beth Joseph, Franklin High School, friends, and children. We laughed a lot and reminded each other of things we hadn't talked about in a very long time. My sisters filled me in on events that had happened before I was born or when I was too young to remember.

It was clear from her attitude that Fedg had been assured that they got all the cancer and she was on the road to recovery. She claimed to love her doctors, to be treated wonderfully by the nursing staff, and to be supremely confident that, just as Lyla had, she would get through this scary time.

Lyla and I went to dinner that second night with Hy who assured us he would keep us informed every step of the way. He told us that Fedg's chances were quite good with the particular type of chemo they would be using. After a brief Sunday morning visit to the hospital, we drove back to Rochester, still worried, but less so than when we had driven to Allentown.

Months passed uneventfully. Fedgie started chemo in Allentown and was able to find a good cancer center in Florida near her winter home-away-from-home in Boca Raton. Of course, chemo being chemo, she did lose all her hair, but she had prepared for the loss, purchasing a blond wig duplicating her own usual hair style. During the harshest months of that winter, she enjoyed Florida sunshine. Because my parents had moved to Florida in the mid-1970s, she spent time with Mum and Daddy when she wasn't weak or nauseous. Their apartment was a 45-minute drive away from hers. Every conversation I had with my parents that winter was filled with Fedgie-talk. She was just leaving. She was just about to come back. We stayed in touch with Fedg too, and relaxed a bit as her treatments were nearing an end.

In July, Michael and I wanted to visit Fedg and Hy in Allentown. Fedg welcomed the idea, but Hy presented a bit of a hurdle.

"I don't want her to tire herself," he said. "I'll let you know when you can come."

"We promise to be helpful," I said. We couldn't understand why, if she was getting better, he wouldn't want us to make a short visit.

Finally he agreed that we could come, but only for one night.

When we got there on Saturday we learned that, unbeknownst to us, Fedg was again on chemo, a new combination that was more poisonous to her system and therefore more enervating. Fedg looked well, however, and seemed to be her cheerful self. I didn't know what to think. Was this happy Fedg real, or were we seeing the actress Fedg, camouflaging her pain for us, her audience?

That night, Fedg gestured to me. "C'mere, Hin, I want to show you something." We went into one of the spare bedrooms and she closed the door. Then she grinned and took off her blond wig. "What do you think?"

There was my gorgeous sister, still totally gorgeous, but with brown and gray hair like a brush cut sticking up all over her head. Some of the hairs were even long enough to have a curl in them.

I giggled. "You look adorable, Fedg. Maybe you should chuck the wig and go natural."

"I don't think I'm ready for that," she protested. "But it's been years since I left my hair untreated and it's fun to see what color, or, I should say, colors it is now." We giggled and she put the wig back on again.

After dinner, as the four of us sat around *kibbutzing*, Hy blurted out, "Do either of you know how to smoke marijuana?"

After a brief glance at Michael, I answered for both of us, "Yeah, we've had a little experience."

Hy leaned in towards us with a pleading look. "Can you please teach Fedg? They say she'll get less nauseous if she uses it, and since she never smoked cigarettes, she doesn't know how to inhale, and I don't know how to teach her."

Hy brought out a small box with many fat marijuana cigarettes already rolled in either red or yellow wrappers. I took one from the box and lit it from a lighter Hy extended towards me.

"Fedg, watch me and see if you can mimic my actions," I said. I had every confidence that she could do it. She was a professional actress; this was just a case of learning a new part.

I inhaled and held the breath in my lungs for a while, slowing exhaling. I handed the joint to Michael who did the same thing. Then he handed it to Fedg who tried to imitate our moves. She coughed and coughed, never getting smoke into her lungs. She handed the joint back to me and we repeated the lesson. This went on for a few more rounds, but, despite our best efforts, Fedg couldn't seem to get the hang of it. Eventually she might have learned, but we became too blasted to help anymore.

We left after breakfast the next morning. The visit had been too short, but very sweet. Michael and I returned to Rochester with hope in our hearts.

Three weeks later, in early August, Hy called Lyla and asked her to share with us the sad news that not only was Fedgie's cancer back, but it was rampant throughout her body. There was nothing the doctors could do for her any more except to make her comfortable. Her time was short. Hy also confessed that he had known from her doctors, even before her surgery, that her chances were slim. He didn't tell her, believing that she would have given up too soon and reject the only chance she had – chemotherapy.

Lyla had the painful task of passing this news on to Mum and Dad. Both of them were in denial. I could tell. In every long distance phone call I had with them they said the same things: "There must be something they can do. She's only 51. They have to try something else."

In the middle of September, after Mum and Dad came north to be with us for the major Jewish Holidays, the six of us travelled to Allentown to see Fedg, knowing it might be the last time we would see her. Once again she was hospitalized, too weak to be at home. But as she lay there, in her pink bed jacket and her golden wig in place, she gifted us with a beautiful smile that took our breath away. We kept the visit short the first day and spent the rest of that day with Hy and Fedgie's daughter, Nancy.

We returned the next day to her room to say our final goodbyes, biting our cheeks to keep from bawling in front of her or making a scene. I felt disconnected from my body, my emotions, even my breath. When it was time to leave, we each said a brief goodbye to Fedg and Hy, not wanting to make the parting even harder for her than it was. Daddy succeeded in reining in his emotions until after he left Fedgie's room and came out into the corridor. He collapsed to the floor, weeping and softly saying, "No, no, no…" We had to get pull up on his feet and drag him out of the hospital. The drive back to Rochester was in total silence.

Hy called a few days later to let us know the end was imminent. Mum, Dad, Michael and I gathered in Lyla and Irv's family room, making small talk and lapsing into strained silences. When the phone rang, we jumped. It was Hy with the news: "Fedg died a few minutes ago. She was in no pain."

Fedgie died on the second day of Rosh Hashanah, the Jewish New Year, when Jews pray to be inscribed in the Book of Life. One prayer we read every year begins, "It is determined this day who shall live and who shall die…" The irony was heartbreaking.

Michael and I decided that the children should not go to Allentown for the funeral. In retrospect, I wished I had let them come. Maybe it wouldn't have been as frightening for them as I feared and we would have all had the comfort of their presence. I sleep-walked through the funeral service, led by Fedgie's dear friend Rabbi Greenberg, who himself wept throughout his eulogy. At the cemetery where we laid her to rest, I held onto Daddy on one side of me and Michael held on to me on the other. I knew I was touching them and yet I was numb.

When we returned to Hy's house for something to eat, we were joined by dozens of Fedgie's dearest friends. I was close to them, having spent time with them during frequent weekends in Allentown during my college years. I found myself trying to comfort them as they tried to comfort me. We all loved her so much. I wandered around and cried with each and every one. Hy spent most of his time with Fedgie's doctors, thanking them for everything they had done and tried to do for her. I didn't worry about my parents. Mum and Daddy were surrounded by Fedgie's friends and her children, feeling their love at this shattering moment.

When we returned to Rochester, Michael's family and many of our friends wanted to pay condolence calls. We allowed our best friends and closest relatives to visit for a few afternoons and then we said "enough." We had to get on with our lives and learn to absorb the pain.

I couldn't be comforted by glib words about Fedg having lived a long life; she didn't. She had been a wife, a mother, and, for the last four months of her life, a grandmother to Mark's son, a little boy who would never remember her, never know her smile, her voice, her kindness.

I changed when Fedgie died. Until that day, although I was also a wife and a mother as well as a professional person, I had looked at my life through the eyes of a child. I had been taking life for granted. I not only believed in "Tomorrow" like Annie, I lived for it. After Fedgie died, I began to understand that all we really have is today, and we must use it wisely.

I became more discriminating in choosing how I spent my time, investing more of it in those activities closest to my heart and dropping others entirely.

I spent the next year looking at the dimensions of every relationship I had – with my husband, daughter, son, parents, in-laws, surviving sister and dear friends. These people were as irreplaceable to me as Fedg had been. My relationship with her was frozen in time; my relationship with the others needed more of an investment from me, more time, sensitivity, forgiveness and patience. I told people I loved that I loved them, frequently, often incessantly. I hugged more and judged less. I remained quiet when a word was misused or a theory quoted as fact. It became more important to me not to embarrass than to be right all the time. I tried to be a better friend, a warmer sister, a more accessible aunt, a more respectful daughter and daughter-in-law, a more patient mother.

Jon was only nine when his Aunt Fedgie died. His age had protected him from the pain we adults had felt. Four years later, much from his insistence, we got a puppy, a wonderful, lovable, cuddly Soft-Coated Wheaten Terrier. Jon was devoted to him. When Briscoe was still a pup, he developed a severe intestinal problem which necessitated many appointments with the veterinarian. Our vet finally put Briscoe on a special diet and advised us to watch him closely because he was in danger of choking.

During the drive home from the vet's one day, Jon said, "I never want to love anyone or anything again because they could die and then I'd miss them too much."

I was slow to respond, carefully selecting what felt like the right words. "You know, Jon, you have that choice. You can choose not to love anyone or anything and never have to feel the pain of their leaving, but then you might not ever feel the joy of their living. Or you could enjoy them for as long as you can and build wonderful memories to comfort you when they're gone."

That answer seemed to satisfy him. I know it helped me.

Everyone expected that, after Fedg died, I would be frightened for myself, having two sisters with breast cancer. I wasn't. I told people who asked me if I was scared, "Cancer is a crap shoot. Sometimes you're the lucky one." I meant it.

But I wasn't foolish. I did breast self-examinations. I went for yearly mammograms. When Michael read an article in our local newspaper about a trial for a new breast cancer prevention medication, I inquired about it. Scientists had found that this medication, tamoxifen, had prevented women who had cancer in one breast from occurring in the other side. They were now investigating what would happen if they proscribed it for women who had not had breast cancer, but had a family history of the disease. They accepted me into the double-blind study and for five years, I took what turned out to be the actual drug and not the placebo. That daily pill reminded me of my sisters and how lucky I was to have been their baby sister.

I have remained cancer-free.

TAKING CHARGE

COLLEGE (check). Marriage (check). Children (check). Lovely house in the suburbs (check). Wonderful friends and social life (check). What next? I'd spent years living as if I had been given a list of "to dos" and checking them off along the way. I felt lucky to be the mother of healthy, smart, kind-hearted, wonderful kids. Caralyn and Jonathan were flourishing; how I wished I was!

In 1979 when the children were both in middle school and I was struggling emotionally with Fedgie's illness and subsequent death, I had the chance to get a paying part-time job. I applied to and was hired at Highland Hospital to reactivate their newsletter and raise funds for and awareness of the hospital. I worked during the hours when the kids were in school. My colleagues were not only paid staff members at the hospital, but also many Highland volunteers. It was a perfect first job back, lasting five years, but eventually the challenges weren't there. Everything became repetitious. January: write stories, take photos, create newsletter. February: work with volunteers on women's event. March: draft brochures for fall fund-raising campaign, and so on. I asked my supervisor to expand my duties, but he didn't want anything to change. Well, I did. I needed a change and fast! I resigned with confidence that I would find something more stimulating and satisfying.

For the next two years, I worked free-lance for a variety of non-profits, helping with public relations, volunteer management and fundraising. It was a challenge each time to walk into a new organization, assess its strengths, and write material to emphasize them. I enjoyed the variety of organizations which employed me, but I always had to search for the next assignment. I never truly felt a part of those organizations because I wasn't actually on staff.

One weekend in late summer 1986, in the midst of deciding on a possible new direction, Michael and I visited a retreat center in the Berkshires. The center offered its guests yoga, lectures, beautiful scenery, Spartan accommodations, delicious vegetarian food and uninterrupted time for contemplation. Between walks, meals and yoga, Michael spent time reading the books he had brought. With all of my physical needs met, I concentrated on my emotional and vocational development, using the time to begin the steps suggested in *What Color is Your Parachute?* the self-help book I had just read.

According to its author, there were four questions I had to answer to determine my future:

What do I really love to do? *I love to be in charge.*

What would I absolutely hate to do? *I hate to spend time around the sick and elderly. I don't like too much repetition.*

In what areas do I excel? *I can write well. I have good interpersonal skills.*

Where do I lack abilities and/or skills? *I don't play an instrument or speak a foreign language well.*

These answers came easily and were a start. More presented themselves while I was doing other things, such as walking or eating. I even dreamed some answers. The list grew longer and more vocationally centered. When I felt I had a sense of my strengths and weaknesses, with an emphasis on the strengths, I began writing myself a job description.

By the third morning of our stay, I had an Eureka Moment: I wanted to head a non-profit organization.

Could it be this easy? Can I really do this?

"Michael, got a minute? I need some advice," I said as we sat in one of the quiet sitting rooms. Up until then, I hadn't shared my process with him.

"Sure, what's up?" he asked, closing his book and giving me his full attention.

I gave him the *Readers Digest* version of my weekend's work. "I want to direct a non-profit organization. What do you think?" I asked, a little nervous about what he would say. Would he think I was on the right track?

"Go for it!" answered my ever-supportive husband.

Even so, I wasn't certain this was an attainable goal. At this point it was all in my head; maybe I was overlooking some important aspect. When I returned to Rochester, I decided to find out if I was on the right track. I knew people who directed not-for-profit organizations. What better place to find out if I was suited for that work than by asking these experts?

Each of the professionals I contacted was gracious in giving me time and attention. With some it was breakfast, others lunch and still others a quick coffee in their offices. Almost every one of them gave me the exact same opinion: "Yes, Hinda, you can do this. Your skills are the skills needed to lead and manage."

Their advice for how to proceed, often using the same words, was: "Get a 'union card,' a degree or certificate, something that proves you can manage a staff, a budget and a board. Why don't you go to graduate school?"

Based on that advice, in January 1987, while still working free-lance jobs, I began to acquire that credential by enrolling in a masters' program in public administration at SUNY Brockport.

One friend questioned my sanity: "You're going back to school at your age? And driving all the way out to Brockport? Are you nuts?"

I answered back in a second: "Yes, I'm going back to school. I intend to live a long life, and I'll live it happier with a master's degree. As for the drive? It only takes half an hour to get to the campus, which I won't do often because most of my courses are offered here in Rochester." I smiled, excited to begin my new adventure. "And, yeah, I am a little crazy."

Things were also changing on the home front. In 1986 Michael was elected to a two-year term as Chairman of the Monroe County Democratic Committee. He now officially had three jobs: lawyer, Town councilman and Democratic Committee Chairman. Caralyn had graduated from Brighton High and was enrolled at Cornell University. Jon had transferred from Brighton High to a private school, Allendale Columbia, and was making a good adjustment. He was even able to travel with the Spanish language students to Mexico, and later, to the Dominican Republic.

It was during this period of time that Michael and I suffered the loss of our fathers. Dad Miller had been weak with congestive heart failure for some time. His physician had alerted Michael that Dad's heart was functioning at only 20% and he wouldn't be able to survive very long. Michael spent part of every day with him, listening to him share stories from his life. Dad Miller became weaker and weaker and died in his home on our 21st wedding anniversary in January 1986. I grieved his death personally and also vicariously through Michael's pain. We were all devastated and tremendously concerned that Mom Miller wouldn't be able to go on without him. After three or four months, she rallied, saying, "If G-d gives me years to live, I'm going to live them." When she moved into a beautiful apartment nearby, she asked us if we would like to sell our house and buy theirs. Michael and I talked about it for a few days. We decided to make the move because we wanted to be able to host the large family holiday gatherings at Rosh Hashanah and Passover that his parents had done for years, and our current house wouldn't be big enough for all the extended family. If we moved there, we would be able to continue the family tradition of gathering all together for celebrations.

When Daddy and Mum visited Rochester that summer of 1986, Daddy developed an illness which seemed like flu. He took a long time to recover and was still somewhat weak when they returned south four weeks later. Eventually he sought treatment in Florida. Phone calls back and forth told of doctors' appointments, tests, and medicines, but my parents were upbeat and unconcerned. They had been assured that whatever he had was temporary, not serious. But whatever it was, it was making Daddy weaker by the day.

A few months after they left, Lyla flew to Florida to check on them. She saw one of his doctors, who appeared baffled. Two months later I flew south to be with them after Daddy had a bronchoscopy. Daddy's doctor came into his room to assure him that tests proved he didn't have cancer. My parents were elated. I was unsatisfied. I followed the doctor out of Daddy's room into the hallway.

"Doctor, you told my father what he doesn't have. He didn't ask any questions so I'm asking. If it's not cancer, what is it?"

With a big smile on his face, he answered, "What are you so worried about? Your father has had a good life."

I saw red and breathed in and out deeply to control my anger before I replied. "Doctor," I said, biting the inside of my cheek so I wouldn't physically attack him, "You look at my father and see an old man. I want to remind you that he is also a husband, a father, a grandfather and a great-grandfather. He may seem old to you or just another patient, but he's somebody very dear to us. And we want to know what's wrong with him!"

The doctor lowered his eyes to the floor. In a quiet voice he answered, "I don't know."

When I returned home, Lyla, Irv, Michael and I sat down to talk about Dad. We were anticipating a dire diagnosis and had lost confidence that the doctors in Florida were giving him proper care. We insisted that our folks come back to Rochester. Within a few weeks, we enlisted the help of Fedgie's son, our nephew Mark, who flew to Florida and brought Mum and Daddy to Rochester. We had arranged for the Brighton Volunteer Ambulance Corps to meet the plane and bring Daddy directly to Strong Memorial Hospital. Within minutes of his checking in, they diagnosed his illness as lung cancer, something Lyla and I had suspected but hated to have confirmed.

Every day I would drive the 3.2 miles to the hospital to visit with Daddy. At first he was placed in a double room and we would watch his roommates come and go as he continually grew weaker. Even when I wasn't there with him, my thoughts were never far away. I tried to use our time together to talk about what was uppermost in my mind and to let him say whatever he had on his mind. Because Mum was there almost all day every day and other family members were there some of the time, and because he was taken downstairs for radiation treatments, our one-on-one time together was limited. Our most memorable private conversation, with Daddy expressing his love for and confidence in my children, was interrupted by a nurse coming in to administer some meds. Daddy turned to me, smiled and winked, and said, "To be continued…" Regrettably, it never was.

The family got to spend a short nine weeks with Daddy, reminiscing, telling stories, jokes and family secrets. Mum was in denial throughout his illness. She would ask, "Doesn't he look well today?" I don't think she could comprehend that her husband of 62 years would die. He was the more realistic of the two and would look up at the ceiling when he heard her say upbeat things like that.

On a Sunday morning in late May, I received a call from the hospital telling me I should come quickly because my father was not doing well. Michael never drove up Elmwood Avenue so fast. He dropped me off at the front door to the hospital and went to park. I made my way to Daddy's floor and was greeted by a handful of nurses, all with tears filling their eyes. I knew. He was gone.

"Do you want to see him?" one asked.

No. "Yeah." I wasn't sure. I had never ever seen a dead person.

I walked to the doorway of his room and looked at the man in the bed. He was so still. I inched slowly to his bedside, reached out my hand to cover his, and moaned. He was cold. With tears streaming down my face, I said, softly so that only his spirit could hear me, "I love you, Daddy. I'll miss you forever." I turned and left the room, only to return to his doorway a moment later when, after parking, Michael arrived on the floor and wanted to say his goodbyes.

I tried to call Lyla from the nurses' office to tell her about Daddy, but her line was busy. I finally called my niece who drove to her parents' home to inform them of Daddy's death. When Lyla called me back at the hospital, she and I agreed that we and our husbands would go together to Mum's apartment to tell her.

As soon as she saw the four of us together when she didn't expect us, she began crying. "No, no, don't tell me," she said, so we literally never told her. Soon after the funeral, Lyla and I went to Florida to dispose of Daddy's clothing from the apartment so that Mum wouldn't have that hard task when she returned in the fall.

I had work and graduate school to keep my mind active. For the next three and a half years, summers included, I took the prescribed courses, almost all of them taught in the evening. The curriculum was designed for graduate students intending to work in government, but most of the courses were applicable to non-profit work as well: budgeting, supervision, organizational management, and computer programming.

Shortly after Daddy died, I applied for a part-time position as Director of Literacy Volunteers of Rochester. I was familiar with its mission because, coincidentally, earlier that year I had taken the training course to become a literacy volunteer. After I went through a series of interviews, Doris Leve, the president, called asking if we could meet on College Avenue in one of the offices of LitVol. I came with both hope and apprehension.

After words of greeting and a little chit-chat, Doris formally offered me the job of Director, the first one of this 22-year-old organization, and I accepted. After welcoming me, she changed tone, warning me that not only was the Board taking a chance on me, but that I was taking a chance on the organization.

"You know, Hinda, those of us who met you are excited about your abilities, ideas and energy," she began. "However," she paused, "you'd better know something." Her face grew serious. "Not everyone is going to be happy that we hired you."

Oh dear. "Should I anticipate problems?"

"Maybe yes, maybe no." She stopped. I could almost see her gather her thoughts. "Not every volunteer will be cooperative. They've been in charge of this organization for 22 years and now here you come. You'll have to implement any changes you see fit slowly and with great sensitivity."

Could you perhaps have told me that before I accepted the job?

I decided to push a little. "Doris, is there anyone specifically who didn't want Literacy Volunteers to hire a director? Someone I should be especially careful with?"

She smiled. "I thought you might ask that, but I'm not going to help you there. Just pay attention and you'll figure it out as you go along."

She took me into the main room of the offices to introduce me to those volunteering that day and showed me my desk. I began work the following week, keeping Doris's words in mind.

Literacy Volunteers had been managed by its volunteers, almost all women. They worked in shifts to answer phones, schedule and teach workshops, interview prospective students, and match students with trained tutors. Others kept records, reproduced handouts, and managed a library of materials. They had been an integral part of decision-making since the Rochester branch of Literacy Volunteers was formed in 1965. If I could get them to work with me, my work would be simplified. But how? An opportunity came from an unexpected source.

I ran into Brenda, an old friend, at lunch one day. After we caught up a little on other things, she asked, "So, Hinda, where are you going to move?"

"Move? Michael and I have just gotten into our new house. We aren't moving again – ever!"

"No, no," she protested, laughing. "Not 'you' personally. 'You' meaning Literacy Volunteers. I heard the building was sold to the United Way, and they want all the offices. Everyone there will have to leave pretty soon."

I was flabbergasted. I thanked her for the tip and as soon as I got back to my office, called a friend at United Way to verify the information. "I'm not supposed to say anything, but, yes, it's true. You're going to hear it from your landlord soon, but in the meantime, you may as well prepare for a move."

I called Doris immediately and told her the news. "I think I can use this move to solidify support from the volunteers, Doris. Some of them can do the site selection with me; others can help with cleaning out and packing up. The Board, of course, will have to set a budget for the move and determine how much rent we can pay for new space." Doris agreed.

Each area of activity at LitVol had a coordinator. I met with each of them to discuss their ideas and concerns about the move and how I could help. The coordinators for the interviewers, matchers, librarians, and workshop leaders were cooperative and excited to have me aboard. They discussed their needs for space such as private rooms for matchmaking and interviewing students, a workshop room large enough to accommodate 20-25 potential tutors, and library space which could be supervised.

Where I met the strongest resistance was from the women who were the first line of contact with the public -- the receptionists. They flung out questions and comments: "Why do we have to move?" "I won't go anywhere if I have to pay to park." "No one will know where we are." I understood their concerns. Many

of them had been working for LitVol since its formation, and the offices had
been on College Avenue almost since its founding. I answered their questions
as patiently and as well as I could, but their negativity was becoming absurd. We
had to move and every potential problem could be remedied.

I asked Virginia, the coordinator of the receptionists, for help. "Virginia,
would you please schedule a meeting of all the receptionists so that we could
talk about the issues?"

"I don't think we'll be able to find a time when we can all meet."

"Try. Please?"

"Okay, but it may have to be on a weekend."

"That's fine," I replied. "I think everyone will want to take part in the decision-making about the new offices."

The offer of decision-making was enough incentive for almost every volunteer receptionist to attend a Saturday afternoon get-together. The Board had
already selected a site on Culver Road, but there were other decisions. I asked the
receptionists to suggest how each of the rooms in the new location should be
allocated, which furniture we could reuse and what we might need to purchase.
They offered to go through 22 years of files to determine which should be moved
and which discarded. They promised to look through their own possessions
for small tables, art work, and bookshelves to donate to the organization. Ah,
success and harmony! The move itself went smoothly and everyone appeared to
be onboard with the new system of management.

Walking into the relocated LitVol offices one day a few months later, I heard
noises from down the hall. Since I was usually the first to arrive each morning, I
didn't expect anyone else to be there. Following the sounds, I found Jill, one of
the receptionists, in the back room, mimeographing something for her church.

"Hi, Jill. How did you get in?" I asked, knowing she didn't have a key.

"Oh," she answered, matter-of-factly, "the last time I volunteered, I made a
copy of the key so I could come and go as I please."

*How do I explain why that's so wrong and how do I do it without alienating her? More
important, how will I get the key back?*

"Well, Jill, let's talk about this a little bit later. I have to get to my desk," I
said, and with that I continued down the hall to my office.

When I reached it, I sat there for a moment. I wanted to cool down; I was very angry. Then I called Doris. I needed her advice on how to handle Jill who had been part of LitVol for at least 15 years. Doris wasn't home. "Damn."

I looked up. Jill stood in my doorway. "You're angry, aren't you?"

"I'm a lot of things: confused, frustrated, and yes, maybe a bit angry."

"You know, Hinda, you're new around here." She was defiant, and since she was in my doorway, I wasn't going anywhere. "We volunteers have always been able to come and go as we please. I don't understand why we can't do that just because we hired you."

I took in a long breath and blew it out slowly. "Jill, because the Board hired me as Director, it was I who had to sign a lease for this space, guaranteeing that I would know all of the activities that take place here all the time."

"So I can't use the copy machine anymore because of that?" Her hands were on her hips.

"Of course you can use the machine. I ask you please to use it only when the office is open for business. Maybe on a day when you're volunteering anyway…"

"Hmmph," she replied.

"Oh, and Jill, I also had to promise the landlord that I'd control the keys. Would you please return yours? We'll gladly pay you for making the duplicate."

She returned the key, didn't ask for compensation, and practically never spoke to me again unless it was absolutely required. I had stood my ground and lost a potential ally in the process. But, even so, I knew I had done the right thing.

Working with the New York State office of Literacy Volunteers, I was able to secure a New York State Education grant, allowing me to go from part-time to full-time. I now had more time to use what I was learning in my courses at Brockport to improve LitVol's operations and outreach. I was still taking one course per semester, as much as I could handle alongside of work and volunteer commitments. One of my degree requirements was to propose a change for my agency and prove how that change would improve the agency's operation.

We had been having a problem for some time. Many volunteers, after starting training or shortly after being matched with a student, dropped out. How could we prevent or at least lessen this? I suggested that instead of having potential tutors show up for the first day of classes, that they be invited to attend a one-hour preview program before the first class, to be certain they really wanted to make this commitment. When we implemented this, the number of drop-outs did decrease, but were they because of the previews? At that point the preview program wasn't mandatory so we had some people coming to previews and others showing up directly for workshops. I created a computer program to compare how long those who came to previews stayed in the program as opposed to those who didn't. My program showed that hosting previews in advance of training was a key to maintaining volunteers. Previews then became mandatory. The synergy between my evening classes and my day job was never more effective.

Another innovation I introduced was a video we produced educating hospital personnel on how to deal with non-English speaking or illiterate patients. It was so successful that the national office decided to distribute it to all the sixty or so affiliate agencies.

For the seven years I directed the local office, my greatest personal development, beyond learning to manage volunteers, came by way of networking with Literacy Volunteers chapters nationwide. One of my downstate colleagues had developed a manual to give newly hired LitVol directors better ways to manage and to raise funds for their organizations. After I was trained in this technique, I was invited to teach it in cities within New York and later in Boston and outside Chicago. I delivered workshops at national conventions in Louisville, Denver, Albuquerque and Virginia Beach and was part of teams to deliver additional trainings in Kansas City, Tampa and Washington D.C. I loved both the travel and the opportunities to teach.

Early in the morning on my fiftieth birthday, May 11, 1989, the telephone rang with calls of good wishes from friends and relatives. When it rang again, my caller ID showed the call coming from an unfamiliar number in the area code I recognized as Washington DC.

"Hello?" I answered with a question in my voice.

"Hello, yourself, and a happy birthday to you!" came back to me in a rich baritone.

It couldn't be. But I think it is. "Burt?" I ventured.

"The very same," was the reply. "You didn't think I was going to miss your special day, did you?"

"You've *got* to be kidding. Out of the blue, you call me on my birthday?"

"Your fiftieth birthday."

"Oh, you would remember that I'm four months older than you," I said, laughing. "But what a surprise. How *are* you?"

"Pretty good." He paused. "Say, I had an idea. We have a lot of catching up to do. Instead of doing it by phone, why don't we get together? I'm planning to be in Rochester for a few days the week after next. Can we have lunch or dinner?"

"That would be great. And, Burt, I just can't get over your calling me today. Thanks so much for your good wishes."

We ended the call by agreeing he would be in touch when he came to town. I was both flabbergasted and elated. After almost 30 years of silence, Burt called. What a great birthday present!

That call led to many lunches and dinners in Rochester when Burt came into town to conduct trials as a federal Administrative Law Judge. We also met when I was in his area for literacy work, first in Virginia Beach, then many trips to Washington. Lunches, dinners, movies, ballet performances, trips to the National Gallery. My old friend was my friend again.

Michael and I were both in robes in May 1990, he becoming a Judge of the Family Court and I walking across the stage to receive my master's degree. Michael had been appointed by then-Governor Mario Cuomo to fill an open term on the Family Court. Six months later, he was elected to a full ten-year term, deciding cases in the areas of child abuse and neglect, custody, domestic violence and juvenile delinquency. Every night during dinner and into the evening, we shared our work days, and I became more intrigued about issues facing children and families. How could I help alleviate the multiple problems that Rochester's families were facing? It would take a few more years before I would begin to see the way.

One downside of being Director of LitVol was that every two years, as in many non-profits, our volunteer leadership changed. As comfortable as I was with most aspects of my job, I constantly needed to adapt to new personalities and peculiarities. After two key members of the Board resigned, people with whom I had grown close, I felt it was time to move on. In May 1994, I tendered my resignation.

When I left LitVol in 1994, I contacted Joe Posner, a community philanthropist whose dearest wish was to help urban children succeed in school. I wanted to know how I could help work on issues which had become close to my heart. Joe and I met for breakfast at The Princess Restaurant, which I later found out was his favorite time and place to entice people into his wonderful web of volunteer activities.

As we sat in a booth at the restaurant, Joe reminded me that one of the best predictors of a child's success was participation in quality early childhood programs. "There aren't enough of them," Joe explained, "and those that exist are too expensive for inner city families." Joe had founded an organization called Rochester's Child to raise dollars needed to fund the best quality pre-school education in the city, but he wasn't satisfied to stop there.

He told me he had a new idea, still in the formative stages. "Did you know, Hinda, that one of the best afterschool programs in the city of Rochester is at Baden Street Settlement?"

Wow, Baden Street. That's the settlement house where my parents got assistance when they first came to Rochester from Europe.

He continued. "What makes their program so successful is that they combine their afterschool sports programs with homework help and tutoring. Kids come to play sports, but they have to keep their marks up in order to stay in the program," Joe explained with a broad smile on his face. "I need help raising dollars to duplicate this program throughout the city. Will you help me?"

"Oh yes!" I told him. I loved the idea of coming in on the ground floor of a project.

Over the next few months we romanced some business people Joe knew and assembled a working committee to look at creating this new endeavor. Joe liked the idea of linking sports with academics, but I knew there were children who weren't at all athletic, but still could benefit from such a program. I fought for them to be included in our plans. That's how the name of the organization was created: the program for the Academic, Athletic, and Artistic Achievement of inner-city children, in other words, Quad A. As a volunteer at first and later as a part- time staff person, I worked with the Rochester Area Community Foundation for both Rochester's Child and Quad A. These organizations worked closely with other child-serving organizations in town, such as the Rochester Area Children's Collaborative (RACC), a child advocacy organization.

After Daddy died, Mum stayed alone in their Florida condominium for four years and maintained a second home, an apartment, near us in Rochester. Through the years, even when Daddy was still alive, she had suffered from high blood pressure, but was otherwise healthy. Occasionally, however, she would have a transient ischemic attack (TIA) -- brief interruptions in the blood supply to parts of the brain resulting in temporary impairment of her speech and movement. Those TIAs would weaken her, but she would recover full function within hours. As she learned to live with these episodes, so did we.

However, in Rochester in October 1991, while having lunch at Lyla's, Mum experienced a full-scale stroke and, after a week's stay at Strong Memorial Hospital, had to go into rehabilitation at Monroe Community Hospital for six weeks. Her physical and occupational therapists cautioned Lyla and me that, because of her loss of depth perception and other functions, Mum should never be allowed to live alone again. We had two choices: if we allowed her to return to her apartment, she'd need full-time care and get little socialization or we could move her to a residential facility where she would be looked after and could interact with other people her age. The decision was agonizing. The only senior facility which served kosher food – a must for Mum -- was the Jewish Home of Rochester, the same facility her mother, our *bubbie*, had inhabited, although in a new location. We decided on Mum's entering the Jewish Home and packed up, sold off, redistributed to relatives and donated to the needy Mum's possessions from both her gorgeous apartments. Eventually the Florida condominium was sold, helping to pay her expenses.

During Mum's first few days in the Home in a shared double room, she stayed almost entirely silent, using as few words as possible. It was obvious she was depressed. Finally she spoke, the words she offered painful to hear. Bent over in her chair, with her head resting forward in upraised hands, she commented, "From two beautiful apartments, one in Florida and one here, this is where I now have to live? In this half of a room?"

It was depressing to see this wonderful woman who had lived so well in such beautiful surroundings reduced to sharing an institutional-looking room with a stranger. Mum's eyesight failing, she could find no solace in books as she once did. Yet she attended some of the arts and craft classes and tried to make a life for herself. One or another member of our family visited her every day. When the weather allowed, we would take her out for lunches, dinners, celebrations, and holidays, but the majority of Mum's time was spent in her room, in her chair, leaning forward, sometimes in the same pose-- her head in her hands. I think she prayed to have G-d take her. I know that I did. This was her existence, not much of a life, for almost five years. Eventually she refused nourishment, lay down on her bed, turned her body towards the wall, and after three days, passed away peacefully.

Fedgie's children came to Rochester for the funeral. The rest of the family lived locally. We met graveside at Mt. Hope cemetery where Mum was laid to rest next to Daddy. The rabbi who presided, one who had known Mum well, seemed distracted and more focused on current political events in Israel than on consoling us. He told us before he began the memorial prayers that he believed that those who had recently passed away were closest to G-d and could intervene on behalf of mortals. As he conducted the funeral, he kept interrupting the service, almost wailing, "Michaela[21], Michaela, please help the Israeli soldiers." We looked at each other, uncomfortable that his focus wasn't on Mum or on consoling us, the bereaved.

When the family came back to our house for a bite to eat after the funeral, we talked about the rabbi's peculiar behavior and tried to put it in perspective. My niece Nancy, Fedgie's daughter, stated it best: "Holy Cow! As if Nonny[22] hadn't suffered enough! Now that rabbi wants her to fight for Israel. I wanted to say, hey Rabbi, let her rest in peace and let Israel take care of itself." We cracked up.

That afternoon together as a family was sweet. We spent hours going through old photo albums, reminiscing about events, and catching up the younger members of the family about things that happened before they were born. All of Mum's living descendants being all together turned a sad occasion into something warm and wonderful.

One day about this time, as Claudia Caldwell, the director of the Children's Collaborative, and I were leaving a presentation we had co-produced for the Chamber of Commerce, Claudia mentioned she had just accepted a new job with the YWCA. The first words out of my mouth were, "How do I get *your* old job?" She laughed at my reaction.

I realized how inappropriate my reaction was and I turned red. "Wow, Claudia, I know I should have congratulated you first about your new job, but I really want to do what you've been doing-- advocating full-time for kids!" Fortunately, we were good friends, and she understood my passion. After a long interview

---

[21] Pronounced Mee-kha-ay-leh, Mum's Hebrew name

[22] What all the grandchildren called Mum

process, I got her job as the new Director of the Children's Collaborative and began work there in September 1996.

The Board was made up of some of the most committed people I'd ever met, seasoned professionals who worked in a variety of child-serving agencies in Monroe County. Our advocacy for children on their issues included speaking out for children wherever and whenever they needed support including at the County Legislature if proposed budgets didn't include adequate resources for day care, health care and education services.

Our name was the Children's Collaborative and collaborate we did with every child-serving agency and local government department serving kids. Through national affiliations with Marian Wright Edelman's Children's Defense Fund and the National Association for Child Advocacy, we learned techniques which had worked in other cities to rally the public to the issues facing children and their families. We held training workshops for parents, supported healthy food campaigns, lobbied state assemblymen and senators, developed a television spot about early childhood education, and stayed current on children's issues through those two national organizations. Michael, in his capacity as Family Court Judge, was dealing with the consequences of poor family life, such as domestic abuse and child neglect, and I was working to improve circumstances and prevent problems. I was proud of our work and the publicity we generated on children's issues. Our efforts gave voice to the youngest and weakest among us.

While paying heed to the issues affecting children and families, the Children's Collaborative did so in collaboration, as our name implied. However, our actions could sometimes not be distinguished from those of overall local promotions for children, at least in the eyes of our primary underwriter. We received a letter in the spring of 2000 telling us that the underwriter had decided to allocate funds elsewhere. Without that grant, we could no longer function. It was a huge blow. The Board and I fought against it, going to see the funder and begging them to reconsider until we could find new funding sources to stay alive. They were steadfast in their position to withdraw support.

As 2000 came to an end, the program closed. I felt guilty. Maybe I should have made RACC stand out as a leader on issues rather than as a partner. I felt that I had failed so many who had faith in me. I should have done something, I didn't know what, but something different or more impactful. It took me months to recover my confidence.

I was unemployed. What would I do now? Could my education and professional experience be combined for another position? Figuring this out would take time and thought.

Returning to my Roots

I had time on my hands. What could I do with it? Perhaps something meaningful for the Jewish community? In the past, I had been a board member for various Jewish organizations, even rising to head the Board of Jewish Family Service. But that wasn't what I had in mind now. I wanted to do something professionally within the Jewish community. As if from heaven, a brochure arrived in the mail describing the Florence Melton Adult Mini-School, a two-year Jewish education program for adults being offered for the first time in Rochester through Jewish Community Federation. The more I read, the more I was certain that this program was going to help me find my new path. I enrolled in the fall of 2000, while still working for the Collaborative but knowing my time there was limited. I began studying Judaism in a way I had never done so before, reading original texts, sharing ideas with classmates and being taught by knowledgeable Jewish scholars.

After six months of study, another idea seemed to appear from out of nowhere. What if I used my interest, knowledge and energies on behalf of my temple? I had chanced upon a brochure explaining that Hebrew Union College in Cincinnati, the educational seminary for Reform Judaism, was offering a course given to train individuals to help their congregations, qualifying them to be called para-rabbis. I knew about para-legals, but para-rabbis? This was a new concept, at least to me. As I looked over the brochure, the training and what it might lead to seemed more and more appealing. The program was offered in three-week segments during two successive summers. It seemed just right for me. I called Hebrew Union for more information which they sent promptly. Para-rabbinics sounded like wonderful, meaningful work, helping my congregation and its congregants. My rabbi encouraged me and, with Michael's blessings, I signed up for the first year's summer program in Cincinnati to begin in mid-July, 2001.

Two weeks before I was to leave, on a hot Sunday afternoon in June, while attending a wedding, I began to feel faint. My heart started beating like a drum, except without keeping a steady beat. It felt erratic, and I felt horrible. As soon as the ceremony was completed, we sped home. Thinking I might just be dehydrated from the heat, I drank glass after glass of water. We both expected I'd feel better as soon as I rehydrated myself. As the afternoon progressed I felt even worse. We called my primary care physician who ordered me to go to the emergency department at Strong.

Because our doctor called ahead to alert the hospital, I was whisked immediately into an examining room, my vitals taken, and quickly moved to an observation floor. I was diagnosed with atrial fibrillation, a type of irregular heart beat caused by inefficient pumping action of the heart. Because a side effect can be blood clots that cause embolisms or strokes, I wasn't going anywhere until they could return my heart to normal rhythm. With medication, I was able to leave the hospital in two days. I was advised to take it easy for a while.

"Okay, but I'm scheduled to leave in two weeks for an educational program in Cincinnati," I told the doctor who signed my release form.

"Sorry, Mrs. Miller. You'd better reschedule," came the answer. "It's just too dangerous for you to leave town." And with that statement, my career as a para-rabbi was put on hold.

Meanwhile, I had completed the first year of the Melton program and couldn't wait for the new year of learning to begin in September. When I ran into someone from my class at the supermarket and expressed my anticipation, she said, "Oh, did you hear that Lily is moving to Florida?" Lily was the director of the Melton program.

"But who's going to be in charge?" I asked. *Me. Me. Me. I could do it.*

"I don't know," she replied. "Lily and her husband just decided to move. Maybe they haven't had the chance to hire anyone yet."

I called Jewish Federation immediately and asked to speak to Jan Katz, the head of the education department, who also had been one of my Melton teachers.

"Hi, Jan. It's Hinda. How are you?" I began. "Are you having a good summer?" We chatted for a little bit before I got to the point of my call. "Jan, I just heard that Lily is leaving," I continued in a rush. "If you haven't already filled her position, I'd really like to talk to you about it."

She laughed. "No, we haven't hired anyone. In fact, we haven't even advertised the position. If you're interested, I'd love to talk to you. Send me your resumè. After we've officially posted the position, I'll call you for an interview." She paused and said, "I want you to know that I'm happy you're re interested in working with Melton. I enjoyed having you as a student in my class." With that we rang off.

Several weeks later I had an interview with Jan which seemed to go very well. She and I talked about many things--our philosophies of education and of supervision, and about how we would work out the dichotomy of having her supervise me as an employee of the Federation's education department while I would be supervising her as one of the Melton teachers. In the short time she and I had known one another, we had built up a trust that we believed would see us through. I was hired and began working as Director of the Melton Mini-School in August 2001.

In many ways, this job was similar to my previous ones in that there was a cycle to what I did and when I did it. I had to deal with various populations of people, both inside and outside of Federation. I was the face of the program to the public, and I had to balance a finite budget. The great blessing was that I did not have to raise funds; student tuition covered all teaching costs, materials and refreshments. My salary and benefits were underwritten by Federation. I could concentrate my efforts on cheerleading for Melton, encouraging adults who felt a lack in their own childhood Jewish education to enroll and fill that gap.

As Director, I made it my business to know every student well. I inter-viewed every potential student and interacted with them throughout their two-year education cycle. I observed classes and monitored student satisfaction. As teachers retired or moved away, I found replacements and, if they were not at the caliber we expected, advised them how they could improve or explained why they would not be retained. I had help in the latter tasks, both from Jan and from the Chicago headquarters of the Melton Mini-School, who sent a representative to visit the Rochester program a few days each year.

Students, for the most part, came to classes smiling and eager to learn, but by March or April of their second year, in many cases those smiles turned to frowns and sometimes even to scowls. Second-year students didn't want to face the end of the adventure of their renewed Jewish education. Fortunately, the national office had created some graduate courses which we began to offer locally to keep our active learners satisfied.

One of the requirements of being Melton Director was to attend an annual conference of Melton directors where we were inspired by outstanding speakers and given opportunities to share techniques with colleagues for recruiting students and retaining them. At that national conference in the fall of 2002 I first heard about a Melton study program in Israel, a two-week text-based course on Jewish history, with classes held at the actual sites of Biblical events. As soon as I heard about it, I wanted to go, not only for myself, but as a *shaliach*[23], so that, on my return, I would know all about it and and encourage Rochester Melton students to attend. I had a second compelling reason to want to go: Sarah had been stricken with cancer and was no longer responding to treatment. I wanted, needed, to see her once more.

In late December I left for Israel, eventually meeting up with 20 Melton students from Sydney and Melbourne, Australia, and two couples from Chicago. I arrived in darkness. I was tired, but alert to the sights and sounds of Jerusalem during the ride to my hotel. In the States we'd been reading and hearing so much about violence against Israelis that it was a great surprise to me and a true pleasure to see life going on as if there were no danger.

I arrived at my hotel to discover they hadn't expected me until the next day. Once we were straightened that out, I was given a lovely room, missing only Michael, my favorite roommate. I called Melissa, a friend, formerly from Rochester, who lived nearby. She came over immediately, and we walked down the block for pizza and salad. A sign of the times: the restaurant had a gate and a guard who checked purses and backpacks before buzzing anyone in.

This trip to Israel continued to be different from previous ones. This was the most religious-based, the most educational and the one most closely aligned with Jewish history. I was able to attend Sabbath services within the Reform tradition, unusual in Israel where Orthodox tradition prevails among non-secular Jews. The first was a Friday night service welcoming the Sabbath where we sang the entire service in Hebrew, and the rabbi's sermon was delivered in English. I found out later that most of the congregants were originally from England, Australia and the United States. The second service was the following morning. I met Melissa again, and we attended Sabbath services at the Reform Theological Seminary.

Bright and early each day after a sumptuous Israeli breakfast, we Melton adventurers boarded buses to visit the sites for that day's classes. Each day was different. One day we might spend at Hebrew University, studying how its

---

[23] (sha-lee-ach) messenger

architecture reflects the conflicts in Israeli identity, European or Middle Eastern. Later that day to an Amphitheatre overlooking the Judean Hills and the Dead Sea where it was not difficult to imagine that this was the view similar to the one G-d gave Moses of the Land. Later still, all the same day, to the site from which the Romans conquered the city in 70 C.E.[24] Whew!

It wasn't sight-seeing. At each location there was a lesson in Jewish history and each evening generally included a summing-up session. One day our text was Psalm 137 ("If I forget thee, O Jerusalem") and we discussed sovereignty over Jerusalem through the ages. Another day we met with David Horowitz, editor of the *Jerusalem Report*, who analyzed the current atmosphere within the country and previewed the Israeli elections which were to be held in two months. The director of Melton International addressed us on how difficult it was to reach peace, something needed by both sides in the Israeli-Arab conflict. Every evening in my room I thought back on what we had done and heard that day. Most nights I couldn't fall asleep for an hour or two after I turned out the light, lying there reviewing what I had learned. How I wished Michael was with me to discuss these issues with.

On various days we had other experiences: We visited the Shrine of the Book to see the Dead Sea Scrolls, and we spent several hours in Yavneh learning about Yochanan ben Zakkia, the seminal rabbinical figure who moved Judaism from a Temple-centered religion to one of study and prayer. I recalled learning about Rabbi ben Zakkia when I was a teenager, and remembered how brave I thought his actions had been in first century Roman Jerusalem. We also engaged with modern history as well, visiting Tel Aviv to wander the neighborhoods of the earliest settlers in what was then Palestine and then spend time in the very building where the State of Israel was declared in 1948.

When we traveled north, we visited a Carmelite Monastery on Mt. Carmel near Haifa we reenacted a section from the Book of Kings about the Prophet Elijah. We also had a study session in Beit Shearim and continued on to Tiberius to a study session about the Rambam, Rabbi Moses ben Maimon, otherwise known as Maimonides.

One of my favorite stops was an evening excursion in the Town of Safed in the north of the country. I had been there before, but this visit was totally different. After we had checked into our guest accommodations at a nearby *kibbutz*, we made our way into town. Slowly, many times single file, we walked

---

[24] C.E. stands for Common Era, sometimes referred to as A.D.

our way along cobblestone streets, past alleyways and muddy roads, climbing weathered stairs, 52 stairs up and 20 down, until we reached the private home of Ronen and Genine Bar-El, who had offered our group hospitality for the evening. Ronen was a fabulous chef, his wife a gracious hostess, and their home perfect to accommodate us for dinner. The only downside was that Michael was not there to enjoy it with me. As if he were somehow thinking the same thing, his call caught me between dinner and dessert.

I stepped out onto their courtyard, under a blanket of stars, to talk across the miles. He and I spoke every day, usually when I was getting up in the morning and he was going to bed at night. As much as I loved being back in Israel, I resolved never to go again without him. I was a jumble of emotions: loving what I was seeing and learning, regretting that I was not sharing it with my best friend.

Back in October, coincidentally on the very day I made my travel arrangements, I heard from Raphi telling me that Sarah had died. When I got to Israel, I called him to tell him when our group was scheduled to be in Tel Aviv. I was anxious to see him as well as their children and grandchildren while there. The night our group was in Tel Aviv Raphi picked me up from a street corner near the site of our last class of the day, the memorial for President Yitzchak Rabin, who had been assassinated. I recognized the pickup spot as being only one city block from my first home-away-from-home in Israel in 1963, the apartment of Sarah's family.

As soon as I walked into Raphi's apartment, I began to sob, feeling Sarah's presence in everything I saw and touched. As I wandered around, remembering the visit Michael and I had made in 1973, I looked up to see her personal artwork hanging over the couch. Near the kitchen was a drawing by our mutual favorite Israeli artist, Shmuel Katz. On the book shelves were books we had both read and discussed long distance. Those shelves also held her beloved blooming plants. I ached not having her there to hug me or for not being able to hug her back.

When I finally got control of myself, Raphi and I sat on the couch to talk before anyone else arrived. He told me there was a video from his son Omer's wedding. "Would you like to see it?"

I hesitated because I knew that this *simcha*[25] had been moved up in time so that Sarah, already gravely ill, wouldn't look the way I remembered her, but this was the only way I could see her one more time. I nodded. I watched the video

---

[25] celebration

of the ceremony and reception, alternating between smiles and tears, the tears coming frequently and abundantly. Every frame showed me how sick Sarah was and how hard she was trying to enjoy this moment. I saw it all; her hair, beautifully styled but in short supply, her wasted frame, the beautiful dress which couldn't hide the pipettes of narcotics muting her pain.

The wedding itself was different from my expectations. I had somehow imagined that Israeli weddings would be formal. I was surprised to see everyone, even the wedding party, dressed more casually than we do in the United States for such an event. Also practically all of the music was contemporary rock, including the Elton John song, "Can You Feel the Love Tonight?" when the bride and groom came down the aisle.

Just as the tape ended, Sarah's daughter Rona arrived with her husband Yoav, their children Noam and Nettie, and her brother Itzhar. I wiped away my tears and made up my mind to enjoy the present, not to dwell in the past. We caught up on what Rona, Yoav and the children were doing, and heard about the new town where they had moved. Through sheer coincidence, their town, Modi'in, had just become a partner city with Rochester's Federation! I was thrilled to learn they were expecting a third child in March. New life. Something sweet to look forward to. Itzhar was enjoying his work, but, perhaps because he didn't have a wife and children yet, he seemed to be the one grieving most deeply for his mother. Time with all of them was lovely, but eventually I had to get back to my group.

The next day, a Friday, I was able to take a few hours away from the Melton group to do some shopping on Ben Yehuda Street, the heart of Jerusalem's shopping district. I wandered around, looking for a specific shop whose owner had been in Rochester the previous Spring, only to find he had closed early that day. With unexpected time on my hands, I decided to go to a nearby café for coffee. Sitting there, I realized that no one in the world knew where I was at that moment; I was totally on my own in a foreign country, sitting in a café that had been previously bombed by terrorists – and yet I felt completely safe! I couldn't explain it then, and I can't explain it now.

When it was time to leave Israel and return home, I wasn't sorry to go. I missed Michael terribly and was sorry to have had this fantastic experience without him. Also I wasn't saying *lihitraot* to Sarah this time, wondering when I would ever see her again. That chapter was forever closed. All the way home I concentrated on one thought: soon I would be able to share this amazing Melton experience with my teachers and students.

Because of the buzz I created about my experience, many students and graduates of the program ventured on their own Melton Israel learning adventures. Many had never been to Israel beforehand, but even those who had been there previously were able to appreciate the enhancement that studying texts at historic sites gave this trip.

Something's Wrong

HAVING surgery is never pleasant, but as a means to an end, well, it can be tolerated. Age was starting to creep up on me and my knees were giving me the news.

I decided to have my knees replaced, one at a time, to improve mobility and give me a break from pain medications. Hospitalization was required, followed by days of rehab in a nursing facility. My vanity prevailed when I announced: "No visitors except family until I get home." What I meant was until I could get my makeup on and my hair looking decent.

I noted to the nurse who took me to pre-op for the first surgery in December 2004, "It takes such a short amount of time to go from being a 'person' to being (and feeling like) a 'patient.' You shed your own clothes, give up your jewelry, remove makeup and there you are: you and yet not quite yourself." With the first insertion of an intravenous port and, especially when the first relaxant is administered, you lose control of everything. Someone transports you, creates your daily schedule of foods, meds and exercise, and controls your comings and goings. For me, someone who liked to be in control of my own destiny, it was a bit much. Before my surgery I prayed not only for a good outcome, but also for patience. Boy, did I ever know my need! I came through both that first and a subsequent knee replacement in March 2009 with flying colors.

I had been blessed with a mother-in-law who treated me like a daughter. When Michael and I were first married, one of Michael's friends asked me out of Michael's hearing, "How do you get along with Michael's mother?"

"Great. Why do you ask?"

He said, "Well, Mrs. Miller was always very possessive of Michael and I thought she might resent you for being the focus of his life."

"You're kidding, right?" I responded, surprised by his remarks. "Mom told me that as long as she sees a smile on her son's face, I can do or say anything I want." In other words, as far as I was concerned, subject closed.

Through the years Mom Miller treated me exactly as she did Joanie, Michael's sister. I was praised when I did something she liked and yelled at when I did something she didn't. In fact, since Joanie didn't enjoy cooking or baking, I became the repository of family recipes. Mom and I were both knitters and readers so we shared those interests as well.

Mom suffered from arthritis, but she didn't let it slow her down much. She taught us family members not to complain but instead to take every day as it comes and enjoy the moment. She continued to drive her large 1985 Cadillac into her 90s, only refusing to drive at night and on especially blustery winter days. Sometimes she relied on her children or a grandchild to shop for her, but for the most part, she was an independent woman.

She was also a Mermaid, as the women in her apartment building called themselves. They met every morning at 8 am. for a daily swim in their heated pool. A few times a day she walked the hallways of her apartment building, holding on to her walker. As Michael accompanied her one day and got a little ahead of her, she called out, "Michael, slow down. I'm not 90 anymore." Her children, grandchildren and great-grandchildren, along with two of Mom's first cousins from Long Island, gathered at Mom's country club to celebrate her 98th birthday in February 2005.

One week later, after Joan and her husband Allan had returned from that celebration to their Florida condominium, they played their usual round of golf. Afterwards, Allan showered and Joan lay down for a nap. When he returned to the bedroom, she was dead, probably from a heart attack. Emergency technicians tried to revive her, but they were unsuccessful. In a flash, our family world turned upside down. Joanie was only 69.

We were all devastated, but Mom took it hardest. This vibrant woman began to lose the will to live, that will she was able to rediscover months after Dad Miller died. This time she couldn't rally. She probably didn't want to.

Even before Mom's slow decline after Joanie's sudden death, I began to sense that there was something wrong with Michael. I couldn't name what it was exactly. I just could see he wasn't himself. Since I had also lost a sister, I understood how grief surprises you with its harshness, even in the midst of enjoying yourself. *Oh no, I can't be having fun. My sister just died.* I'd been there, in that what-do-I-do-now and how-can-I-make-this-all-go-away when Fedg died, but these circumstances were different. I had lived through months of knowing that my sister was terminal. Michael had no time to prepare for Joanie's death.

And, thank G-d, I had a surviving sister, someone with whom to share the loss, as only a sibling could. Joanie was Michael's only sibling.

One evening in late March, Michael suddenly began a rant about how poor we were and how were we ever going to pay our bills. I tried to assure him that we weren't poor and we had no outstanding bills. Then it hit me. We had had this exact conversation every day for more than a week and nothing I said had made a difference. I became alarmed. What was happening to this man I loved so much? When in doubt, get help, I told myself, and picked up the phone to call a dear friend who was a psychiatrist.

"Eric, I need help," I began. "Something's very wrong with Michael and I don't know what to do."

He, the consummate professional, calmed me down just by the soothing manner he used. "First tell me what you are experiencing."

I described the concern Michael had expressed about our finances and told Eric that, although I had assured Michael there were no problems, he couldn't seem to let the topic go.

Eric took a deep breath and then said, "Hinda, he's depressed. I've seen it before and it's usually brought about by some kind of trauma, like Joan's sudden death. Whether it will subside or not without treatment, I can't say."

At least I now had a name for Michael's behavior and that was a start. "So now what do we do?" Eric, as a friend, didn't believe he should treat Michael personally, but he prescribed a drug to calm him down temporarily and contacted another psychiatrist, asking him to see Michael as soon as possible.

I escorted a shaky, shaken Michael to this appointment, hoping for the best. As expected, the diagnosis was clinical depression. After that one hour appointment and a trip to the pharmacy, Michael began taking the drug prescribed. We were told it would take at least six to eight weeks before we would know if that antidepressant was working. We had high hopes.

Six weeks later, it was obvious that, not only wasn't the drug working, but that Michael had slipped even further into depression. And so another drug was prescribed. And after six weeks of that and two weeks to have it clear his system, another. And another. And another.

Meanwhile Mom Miller was getting weaker, too. By August of that year, after a two-week stay in the hospital, she died, leaving an enormous hole in the lives of those she left behind and compounding Michael's grief. He now had no one from his nuclear family still alive. He still went downtown to his law office, but from what he told me, when he got there, he stared at his computer screen and did no work. He didn't trust his judgment to do anything. Blessedly his law firm was supportive and asked little of him during that time.

During Michael's downward skid he lost faith that the right drug would ever be found, that his life would turn around. I, on the other hand, wouldn't allow myself to think that way. When someone would ask about Michael's health I would say, "Well, they haven't found the right drug yet, but I'm sure they will – soon."

It was a roller coaster ride, the worst possible version of one actually. After a few weeks of his being on a new drug, I would think I saw some lightening in Michael's mood and improvement in his functioning. Each time it was hope, not reality, making me see changes. What to do next?

Because of all previous options failing, in the summer of 2006, a year and a half after Michael's original diagnosis, his psychiatrist decided it was time to try electroconvulsive therapy (ECT). In other words, they would shock his brain with a controlled electrical impulse until he experienced a brain seizure. I remained upbeat with Michael, but I kept thinking: *Has it really come to this? He's going to have to live a scene from* 'One Flew over the Cuckoo's Nest?' But there were no other options so I drove Michael to the Strong twice a week and escorted him up to the special psych unit devoted to ECT. I waited for the initial injections to take hold and a nurse to take him into the special room for treatment.

For the first two weeks, I stayed in the waiting room while he was receiving treatment. One by one seriously depressed patients came in to get their pre-treatment injections, often with caregivers who looked even more depressed than the patients. I couldn't stand it. If I was going to maintain my positive attitude, I had to get away from that environment. So, after Michael's fourth session, I left the hospital after he was taken into ECT, and drove to a nearby Starbucks.

Even away from the hospital, my mind stayed focused on Michael. Where had my darling friend gone? Where was the man with whom I'd toured London three times? The fun companion from a week in Bermuda?

I left my cell phone number with the woman in charge of the ECT department and waited for her call to tell me when he was ready to go home. Then I drove back to the hospital and sat in the car in front of the psychiatric unit. Michael would be wheeled out, his head almost touching his chest, exhausted, needing the help of both his attendant and me to get him into the car. He would sleep the entire afternoon following each treatment. After ten weeks it became obvious that the treatments weren't helping.

Friends and family were supportive of both of us throughout his illness although it was hard to be in Michael's company. He was a shell of himself, sitting quietly and solemnly, never contributing to the discussion unless directly asked a question, and then answering in as few words as possible. Everyone wanted to help and no one knew how. That is, until we were invited to dinner at the home of cousins.

While we were enjoying appetizers in their living room, and Patty was fussing in the kitchen, Bob told Michael, "You know, I've been on a combination of a couple of drugs since I was diagnosed with PTSD. I wonder if that combination would work for you, too." Michael hadn't taken either drug previously.

When we went to the next appointment with his psychiatrist, Michael told him about Bob's suggestion. "What do you think?"

His shrink replied. "It's certainly worth a try. I've prescribed just about everything else for you. Let's try it."

It didn't even take the full six weeks for us to begin seeing improvement. Michael was becoming Michael again.

While he was ill, I had continued to work part-time in the Melton program. I felt guilty about leaving him alone, but I needed the distraction from watching him either nap or spend his conscious hours like a zombie. Once he was feeling better, and we began to enjoy each other's company again, I wanted more time to spend with him. Even though the job as Melton Director had been the best job I ever had, I knew I was ready to leave. I retired.

It didn't take long for a new opportunity to present itself. Michael had, since his days as the first Democrat elected to Town Council of Brighton, been a well known figure. His years on the Family Court bench enhanced his reputation as a respected public figure. His triumph over depression became a story that many people wanted to hear. He was asked to speak to various groups and, now that I was retired, I attended each time.

Meg, a woman we knew from Red Wings baseball games, had told me at one game that her husband Howard had suddenly and inexplicably sunk into depression. I told her to try to bring Howard to an upcoming speech Michael was giving at the JCC. They did, sitting unobtrusively in the very last row of seats. During the question and answer period following Michael's talk, some of the questions were directed to me. I learned that people, like Meg, were anxious to hear my story, the story of a caregiver for a severely depressed person. As people left the room, Meg approached me, thanking me for telling her about Michael's talk and saying that it was helpful.

"But what I really want to know is your part of the story," she continued. "How did you manage to get through this hell?" Standing there with her, I gave her my best advice and told her she could call me with any other questions. We parted with a warm hug, sisters in caring for our loved ones.

When I got home, I wrote down everything I had said that day to Meg, what I might have added if I had had more time to think about her questions and what other caregivers might need to know. From then on, Michael and I both addressed audiences even if he was the only one invited to speak. I spoke honestly and from the heart, sharing things I wished I had known from the first signs of Michael's illness. I told listeners to recognize a problem when they see, hear or experience behavior which is out of the ordinary.

"Get professional help. Don't try to solve the problem, and don't try to talk your loved one out of his or her feelings," I told them. "You can't minimize their pain." I urged them to go to all doctor's appointments, to listen and remember what the patient cannot retain, and to remain positive. "If you have to cry, do it in the shower. Keep your pain away from your loved ones. They have enough to deal with." I urged caregivers to keep their own spirits up, to go out with friends, even if their depressed loved one cannot join them, and to share what they themselves are feeling with those closest to them. I wished someone had told me these things when we began our journey through depression years before.

Life gradually returned to normal. While looking for activities to fill my hours and challenge my brain, I joined a group of women to study Jewish texts each week and also returned to Sabbath worship at my temple, which both Michael and I stopped attending for those years. We started to go there early to meet with a group of adults studying the Torah portion to be read during services that morning. I began to volunteer to assist in elementary school-age classrooms at a local charter school. I also took an 8-week course in memoir writing offered at Writers and Books, a local nonprofit organization. That course led to a writing group and gradually developed into this book.

WHO DO I WANT TO BE?

HOW fast it all seems to have gone! Seventy five years of love and loss, ups and downs, high- and lowlights.

Most of the best moments I experienced are connected to family. Our daughter Caralyn graduated from Cornell and went on to Syracuse University when she studied both law and public administration. I teased her that she wasn't content to get the graduate degree of only one of her parents; she had to get them both! She graduated magna cum laude in 1992 and returned to Rochester where she found employment writing legal articles with Thompson Publishing.

There she met Alan Ross, another attorney. After a year-long courtship, they were married in July 1995. At Chanukah two years later, we were sitting at the dinner table having had dessert, when they presented us with small wrapped packages.

"This is a surprise," I said. "You know gifts are for the children, not for the parents."

They both smiled. Caralyn said, "This year we made an exception. "

Michael and I opened the wrappings to find a pair of picture frames with the words "Grandma" and "Grandpa" written on them. We got the message. "When do you think we'll have photos for them?" I asked, smiling.

"In June," Caralyn answered, smiling back. We exchanged hugs and kisses. We were ecstatic.

The day Emma was born, I went to see my new granddaughter and Caralyn in the hospital. I held the baby and smiled down at her, experiencing something deep inside me that I'd never felt before, even when I held my own babies for the first time. This was eternity, continuity. Our family was going on for another generation at least. I was lost in my thoughts when Caralyn called me back to reality.

"I'm chopped liver now, aren't I, Mom?" she asked.

"Yeah, pretty much," I answered. But in reality, no one could ever displace the feelings I'd always had for my daughter. Caralyn still works for Thompson

Publishing, but ever since Emma's birth, she does so from home. Somehow she also cares for her family, multiple pets and chickens and she also knits, weaves and writes a blog, the very definition of a multi-tasker.

Jonathan, who prefers to be called Jon, graduated from Eastern Michigan University in Ypsilanti. He had always wanted to work in real estate and, after doing research on various colleges, discovered that at EMU he could major in business with a concentration in real estate. After another year of living and working in Michigan on a project to retrofit an old vodka factory into a convention center, he returned to Rochester and, a few years later met Renèe, the woman he married in March, 2000. Today Jon works for the Monroe County Board of Elections while also managing apartments he owns. Renèe teaches neuroscience at the University of Rochester. She and Jon are divorced.

Grandchildren came in waves. Caralyn's Emma in June 1998 was followed in May 2000 by her sister Isabel (Isa). In November 2002, they welcomed a brother, Nathan (Nate) and in January 2006 another brother, Matthew (Matty). Jon's family expanded during the years with Teddy arriving in April 2002 and then Dustin in May 2004. I am Bubbie to six grandkids and the best part is that all of them lived locally.

Michael and I share an undying love for baseball, although we are also devoted fans of "The 'Cuse," Syracuse University basketball. Back when we were dating and continuing after we married, we frequently drove cross-town to Red Wing (later Silver) Stadium to see games. Of course, we took Caralyn and Jon to games, but it was "our" thing to do together.

We saw some of the greatest players ever to play the game, chief among them Cal Ripken Jr., who played for the Red Wings in 1981, his last stop before the big leagues and, ultimately, the Baseball Hall of Fame. Ripken in 1995, playing for the Baltimore Orioles, broke Lou Gehrig's record of continuous games played and earned the title of Iron Man. He was an Energizer Bunny who played game after game, eventually 2,131 before finally sitting one out.

By 1994 I thought we needed more baseball in our lives. An occasional trip to the stadium didn't seem like enough. As an anniversary present for both of us I bought a pair of season seats at Silver Stadium. We didn't go to every game, but we went to most of them. For the first three years that we had season tickets, the

Red Wings played in that stadium while a new one was being built downtown. That last home game at Silver was something I'll never forget.

During the game itself, emotions ran high. It was the largest crowd in more than a dozen years. We cheered every time a Red Wing was at bat, at every hit, for every catch a Rochester player made. When the game was over, our team losing to the Ottawa Lynx, nobody moved to leave.

Michael and I stood through the closing ceremony, but not by ourselves. Joining us was Arthur Kolko, one of Burt's younger brothers. Arthur told us how much Burt wanted to be there, but he couldn't get away from work. It was fitting that a Kolko was at my side, even if it wasn't the one with whom I had shared my childhood love of baseball.

Dan Mason, Red Wing general manager, took the field and, with much emotion evident in his cracking voice, thanked the fans for their support and invited us all to join him and the team at the new stadium in the next spring. Home plate was dug up to be transported there where it would be mounted on the wall of the club owners' suite. Then we heard the voice of Frank Sinatra on the public address system, singing "There Used to be a Ballpark." There were no dry eyes. As much as we looked forward to the new stadium, we were going to miss this one, the one we had known as children, the place where we discovered the game and began our love affair with it. When the music ended, the lights on the field dimmed and then went out completely. There was just enough light in the stands to get us safely out, although no one really wanted to leave.

Michael and I took our love of baseball as motivation to visit some major league cities. We had a lovely visit to Kansas City, enjoying a game at Kaufmann Stadium and, on another day, visiting the Truman Presidential Library in Independence. When the Red Wings changed their major league affiliation to the Twins, we visited Minneapolis. We also saw games in Phoenix, San Francisco, Oakland, Cleveland, Baltimore, Toronto, Washington and Seattle. We made many trips to New York, watching the Yankees in both old and new Yankee Stadium and our beloved New York Mets at Shea.

I learned many life lessons from baseball. To succeed, a player has to take one game at a time and concentrate on only one play at a time. This taught me that I should focus on each aspect of my daily life, doing each as well as I can.

To be good at baseball, it isn't enough to be able to hit the ball and play your position, whichever it may be. Sometimes you have to cover for others when they're pulled out of their position. Life requires anticipating changes and adjusting to changing circumstances.

Baseball, like life, is unpredictable. Games can change on a crazy bounce, a heroic catch, or a fluke ground ball. You think you know what's ahead, and you may be wrong. Many times the surprises are good ones, but you find yourself able to sustain the bad "bounces" as well.

I also learned lessons from my faith. My sense of myself as a Jew was formed early in a religiously observant home and an orthodox synagogue. It was finely tuned as an adult, especially with my experiences in Israel and working as Director of a Jewish studies program. I learned that we are almost the only ancient people to retain our history, language and customs. Although Hitler planned the annihilation of the entire Jewish people, most of us not only survived, but thrived. I am proud that that there exists today a vibrant, flourishing State of Israel.

Okay, I didn't fulfill my desire to become a para-rabbi. I still have chances from time to time to deliver a homily at a Shabbat service and have, since 1986, written the *haggadah*[26] our extended family uses for Passover *seders*.

My friendships through the years have been fulfilling and lasting. Many people I met at summer camp and in school -- Wendy, Tala, Danny, Lewis, Judy, Wendy & Morley -- are still in my life today. The exception, regrettably, is Burt. He and I had rekindled our friendship after thirty years of non-communication. When we spent time with one another, we just picked up from wherever we had left off. When he and his family came to Rochester, in November 2004 for the burial of his mother, we had a chance to spend an hour or so together. It was the first time I met his two grown sons who quizzed me about what their father was like when he and I were children. Although this was a sad occasion, there was also levity as we talked about life way back when.

But I could tell something was a bit off. I had heard from mutual friends that Burt had been ill and was seeking treatment for whatever it was. When I approached the subject, he deflected my question into another line of conversation. He wasn't going to discuss this with me, no matter how much I asked, so I stopped asking and simply enjoyed his company.

Burt died ten months later, two days after his 66th birthday. To me, he will always stay alive as my first and dearest best friend.

---

[26] The service read before the Passover meal

Most of the lessons I learned in life came from observing my parents. The deprivations and hardships my parents experienced as children and shared with me were life lessons not available to many of my friends whose parents, and sometimes grandparents, were born in middle-class America. Mum and Daddy taught me how to be happy without an abundance of material possessions, but with abundant love. They taught me that with the right attitude, a strong family, and a deep faith, you can endure catastrophe, triumph over tragedy and find joy.

When I grew up, I thought the most important question I would have to answer was <u>what</u> I wanted to be when I grew up. Now that I am all grown up, I know that the real question is: <u>Who</u> do you want to be? I think I've become that "me," the one I always wanted to be.

POSTSCRIPT

To my grandchildren:

I hope to share many important events in your lives, graduations, weddings, perhaps even the births of some of your children. If not, and if you don't remember all we talked about when we were together, this book will remind you of what your Bubbie learned and wanted to share with you and yours.

While your mother and father were growing up, Poppa and I talked frequently about how our lives were so very different from those of our own parents. We realized we couldn't know what life would be like for our own children when they grew up. We decided, as best we could, to prepare our children, your parents, to be flexible, to be able to adapt to the world however they found it. It's a good lesson for you to remember for your own lives. Don't see only one way of doing things. Don't hold onto one stance that isn't working. Be flexible.

That leads to another adage: Be likeable. You're going to encounter many types of people. Many will respond to a smile and a warm gesture. Unfortunately, some won't. Try to see things from another's point of view and anticipate what he or she might need. If you do, someone might be more willing to see things your way and meet you halfway.

Remember that being likeable doesn't mean you should compromise your values. Being liked by the wrong sort of people can bring trouble. Choose your friends wisely, not based on who they like or dislike, or what they like or don't like to do. Your choices should be about what and who they value. Do they have good relationships at home? Are they generally kind and friendly to everyone? Can they be trusted to do the right thing? Would your parents be proud of the things they do and say?

You are fortunate to be the children of good people. You enjoy an enviable standard of living and have all the necessities of life and even some of the extras. There are many people who are not so fortunate. Give some of yourself to them, whether goods, money or time. You have been blessed from birth. You did nothing special to deserve that blessing – you must pass it on. Good fortune obligates.

Above all, remember who you are and who you come from. You are yourselves, as well as the children of Caralyn and Alan, Jon and Renèe, the grandchildren of Marilyn, Arthur, Linda, Tom, Paula, Hinda and Michael. That's where you came from – where you go are your choices.

I love you for what I see in you that reminds me of your parents, but mostly for what I see in you that is uniquely yours.

Bubbie

ACKNOWLEDGEMENTS

BY now you should have some sense of who I have become. I have more stories to tell, many more memories, but I believe that every little last bit of your life doesn't need to be revealed so that someone out there can get to know the essential you.

Many people helped me to shape what I have shared and to mold my words into a book. I appreciate each and every one.

For baseball memories, thanks to the voice of the Rochester Red Wings, Josh Wetzel,

For encouragement and unflagging enthusiasm for this project, hugs to my stalwart writing group: Shirley Gray, Cathy Dayan, Newcomb Losh, Marilyn Belle-Isle, Jen McLernon and Anäis Salibian and also to the Brighton branch of Canandaigua National Bank which hosted our weekly gatherings through the years,

For reading my manuscript and offering wisdom, deep appreciation to Scott Pitoniak,

For cover photography which makes me look more attractive than I rightfully deserve, everlasting gratitude to Stephanie Albanese,

For cover design wrapping my book in her amazing artwork, I am much beholden to M. Wendy Gwirtzman,

And, most of all, I want to acknowledge the singular person who was here throughout the entire process of making this book happen, my helpful, patient, tolerant and encouraging husband. I couldn't love you more.

CPSIA information can be obtained at www.ICGtesting.com
Printed in the USA
BVOW09s1604280914

368526BV00026B/557/P